CLASSROOM CONVERSATIONS

ALSO BY MAUREEN MILETTA

A Multiage Classroom: Choice and Possibility

CLASSROOM CONVERSATIONS

A COLLECTION OF CLASSICS
FOR PARENTS AND TEACHERS

EDITED BY

Alexandra Miletta and Maureen Miletta

THE NEW PRESS

NEW YORK
LONDON

Requests for permission to reproduce selections from this book should be mailed to:
Permissions Department, The New Press, 38 Greene Street, New York, NY 10013.

Published in the United States by The New Press, New York, 2008
Distributed by W. W. Norton & Company, Inc., New York

ISBN 978-1-59558-157-0 (pb)
CIP data available

The New Press was established in 1990 as a not-for-profit alternative to the
large, commercial publishing houses currently dominating the book publishing
industry. The New Press operates in the public interest rather than for private
gain, and is committed to publishing, in innovative ways, works of educational,
cultural, and community value that are often deemed insufficiently profitable.

www.thenewpress.com

Composition by NK Graphics

Printed in Canada

2   4   6   8   10   9   7   5   3

To Ellen Gordon Reeves, our brilliant friend,
who suggested we write

CONTENTS

PART IV. ON EQUITY AND ISSUES OF SOCIAL JUSTICE

PART V. THE FINAL WORD: PURPOSES OF EDUCATION
IN A DEMOCRACY

ACKNOWLEDGMENTS

We wish to thank our friend and editor Ellen Gordon Reeves for proposing the idea for this book and helping us see it through to completion. Her support and constant helpful feedback have been invaluable, and her patience is limitless. We are also grateful to other early readers, including Michaela Daniel, Jennifer Miletta Adams, Kathy Morris, and a group of insightful students at Hofstra University. We are indebted to the authors in this anthology for their contributions as scholars and writers, and for granting us permission to include their work. Thanks also to Marty Umans for photographing our portraits. Finally, we must thank the colleagues, students, and parents we have worked with over the years, for they have shaped our thinking and given us many memorable experiences and rich conversations that continue to inform our beliefs and our practice.

INTRODUCTION

These are challenging times for educators, parents, and their children. The litany of problems with education are all too familiar—high-stakes testing, the achievement and education gaps, segregated schools, tracking, school violence and bullying, teacher attrition rates, hard-to-staff schools in urban and rural areas, inequitable funding, and the political turmoil spiraling out of control in the wake of the No Child Left Behind legislation. Education is at the center of many public debates, and more than ever before, politicians are engaged in developing policies at the state and federal levels that are changing how teachers are trained, recruited, and supported; and how students learn, are evaluated, and promoted. Demographic changes in public education have also meant increased scrutiny on issues related to teaching second-language learners, students with special needs, and students who are retained and repeat a grade.

Yet in the midst of all this attention to the problems of education, what happens behind closed doors inside the classroom continues to remain largely a mystery to the public at large. Reporters rarely venture there, and even in fictional movies and television programs featuring schools, the action always occurs after the bell rings and the class is over. Parents may sometimes succeed in extracting bits of information about what happened during the school day, but assembling these pieces of information still won't suffice to convey the complexities inherent in the work of teaching. Visitors to schools can get some clues from hallway bulletin boards and displays of work inside classrooms, but the picture is incomplete. Each classroom has its own culture and community, with active participants who talk, listen, and engage with each other in ways that are meant to promote moral and intellectual development. As adults, we can reflect back on our own schooling experiences, memorable teachers, and childhood friendships as a partial window into today's classrooms. However, things are changing so rapidly in the information age that comparisons are getting harder to make. The fact that we have watched teachers throughout our own schooling experiences does not necessarily mean that we have insights into the invisible aspects of teachers' work.

Because it is so difficult to know what happens inside classrooms, we find ourselves now in a quagmire of policies that constrain, prescribe, and punish, denying students and teachers of basic freedoms to pursue their interests and questions in ways that they find meaningful. As teacher educators, we are particularly troubled because it is our job to inspire, educate, and create high expectations for the next generation of teachers, yet we are just as susceptible to feelings of overwhelming despair as those we are seeking to teach. For our own well-being and in order to forge ahead, we often turn to our favorite writers, whose wise words and thoughts fill our bookshelves and files. These are people whose work stands the test of time. As educational fads and jargon come and go, we feel a strong connection to these great thinkers who have shaped our beliefs and practices in education and who continue to have an influence in the field.

We are both teachers, and like many other teachers we've encountered, the profession runs in our family. We have been talking about educational problems around the dinner table for as long as we can remember, and our cross-generational perspectives have helped to enrich our respective knowledge of research on teaching and the preparation of teachers. When we were both elementary teachers, we talked a lot about children, about curriculum, and about life in our classrooms and school. Now that we are both teacher educators, we tend to talk more about our teacher candidates, both graduate and undergraduate, and their experiences in schools. Our conversations with each other and with our current students are grounded in the essential issues: knowing children, understanding subject-matter content and the work of teaching, and helping our students know that teachers can make a difference in the public's struggle for social justice and equity of opportunity for all.

Our purpose in writing this book and in gathering these writers for an anthology of classic and lesser-known readings on Western education with our commentary is to share our sources of inspiration with parents, teachers, and those considering teaching as a profession. We hope to provide insights into how and why these writers have been influential thinkers in the field and for us over time. We also share the personal meanings we've derived from these selections and the relevance of these authors' ideas given current reforms in education. We have tried to make evident the ways in which the ideas found in these writers' works can help parents and teachers work together toward common goals, to understand their respective roles in educating the young, and to talk together about fundamental ideas about how children learn. Parents can be reluctant to talk to teachers for fear of having the wrong influence on their child, and teachers sometimes shy away from contact with parents for fear of criticism. We would urge all parents and teachers to stay in close communication, and when possible, to find ways for parents and family members to become active participants in the education of children. Participation does not necessarily have to mean volunteering time in the classroom or school, but rather that parents and relatives are co-constructing the child's learning together with the teachers in a partnership that is mutually beneficial and relies on open, honest communication.

The selections in this anthology are written by academics and scholars. Although we tried to select pieces we felt were accessible to a lay audience, we are aware that some readers may find certain writing challenging at first. We feel that those who work through these challenges, perhaps by talking with others who read these selections, will be rewarded with insights rich with important ideas that have enduring value and are not just trendy "fix the problem" approaches found in many parenting and education books. We carefully selected these authors because we felt their writing was inspiring, meaningful, and not always as well known as it deserved to be.

There are many people who believe that learning to teach is about acquiring a certain set of skills and having sufficient subject-matter knowledge, and that these requirements can be measured by standardized test results. We hope to show that teaching is far from merely technical in nature, that the complexities of the work are profound and challenging, but also that the work of teaching the young is infinitely rewarding. Teachers and parents are partners in this thrilling endeavor, and with the good ideas found in this collection as common ground, it is our profound hope that they can forge ahead together, finding new pathways, new dialogue, and always keeping their eyes on the prize: the learning of children.

CLASSROOM CONVERSATIONS

▪ PART I ▪

UNDERSTANDING CHILDREN

We begin this collection with a central focus on children because they are at the heart of education. Introductory courses in education often ask students to engage in a child study, a sustained investigation of one student, that entails observation, conversation, and analysis of that student's work in school. This is because studying children is at the heart of good teaching. Teachers must know how to make sense of the learner's point of view, and not just in an academic way. Parents need to consider this, too. These authors highlight the need for moral, cultural, and artistic insights into children as well. Only when we begin to assemble portraits of children in the full complexity of their humanity, in and out of school, can we envision the paths of exploration and learning that will lead from childhood, to adolescence, and on to adulthood.

• 1 •

Patricia Carini

A LETTER TO TEACHERS AND PARENTS ON SOME WAYS OF LOOKING AT AND REFLECTING ON CHILDREN*

MAUREEN: As I write, I am sitting on a Tuscan beach watching a group of children playing tag with the waves of the Mediterranean. They are a lively group, even though they have only known one another for a few days. Beaches and waves tend to help form relationships rather quickly when sand castles and kite flying replace basal readers and multiplication tables. They also provide the best possible observation point for parents and teachers who want to make discoveries about children and open windows to view them with greater sensitivity and deepened insight. These children are a microcosm of the world. Differences of age, color, language, gender, and economic status are unimportant to them as they run in and out of the pounding surf. All conflicts disappear in the joyous pursuit of projects and the inventiveness of their games. What strikes me immediately is the freedom they are afforded by the watchful adults, and I am reminded of this insightful article by Patricia Carini, co-founder of the renowned Prospect School in Vermont in 1965. Many educators and parents use the Descriptive Review process established at her school, which asks us to view the children under our guidance with depth and intensity, and her influence as an author, speaker, and independent educator is widespread. How often, I ask myself, have I made a quick decision about what is best for children based on insufficient knowledge of their connections to others or their strong interests and preferences?

Carini helps us think more carefully about the many facets of childhood and the complex learning mechanisms children employ. I use this article with beginning teachers as they work to know and understand the children in their

*From *Another Angle: Children's Strengths and School Standards*, ed. M. Himley and P. Carini (New York: Teachers College Press, 2000), 56–64.

classrooms. I have also recommended it to parents struggling to understand the
dilemmas that both they and their children experience as they negotiate the
complexities of schooling in these days of assessment in the form of high-stakes
testing. We all need to take the time to look beyond the prescribed measurements
of ability and progress to examine and enhance the imaginative worlds of our
children.

———————

Dear Parents and Teachers,

I have chosen a letter as the way to talk with you about looking at
children and reflecting on what you have noticed for the reason that letters can be personal in tone and rather informal. And that fits with what
I want to say about observing—an attitude or way of looking that I prefer to think of as *attending to children with care*. Parents and teachers are
interested in children. They are with children a lot. Through that continuous immersion, parents and teachers possess thick layers of working
knowledge about children. Parents and teachers care *for* children and
they also care *about* children. Parents and teachers share the responsibility for educating children. And yet, often teachers' and parents' knowledge of children is neither recognized nor valued.

This letter describes an exercise that is meant to do just that: to value
and recognize your interest, caring, and knowledge and to build upon it
for the benefit of children. The exercise I propose asks teachers and parents, or others with children close to them, *to form a habit of regularly re-*
viewing them—that is, calling them to mind; picturing them in particular
settings or locations; remembering them in a variety of postures and
moods; listening with an inner ear to their voices. The purpose of this re-
viewing is the deepened recognition of children. It is meant to give you,
the important grown-ups in a child's life, a way to recognize fully how
much you already know and understand. It is meant, too, to expand those
understandings and to create a context of memory, ever growing and
deepening, that will inform your own responses to children as individuals.

If your experience with this exercise turns out to be something like
my own, you will also find as you visualize a child in your mind's eye—
or listen to the child's remembered voice and words—that there are blurs

and gaps in the picture. Some of these will make you wonder, reconsider, and take a closer look. In this way, for me, recollecting leads to more attentive looking and listening. It is also important, though, to keep in mind that the purpose of attending isn't to scrutinize children or even to "figure them out"—and certainly not to change them into someone else. The purpose is simpler and more ordinary: to be more sensitively attuned to who they are and are becoming, so that, recognizing them as persons, we can assist and support their learning better.

To do this exercise, cast your inner eye on a particular child. If you want to re-view several children, perhaps all the children in your family, or a group of children in a classroom, it usually works best to do this one at a time. At least in my experience, if I try to do several at once, they blur or one child takes center stage and calls the tune for others. Then, instead of seeing each child as who that child is, I find myself comparing them according to what stood out to me about that first child who caught my attention. What does work is to develop the picture of one child, allow an interval of time, and then move on to others. The first few children will take quite a lot of concentration; as you form the habit of attending carefully, you will find yourself noticing more and remembering more. As your memory strengthens, you will grow more attuned to subtler and broader aspects of children's expressiveness. As you notice more, *and attend to what you notice more consciously*, the picture of a child will form with greater ease, and your capacity to keep a number of children in mind at the same time without blending them will increase.

As you are recollecting a child, also form the habit of making notes to yourself about what you are remembering. The notes are raw material that you can go back to later to review in preparation for a parent-teacher conference or in order to present (or write) a portrayal of the child. Other raw materials you might keep along with this folder or journal of notes are photographs, drawings, or other things that child makes, or even, if you wish, audio or videotapes.

Another help in recollecting a child is to think of the child in a variety of settings and locations. Every parent knows how surroundings and time of day influence a child; so do fatigue or illness. Teachers are often aware that a child who is free and open outdoors on the playground may look less so in the confines of a classroom or even seem subdued or withdrawn. Also children (and adults) have favorite places to be and other strong preferences; for example, feelings about how quickly or slowly they want to start or end the day or an activity; how many people they want around and how much time they need to be alone; how long they can sit in one place and concentrate on the same thing and how much variety and change they can comfortably tolerate, and so forth.

The following paragraphs use headings of the *Descriptive Review of the Child* as a sort of organizing device for recollecting. Use them as they seem helpful, but please don't feel bound by them. They are meant to prime the pump of memory, but not to be confining or predetermining.

Thinking of a child's *Physical Presence and Gesture*, be attentive to what stands out to you immediately. Then, take note of size and build, but also of style of dress, color preferences, prized possessions, and so forth. Visualize how the child moves, with attention to pace, characteristic rhythm and gestures, and how they may vary. For example, you might think about how the child tends to enter the classroom or the child's pace at home first thing in the morning or at the end of the day. You might think, too, of how much space a child occupies, where the child tends to position him- or herself in a group, and so forth.

Locate the child in motion, physically engaged, both outdoors and indoors. For example, you might think of what the child likes to do outdoors (such as bike riding, exploring, sports, etc.) and notice to yourself the energy, pace, and gestures involved. Do the same for active indoor play, such as dress-up, block building, and other construction. Then think of the child quietly occupied; for example, drawing, reading, observing, conversing. What pace and gestures are characteristic in these occupations? Think about where the child seems most at ease and how you can tell that is so; then take it other side round and think of where the child seems least comfortable or most constrained.

Other slants you might take on the child's presence include the voice, its inflection, volume, and rhythm; characteristic phrases and ways of speaking; the expressiveness of the eyes, hands, and mouth; where the child's feelings can be read (and how easily); where and when energy flows most easily and smoothly; where energy seems to be concentrated; how tension shows itself; and so forth.

Attending to expression makes a natural bridge to the child's *Disposi-*

tion and Temperament. You might start by reflecting on how the child usually greets the world. Or to say that a little differently, you might think of how you would describe the child's most typical attitudes toward life.

With these characteristic feeling tones at the center, picture to yourself the sort of emotional terrain the child covers in the course of a day and also according to a variety of circumstances: Some children (and people) tend to maintain an even, steady emotional balance; others are quick to laughter and quick to tears; still others are likely to be inward turned and unlikely to display their feelings.

Think, too, about what the child cares for deeply and what stirs deep feeling. Similarly, reflect on what goes against the child's honor or sense of rightness or justice and where the child has deep loyalties and strong personal commitments. Reflect, too, on how these deep feelings tend to be expressed.

Connections with Other People are not easily separable from disposition and temperament. First, gather in your mind some examples of the child in the company of other children. In the classroom or at home, think about the location of the child in relation to the larger community of children. That is, reflect on where you usually see her or him; how she or he goes about making a place for her- or himself; how she or he tends to move into a new group or to respond to unfamiliar children.

Picture to yourself the range of the child's relationships with other children; for example, think about any children with whom the child has formed a close, enduring relationship, but also think of how the child falls in with more loosely connected groups that may form around games or other classroom or neighborhood activities. Reflect on what the child's role is within friendships and small groups; with brothers and/or sisters or other close relatives; within larger groups.

Give some attention to how the child responds if difficulties arise in a group or with a friend or if she or he, or another child, is in distress or left out, and so forth. Also think about when the child prefers to be alone or left to his or her own devices.

Now you might shift your attention to the child in relation to you or other adults. Think first of the child's characteristic responses and ways of connecting with adults and also the range of these. Picture, for example, how the child greets familiar adults and the kind of contact the child establishes in the course of the day. For example, if there are adults who are sought out, reflect on what draws the child to them; if there are others who are ignored or avoided, think about what keeps the child at a distance.

Think, too, about the child's preferred ways of being with you or with other adults and what the child expects back from you. Another point of reflection might be the way the child negotiates the transition from one adult to another. Yet another might be your sense of what makes the child feel safe, trusted, respected, and secure with adults (or not).

Now give some attention to how you and other adults tend to welcome the child and generally respond to him or her. Think about how easily you or other adults recognize and value the child and how you or others express that to him or her. If the child is hard to see, give some thought to what keeps the child hidden from you or others. Reflect, too, on what adult responses, interests, and ways of being hold the child's interest and win her or his respect and, alternatively, which kinds of responses or attitudes are likely to put the child off or lead to anger or conflict.

Children, like adults, tend to have *Strong Interests and Preferences* that are absorbing and long lasting. From my experience, these are likely to offer much valuable insight in terms of the child's entries into learning and particular talents to be nurtured. I like to start by making a list of all the things I know a child really likes, such as particular foods (or eating in general!), colors, people, animals, places (indoors or outdoors), and a parallel list of what I know the child dislikes or finds repellent. Quite often when I look at these lists, patterns emerge of which I wasn't previously aware. Think, too, about the ways the child expresses these likes and dislikes and how likely they are to change or to be sustained.

A next step is to make a list of any questions, wonderings, or curiosities that have stirred the child's mind and imagination, giving special attention to those that persist or are recurrent. Here, too, it is interesting to look for patterns among these—for example, connections and contrasts—and also for range. Reflect, too, on how these questions and interests are expressed; for example, in play, in choices of books or films, in conversation, in drawing or construction.

Closely related to this, picture the media and the play that most capture her or his attention. I find it helpful to start by recalling what the child is likely to do if she or he has choice and plenty of time; for example, listening to stories, reading books, building with blocks, making "small worlds," drawing, writing, painting, junk construction, sand or water, video games, the natural world, games and sports, making large-scale forts or houses. Here, too, lists are often useful and again usually yield patterns and give a good sense of the range of play and media in which the child finds satisfaction. I often start this listing with favorite stories and books, television programs, and movies, and turn next to play, games, and activities that are absorbing.

Other interesting points of reflection are the kinds of props that are part of a child's preferred play and activities (dress-up clothes, boxes, miniature figures, balls, wheeled vehicles, etc.); the ways that play or activities may be linked to particular seasons or times of day; or the role the child tends to assume in keeping group play and activities going and developing. Sometimes, too, there are particular figures or especially interesting topics or themes featured in the play a child prefers; for example, superheroes or knights or battles or space or dinosaurs or ninja turtles or olden times or disasters or fairy tales or . . . (this list is virtually endless in its possibilities).

Think, too, about what seems to you to be really satisfying and fulfilling about these kinds of play, interests, and activities. And reflect, too, on the standards the child observes around this play; for example, what makes it go right, what spoils it, what rules or customs other children have to observe in order to be part of the play.

In my experience, the child's preferences, interests, and choices are windows to the child's *Modes of Thinking and Learning*. Through these windows it is possible to glimpse how a child goes about making sense of the world and his or her own experience. Or, to say that a little differently, from noticing those world themes that fascinate a child, it is possible to intuit fields of study that will have a strong appeal. In a parallel way, attention to play—as a sort of thinking space of the child's own making—yields insights about the child as a maker of knowledge.

A good place to start is to think of things, ideas, or media for which a child has an inner sense or "feel"; for example, machines or music or language or people or throwing a ball or animals or drama or number or color or paint or the piano or building or . . . (again the possible list is virtually endless). Another way to approach this is to reflect on what the child has always done or does with great ease.

Think, too, about how, through what situations and experiences, this "feel" or inner sense is observable to you and others. Give some thought to whether the child recognizes these talents. This is important to consider since often people take their greatest strengths as givens and, although they rely on them, are not aware of them. I don't personally think that it is always a good idea to point these strengths out to another person, since for some that could be inhibiting or embarrassing. I do think, though, that having a sense of where children stand in relation to their own abilities is useful to a parent or a teacher. Then it is a matter of judgment, based on your other knowledge of the child and the nature of your relationship to him or her, to make the decision on what will best support and assist the child's development of these strengths.

Looking in another direction, think to yourself how the child gains a firm understanding or internalizes knowledge or is inclined to figure things out. For example, there may be an inclination to map or sketch or draw or construct a graph. Or, equally, a child may rely a lot on a strong capacity for observing and remembering. Or perhaps the child gets to know something by talking it through or dramatizing and enacting it. There may be interest in taking things apart and putting them back together; or looking at things or ideas from many angles; or counting, ordering, and creating patterns; or discovering what makes something happen by trying different combinations; or looking things up in books; or studying pictures or photographs . . . (again, the possible list is virtually endless).

Since we all have many ways of figuring things out, spend some time reflecting on when the child is likely to prefer a particular approach and when that may be discarded in favor of another. I have noticed, too, that usually there are observable connections among the range of approaches. For example, a 5-year-old child of my acquaintance, much interested in nature and natural objects, was a close observer and an astute connector of events. ("Grown-ups . . . mow down the dandelions because they grow bumblebees. I know. I saw them together and they were both yellow.") While the conclusion is faulty, the logic is sturdy. He was also an able tree climber, using the trees as an observation point that gave him new and different perspectives on the world.

Sometimes, and especially from children's questions and wonderings, it is possible to glimpse what I think of as a sort of bent or inclination. Some children incline toward imaginative, poetic comparisons with an eye to surprising likenesses between objects or events that on the surface are quite different. To offer one example, I once overheard a child of about 3 say softly, to herself, "rain" as she observed her mother's long dark hair to fall back, catching the light and shimmering as it flowed. Both the comparison and the image that captured it were apt. Or there may be a philosophical, reflective, and speculative talent, or the child may have a religious or spiritual bent. There may be an attraction to the big picture and big ideas, or the child may be adept at seeing the outline or structure that holds things or ideas together, or there may be an attraction to textures and small detail. There may be an experimental or problem-solving slant on the world and an interest in causal relationships.

However, it's important to keep in mind that in life children draw on all these and more. So, even if there is a strong bent in one direction, don't overlook others that may be there. One of the things about us humans is that we are complicated. Given that complexity, in my experience, creating types or categories of thinkers and learners tends not to do a child (or adult) justice or to be especially helpful in the long run to the parents and teachers responsible for that child's learning and education.

From this bigger picture of the child's ways of making sense of things, you might focus in on the narrower piece of the child learning something specific; for example, a task or skill. I often find it useful to think first of how the child positions her- or himself as a learner. Some children (and adults) tend to plunge right in or take some other "I'll do it myself" approach. Some children (and adults) want a lot of time to observe and to practice privately on their own. Some of these same persons value the chance to sit alongside someone else doing the task and follow along, sometimes asking questions. Some children (and adults) want one-on-one instruction; others shy away from any direct contact with a teacher. Some children (and adults) like working on something new in a sort of social, cooperative group; others like to be on their own.

Again, the picture that emerges is complex. Much may depend on what is being learned and much may also depend on the degree of trust that exists between a child and a teacher or among a group of children. A way to get at this complexity is to think of how the child positions her- or himself when the task or skill to be learned is self-selected; next to that picture, reflect on how the child positions her- or himself when the task is assigned or has a strict time limit or is in other ways pressured. The contrast in these circumstances contributes nuance to the portrayal of the child as a learner.

Other slants you might try include picturing the child's responses when mistakes or accidents happen, when it is necessary to rework or do something over, when there are interruptions, when the situation is highly competitive, when the child has options about leaving and re- turning to a task as compared to start-to-finish expectation. Or you might think of specific skills the child has easily mastered and those that have been more difficult, giving particular attention to surrounding cir- cumstances and other factors that have helped or hindered the child.

Thinking again more broadly, reflect on the subject matters or fields of study to which the child gravitates; for example, science, history, lit- erature, art, drama, music, geography, math. Note to yourself what seems to make these attractive and also how the child engages with these modes of thinking and learning. Think, too, about how these interests might be supported, deepened, and expanded. It is also worthwhile to give thought to the future and the learning opportunities that need to be sustained and others that should probably be made available as the child grows older. If there are disciplines the child finds boring or actively dis- likes, reflect on those with particular attention to what seems to distance the child.

Finally, reflect on the standards the child tends to hold for her- or himself and how these may vary depending on circumstances. Think first about the child's own pride of work and in what places and circum- stances that is visible and observable. A useful way to approach this is to think of times and pieces of work that have been really pleasing to the child as well as the converse—times and pieces of work that have been displeasing.

In a more general way, reflect on what seems to influence the value a child accords to his or her own work, when the work and learning are the child's choice. Think, too, of how that may be the same or different when the child finds the task to be mastered boring or distasteful or hard. Taking a slightly different approach, call to mind any situations that would allow you to glimpse how outside expectations and standards affect the child's learning and self-evaluation. It is also useful to give thought to how the child's standards mesh (or don't) with external standards held at school or at home.

What I have outlined above asks for a lot of thinking and reflecting. It isn't necessary to do this all at once, nor is it important if there are sections under each heading that don't ring any bells. Ignore them. Equally, this is an outline and there is a lot that isn't touched on. Add in anything that comes to mind—including other headings, if that seems useful. Remember, this is an exercise and an organizing device. Use it only in the degree that it is helpful to you in picturing the child and expanding your understandings of him or her as a person.

As a conclusion to this exercise, and especially if the picture of the child has become very full and complex, I find it useful to write down words or phrases the child brings to mind. Some of these turn out to be images; others are simply vocabulary that seems particularly apt for describing the child. Quite often, among these, there are ones that seem especially to capture the sense of the person. I remember, for example, a teacher's description of a child's way of moving *and* his way of thinking as "quick-silver"; or an image of a child's warmth and clarity that was made vivid by likening her to her own drawings and paintings, in which there was often a suffusion of yellow light or a figure was seen through a transparent surface. I mention these because one of the yields of doing this kind of exercise is the discovery of a vocabulary that is *particular* to the child: not jargon, not labels, not categorizations or stereotypes, not empty generalizations applicable to virtually anyone and everyone.

I find this kind of recollecting of children refreshing and renewing of my faith in our humanness. I hope you will, too. It is always easy to criticize and find fault with children (or other adults), to point out what they can't do and how problematic they are. It takes more time and patience to paint a fuller picture in which the person is understood to be not the sum of unchanging traits but in process, in the making. Understood as active and open-ended, each of us is at any moment in our lives, and in all taken together, a complex blend of failings and virtues, of strengths and vulnerabilities. It seems to me that this is what makes us interesting and what makes education (and not merely training) a possibility. I hope you will find the time it takes to look at children (and adults) this way worth the patience it requires.

I won't give this letter a formal closing, but simply extend my best to you and to all the children you attend to with care.

———————

ALEXANDRA: Whenever the inevitable talk about the "theory and practice divide" comes up among educators, I feel compelled to talk about Patricia Carini's Descriptive Review of the Child. In my experience, theory becomes powerful and meaningful when I can see it and use it in my practice as an educator, with children and with adults. Theory and practice are therefore not separate, not in conflict, and not on different levels of importance, as some would have us believe. Carini has created a framework, a way of organizing our thinking about a child we wish to know, to study, to learn about, that is at once theoretical and practical.

In my graduate teacher education courses, students find that when they work with Carini's five categories for a Descriptive Review, it helps to reveal holes in their knowledge of the students in their charge, and this makes them work harder to fill in the gaps. For those doing research or child study projects, the Descriptive Review process becomes a tool for talking with peers and colleagues to collectively sort through, for example, puzzling moments of interaction, student work whose meaning is hard to decipher, and personal information revealed in private conversations that may contain helpful clues to knowing more fully the students under study. They tell me that these sharing sessions stand in marked contrast to the typical sessions of professional development they are forced to attend at their schools, because they are talking about something they really care a lot about, and they are working on compelling and challenging cases.

If I could somehow magically mend the rifts that exist between parents and teachers, particularly those that seem to exist for no good reason, I would ask them to read this letter, to talk with each other about the children both care about, to collaborate on painting together the richest portraits imaginable, and to find ways of being, as Carini says, "sensitively attuned to who they are and are becoming" (p. 5) in partnership with each other.

· 2 ·

David Hansen

UNDERSTANDING STUDENTS*

ALEXANDRA: David Hansen, a professor at Teachers College, Columbia University, is the kind of philosophical writer I admire because he works at untangling complex ideas in prose that is clear without being watered down intellectually. Author of The Call to Teach *(1995) and* Exploring the Moral Heart of Teaching: Toward a Teacher's Creed *(2001), his scholarly interests include philosophy of education, moral and ethical issues in educational practice, and teaching and teacher education.*

I have to think hard about issues when I read his writing, but I don't have to go back and reread a sentence three times to figure out if there's something to think about, as is the case with many academic writers. I find I am quickly in agreement with many of his fundamental ideas, found in this article:

- *"At teaching's core is the commitment to serve students' intellectual and moral growth." (p. 19)*
- *"Teachers' regard for students reaches beyond the need to say it but rather materializes in their daily work." (p. 20)*
- *"Being intellectually attentive means getting as close to students' responses to subject matter as time and opportunity afford." (p. 22)*
- *"Each [student] is a unique and unprecedented human being. . . . Each incarnates a distinctive and evolving set of capacities, inclinations, dispositions, and attitudes." (p. 26)*
- *"Teaching and learning are processes of using and developing mind." (p. 28)*

But Hansen's work cannot be reduced to well-phrased aphorisms that might be found in a philosophical fortune cookie. What he does so successfully in this rel-

*From the *Journal of Curriculum and Supervision* 14, no. 2 (1999): 171–185.

atively short piece is link the unique purposes of teaching to the partners of moral and intellectual attentiveness that he argues teachers must work to develop if they are to have meaningful relationships with students that will promote their learning. This attentiveness requires not just watchfully taking note of students but seizing opportunities to help guide them into new territory. As he argues in the case of moral attentiveness, there are two aspects to alertness—to students on the one hand, and to the teachers' own "regard for and treatment of students" (p. 26) on the other.

What I find most provocative about this piece, however, is an idea explored in the final paragraphs. Teachers talk about their students a lot. Often in their talk, they label students, typecasting them in various ways: athletic, sensitive, popular. Hansen explains such classifying as perhaps an entry or "provisional way of 'seeing' a student" (p. 30) and notes that it is virtually impossible for a teacher to be so perfect that he or she can stay abreast of every way in which students are growing and evolving as human beings: "No teacher will ever be so observant that he or she can accurately say: Jane became a patient human being today during third period. However, the teacher can say: Today, in third period, marks the first time I have recognized patience in Jane" (p. 30).

Such a stance requires that teachers be open to revision of initial impressions, and Hansen helps show that moral and intellectual attentiveness are ongoing processes of studying students who are in flux, who change from day to day, and whose personas vary in different contexts. Hansen's ideas give me hope that in the future we might have fewer teachers jumping to conclusions about active children who they feel should be diagnosed as having an attention deficit disorder, or having low expectations of a student whose first language is not English, or writing off a student as having a negative attitude toward school because of a nose ring, dreadlocks, Mohawk, or tattoos.

In the preface to his influential book *Émile*, Jean-Jacques Rousseau exhorts readers to take childhood seriously on its own terms:

> Childhood is unknown. Starting from the false idea one has of it, the farther one goes, the more one loses one's way. The wisest men concentrate on what it is important for men to know without considering what children are in a condition to learn. They are always seeking the man in the child with-

out thinking of what he is before being a man. . . . Begin, then, by studying your pupils better. For most assuredly you do not know them at all.[1]

In the centuries since Rousseau penned these (for his time) revolutionary words, many educators have sought to understand students. They have endeavored to regard girls and boys not as miniature or unformed adults but as developing persons in their own right: persons who, as Rousseau's contemporary Immanuel Kant put it, deserve to be treated as ends in themselves rather than as a means to others' ends.[2] A central part of such treatment is listening to and heeding children's questions, concerns, and ideas. That approach has been made concrete in numerous educational innovations, from kindergartens to child- and student-centered curriculums, which have emerged thanks in part to Rousseau's path-breaking, powerfully argued call.

However, the demand to deal with students as the children and young people they are has presented teachers with a hitherto unimagined problem: addressing what it means to "understand" students in the first place. The question requires careful consideration. If students are not, after all, empty vessels to be filled mechanically with adults' knowledge, then teachers face a complicated intellectual and moral challenge. Every teacher who has hearkened to Rousseau's advice knows something about that challenge. What serious-minded teacher, at any level of the educational system, has not felt at one time or another that her students remain "unknown" to her, to employ Rousseau's term? What teacher has not felt at one point or another that he simply does not understand his students—their conduct, their ways of thinking, their response to subject matter? If experienced practitioners harbor such questions, what about new candidates facing classrooms full of young people for the first time?

Thinking about what it means to understand students can be valuable to teachers. It can help them address a related, and perhaps more visceral, concern that some bring to their work, namely: What kind of relationship should I form with students? Will I like and respect them, and will they like and respect me? Many teachers wonder how close or how distant they should be with students, whether and to what extent they should be friends with them, how much of their personal lives they and their students should disclose, and more. These pertinent and often deeply felt questions attest to teachers' appreciation for the human dimensions of pedagogy that many educators have articulated and embraced during the last two centuries. At the same time, however, such concerns are difficult to address without an awareness of the distinctive aims of teaching—aims that, among other things, distinguish the work from other social endeavors such as doctoring, parenting, counseling, and nursing. Such aims characterize teaching as a unique practice with its own recognizable activities and obligations.

The process of understanding students brings teachers into the heart of the practice. At teaching's core is the commitment to serve students' intellectual and moral growth. That purpose helps give teachers their overall bearings. It provides a vantage point, a place to stand, in determining how to perceive and teach students. Parker Palmer argues that the word *understand* "suggests that we know something by 'standing under' it." Understanding implies "submitting ourselves to something larger than any one of us, something on which we all depend."[3] To use Palmer's terms, understanding students involves depending on the aims of teaching for guidance, rather than seeking a standpoint from outside the practice. It means recognizing that understanding students is necessarily an ongoing, open-ended affair. The process has no terminus because students are always changing as persons, even if such changes may be difficult to detect. As teachers learn how to engage in the process of understanding, issues of personal relationship take on contextualized meanings. Teachers learn to view them through an educational lens rather than through a perspective defined apart from the purposes of the work.

At the center of understanding students is learning how to be intellectually and morally attentive as a teacher. My interest in these forms of attentiveness, and in the larger process of understanding students that these forms serve, derives in part from a study in which I sought to understand the views and practices of four highly regarded teachers who work in an urban setting.[4] I found that the language of *calling*, or *vocation*, helped capture their underlying motivations and conceptions of teaching better than the contemporary languages of *profession*, *occupation*, or *job*. The language of calling illuminates the sustained and deep regard the teachers have for their students, a quality perhaps shared by dedicated practitioners everywhere. Moreover, that quality appears to be more educationally promising than what is suggested by terms like *personal relationship*.

Over the course of several years, during which time I observed more than 40 of each of the teachers' classes, I rarely heard them say explicitly that they liked or respected their students. This is not because they brought an unfriendly or steely-eyed demeanor to their work; they did smile before Christmas! However, based on what I observed in their classrooms, as well as on what I learned from extensive formal and informal conversation with them, I believe the teachers' regard for students reaches beyond the need to *say it* but rather materializes *in* their daily work. It is manifested in their intellectual and moral attentiveness. These allied forms of attentiveness bring to life what it means to understand students.

INTELLECTUAL ATTENTIVENESS IN TEACHING

The question "What are the purposes of teaching?" is obviously too big to come to grips with here. Nevertheless, it must be asked in order to make sense of the idea of understanding students. The brief and admittedly cursory response that follows paves the way for examining the notion of being intellectually attentive as a teacher. The second half of the article addresses its closely related partner, moral attentiveness.

Teaching exists in a distinctive space of questions and concerns about the meaning of becoming human.[5] Teachers do not invent either the questions or the concerns. Posed differently, teachers do not invent the terms of the practice. Rather, they take on these terms; they embrace them, they enact them. For example, teaching entails leading or guiding others to know what they did not know before—the course of historical events or the structure of the solar system. It means helping students to articulate or apprehend what they did not know they knew—for example, elements of logical and persuasive argument that they may have learned unawares through years of talking and playing with friends. Teaching means assisting or coaching others in how to do things they could not do before—for instance, how to prepare a science experiment or how to play a musical instrument. Teaching involves promoting or encouraging attitudes students did not embody before—for example, to enjoy reading or to enjoy discussion with peers rather than just looking for "the answer." Still another term or aspect of teaching is spurring students to reconsider old beliefs in favor of potentially better ones—for example, that they can think for themselves and that they can accomplish things through their own initiative and effort.

These purposes share a common element. They involve drawing or guiding students into new intellectual and moral terrain. Serving as such a guide—Sockett considers teachers to be "guides through difficulty"[6]— obliges the teacher to be intellectually attentive to students. This attentiveness involves teachers becoming as close to students as they possibly can. However, the kind of "closeness" teachers seek with students differs from what they might cultivate with a colleague, a spouse, a son or daughter, a parent, a doctor, a counselor, a pastor, and so forth. Furthermore, this stance does not constitute a middle ground between the intimacies of friendship, on the one hand, and the distances sometimes associated with professionalism, on the other hand.[7] Intellectual attentiveness takes its meaning from the distinctive ground that teachers occupy. That ground renders their work into something other than "helping" young people. Barcena and colleagues argue that

> it is not enough to define the educational relationship as an assistance-based one. The important thing is not merely to be of assistance, but to be of pedagogical assistance. This is what distinguishes an educational relationship from other forms of assistance or help, such as psychological or therapeutic.[8]

Adults can be helpful in many roles—for example, as parents, ministers, nurses, or counselors. But neither parenting, ministering, nursing, nor counseling places both intellectual and moral development at its center in the uniquely formal and public ways that teaching does. In the usual course of events, parents, ministers, nurses, and counselors are not formally responsible for educating other people's children. Teachers are. Moreover, because parents or social workers may have achieved success in their respective endeavors does not automatically imply that they would be successful teachers. Teaching has its own characteristic set of responsibilities and obligations.[9] Consequently, teachers' understanding of students has dimensions of meaning that are different from, although not necessarily antithetical to, the ways in which parents, friends, or counselors might understand those students.

The kind of closeness embedded in the idea of intellectual attentiveness centers around factors that in educational practice are virtually indistinguishable: the subject matter, the classroom setting, and the persons students are becoming. Being intellectually attentive means getting as close to students' responses to subject matter as time and opportunity afford. Those responses can pertain to mathematical understanding, historical or literary interpretation, scientific experiment, artistic creation, or athletic development. Intellectual attentiveness also involves teachers' being alert to aspects of student conduct that influence students' engagement with subject matter. Such aspects include those that enable and support students in using their minds—concentration, signs of emerging confidence, and persistence. Other aspects of student conduct discourage their use of mind—for instance, interrupting others, not taking their time or their energy seriously, and giving way to excessive self-doubt. In short, being intellectually attentive means focusing as closely as the teacher can on what students know, feel, and think about the subject at hand, all with an eye toward their building both knowledge of the world and a sense for how to continue learning about the world.

This process, furthermore, is moral. It entails teachers' care and concern for students in their relation to the subject, not to the teacher per se, and whether or not that relationship is productive and meaningful. The process is intellectual because it presumes the teacher's familiarity with the subject, including its logic and structure. It presupposes a sense of the values that inhere in subject matter. For example, teaching and learning mathematics involve developing qualities of imagination and curiosity.[10] Studying literature includes cultivating disciplined respect for language and for choice of words.[11] Teaching and learning history involve appreciating critically what different people have found important in life.[12] To be intellectually attentive means being alert to the emergence of such qualities of mind in students. This process entails more than teachers' checking whether students have ingested a particular group of facts. It means appreciating that facts are pedagogically relevant in light of students' development of their intellectual capacity and perspective.

At this point, another factor in intellectual attentiveness comes into play: awareness of the persons students are becoming. To understand students, the teacher seeks closeness not solely to the persons they are now, but also the persons they are becoming and are capable of becoming— for example, individuals who can read and write critically, think and act independently, relate efficaciously with others, develop and pursue interests, and more. This awareness does not necessarily mean that teachers must anticipate what students may be like as adults, although that prospect could be relevant, especially with adolescents. To be intellectually attentive means considering the persons students may be becoming in the very next moment. It means being on the lookout for signs of students' incipient interests, strengths, and capacities. It means not just noting such signs but seizing upon them in order to help guide students into new terrain—to come to grips with subject matter and with issues of personal conduct as they bear on learning in social settings like the classroom. This intellectual attentiveness, or closeness, takes its identity not from thinking about issues of personal relationship, but rather from the larger purposes of teaching touched on previously.

Educators have amply documented the knowledge and background teachers need to serve those purposes. In addition to their knowledge of subject matter, teachers' intellectual attentiveness draws on their mindfulness and understanding of psychological, cognitive, cultural, and social aspects of their students' learning. Depending upon the situation, a teacher's lens may be cultural ("I wonder if Rachel seems tense because she's not comfortable with our classroom procedures"), or emotional-developmental ("Now I appreciate our counselor's take on why Alex has such a short fuse"), or cognitive ("Shawn may be struggling simply because she's never been asked to think in the ways these questions lead us to"). More typically, the great variety of pedagogical situations oblige teachers to be open to an always shifting combination of such lenses.

Concern for appropriate "lenses" attests to the fact that what I have been calling intellectual attentiveness involved perception. To attend as closely as one can to students' responses to subject matter literally means being alert and watchful as students tackle various challenges. It means, for example, noting frowns of doubt and confusion, smiles of curiosity and delight, and gestures of resignation or determination. It involves awareness of how students respond to and treat one another, especially with regard to one another's ideas and endeavors. What scholars have called the "enacted curriculum" becomes much richer and deeper as teachers attend to student responses to subject matter.[13] Teachers' perceptions of what students are about and of what is unfolding in the classroom are central to the task of intellectual attentiveness.

MORAL ATTENTIVENESS IN TEACHING

These remarks about the importance of perception provide a bridge to a second, closely connected concept: moral attentiveness. It bears emphasizing that everything said about intellectual attentiveness thus far has moral overtones, with *moral* understood to pertain to what it is good for human beings to do and to be. The purposes of teaching outlined previously are themselves moral as well as intellectual. They are moral because they presuppose that human development is a good thing. They presuppose that a person's life will be better rather than worse for learning the kinds of things teachers are charged with teaching: for example, thoughtful reading, writing, numerating, thinking, and problem solving. Moreover, the qualities of intellectual attentiveness examined above— identifying students' responses to subject matter, seeing what they can and cannot do, and discerning what they think and feel about ideas and activities—all presume a crucial moral disposition on the part of the teacher: the willingness to attend closely to students in the first place. That process can be time consuming ("Robert is so quiet, I still haven't figured out what he's grasping"), fraught with uncertainty ("Am I right to conclude that Diane is an adequate writer given her age and experience?"), and often frustrating ("John acts so confidently, and yet his work is not up to par; I wish I knew how to deal with this"). Because of these facts, being intellectually attentive to students presumes a certain moral tenacity on the part of the teacher, which translates into not giving up on or prejudging young people.

It also presupposes what I want to call moral attentiveness, a term with roots in contemporary moral philosophy and in educational scholarship. Some philosophers have argued that the moral life is more a matter of paying attention to particular contexts and persons than it is a matter of articulating and applying general ethical principles or rules of conduct.[14] Without dismissing the value of considering such principles, these thinkers argue that virtues such as patience, respectfulness, humility, and so forth are more dynamic and decisive in the everyday business of dwelling morally with other human beings. Some educational scholars have recently argued that what they call "moral perception" or "situational appreciation" is crucial to the enactment of morally and intellectually sound teaching.[15] The terms they employ highlight the teacher's capacity and willingness to pay fine-grained attention to classroom contexts and student individuality. *Contemplation*, *discernment*, *disposition*, *orientation*, *sensibility*: this is the language such scholars suggest is indispensable for helping us to understand what serious-minded teachers do.

What does being "morally attentive" to students mean, and why is this concept relevant to teaching? Being morally attentive to students does not entail articulating and then applying a moral theory to one's work in the classroom. Nor does it mean articulating and then applying a set of moral or ethical principles of conduct. At first glance, these claims may seem dubious or discordant. Who can doubt the value of pondering and employing ethical principles when one is genuinely unsure about how to handle a difficult situation? In such circumstances, it can surely be helpful to weigh in a detached fashion principles such as truth-telling and fairness with the likely consequences of choices of action. A number of scholars have demonstrated how this is so when teachers are faced with thorny dilemmas in which every course of action seems to have negative aspects.[16] According to the literature, ethical principles and standards can help a teacher survey his or her choices more comprehensively and intelligently, all with an eye on the desired aim of helping rather than harming students.

However, moral attentiveness pertains not to resolving dramatic classroom or school dilemmas, the kind that both scholars and teachers often emphasize and that seem to invite talk of decontextualized principles. Rather, like its close partner intellectual attentiveness, moral attentiveness takes its meaning from the everyday work of teaching and learning.

Most teachers do not confront eight hours a day of nonstop crisis. Even in challenging institutional settings, the bulk of their classroom time is given over to the ordinary and familiar business of teaching and learning. *That* business is infinitely complex and demanding in its own right, and here moral attentiveness comes into play. Teachers' moral attentiveness has two components: alertness to the development of their students' character, and awareness of their own regard for and treatment of students. These components are so thoroughly intertwined in actual practice that I will examine them together.

Being alert to students' character does not imply that a teacher should bring to the classroom a moral checklist composed of, for example, "liberal" or "conservative" values. Such an approach is exactly the opposite of what is meant by moral attentiveness. Those terms suggest, instead, a recognition on the teacher's part of the nature and limitations of any predefined set of societal values or, in broader terms, of predefined category systems of any kind that might influence how one perceives students. Understanding students ultimately begins where such categories and the perspectives they represent leave off. The historian and social critic Tzvetan Todorov casts the matter this way:

> Reducing the individual to a category is inevitable when one wants to study human beings; when one is interacting with them, however, the practice is dangerous. A category can never stand before me in the flesh; only a person can.[17]

Students are the persons who stand before the teacher. In one way or another, each is a unique and unprecedented human being. Each student has witnessed, heard, and learned things nobody else has. Each incarnates a distinctive and evolving set of capacities, inclinations, dispositions, and attitudes.

Being morally attentive to students means taking seriously these familiar if perhaps easily overlooked realities. Such a stance differs from sentimentalism, which represents a non- or even anti-intellectual orientation toward teaching. That posture is not what Rousseau had in mind in urging educators to take children seriously. However, to echo Rousseau again, nor does such a stance presume that the teacher must be alert for what is morally "lacking" in students. It does not mean measuring stu-

dents' individual character against some preset standard of what respectfulness, for instance, entails as a factor in learning. Like other virtues
such as patience, persistence, open-mindedness, honesty, and courage,
respectfulness can be enacted in many different ways that depend heavily on the particular context. In a school where tardiness is the norm, for
example, it may be a sign of respect for learning when students show up
promptly to class. In another setting, respect may manifest itself more
relevantly, at the moment, in the seriousness with which students take
each other's ideas. Moreover, the meaning of these and other virtues can
evolve as students grow and change. For example, it may have been an
act of courage in September when young Yvonne spoke up in discussion
for the very first time. In March, courage for Yvonne now means attempting to give her first formal presentation to the whole class. For
another student in the same group, Andrew, courage might mean volunteering for the first time in November, and in March serving as a note
taker rather than public speaker. For teachers, being morally attentive
means being mindful that all the young Yvonnes and Andrews in the
classroom are becoming persons of one kind or another, and they are
doing so before teachers' very eyes. This implies that teachers need to
develop eyes for such matters. To cultivate this perceptiveness is less a
matter of articulating abstract principles of moral conduct than it is of
learning to attend to the particulars of students' words and deeds.[18]

I have suggested that a moral quality such as respectfulness can take
many different forms. But, importantly, it cannot take just any form. My
argument is not a brief for an uncritical relativism. On the contrary,
virtues cannot be defined in any way one pleases. Put differently, their
nature presupposes the existence of their opposites: willful lying to others, stealing from them, physically harming them, and so forth.[19] The
cliché notwithstanding, there is no honor among thieves as we typically
employ and esteem the concept of honor. To make the point in dramatic
terms, no serious-minded teacher or student welcomes physical violence
as a "respectful" solution to a disagreement about the interpretation of
a poem or about the correct answer to a test question. In short, although
the actual, living form that the virtues take varies a great deal, they have
a characteristic shape and boundary that makes it possible to discuss
them in the first place.[20]

The virtues also accompany intellectual growth, which is why intellectual and moral attentiveness can be treated separately only for heuristic purposes. For example, patience as an aspect of learning does not exist in an intellectual vacuum. It takes its meaning in contexts such as waiting one's turn to speak, not overlooking crucial steps in an experiment in one's excitement to learn the results, and practicing chords so one can play a guitar piece. But all of those activities, each intellectual in its own right, also do not take place in a vacuum, in this case a moral one. They can only materialize *with* the enactment of patience. The moral quality accompanies the intellectual process, or there will be no such process, period.[21]

Earlier I suggested that intellectual attentiveness means focusing on students' conduct as it facilitates or undermines their learning. In light of the present remarks, such a focus clearly entails moral attentiveness as well. A student who acts *im*patiently may be thwarting his or her opportunities for new educational experience both in the immediate moment and possibly in future ones as well.

UNDERSTANDING STUDENTS AND GROWING AS A TEACHER

Rousseau's appeal to educators to regard children *as* children rather than as unformed or deficient adults has helped trigger an educational revolution over the last several centuries. It has helped create a contemporary ethos in which, unlike in the days when Rousseau wrote, few educators are surprised by talk of "showing concern" for students or of "supporting" students in their learning. It is also no surprise that many of today's teachers approach their work troubled or unsettled by the question "What kind of relationship should I form with students?" In posing that question they are tapping into the notion that teaching is at once both an intellectual and a moral endeavor. Whether mindful of it or not, they are attesting to the fact that teaching and learning involve more than transmitting or ingesting facts. Teaching and learning are processes of using and developing mind. Teaching and learning in classroom settings oblige teachers and students to fashion ways of communicating and interacting. Recent research has shown how morally complicated, ambiguous, but also significant that process can be.[22]

Fortunately, teachers and students do not have to invent ways of communicating out of whole cloth. With the exception of very young children, they bring to the classroom a broad array of expectations about what is supposed to happen in such settings. Nonetheless, each teacher and each group of students must develop their own particular way of communicating. Nobody else can find the way for them. It also holds true that the teacher remains the single most important figure in this process, even if he or she seeks to stay out of the classroom spotlight. Teachers committed to sharing decision making with students, for example, do not abandon teacher authority. Rather, they employ their inherent authority to disperse decision making throughout the classroom.[23] Their willingness to do so is itself a moral stance. Teachers who are concerned about their relationship with students are, perhaps unawares, tuning into these classroom dynamics.

In studying ways of thinking about students, teachers might replace concerns about personal relationship with reflection on the process of understanding them. At the heart of that process is learning to be intellectually and morally attentive to students. As we have seen, these forms of attentiveness accompany one another. Intellectual attentiveness entails closeness to students' responses to subject matter. Moral attentiveness involves closeness to students' responses to opportunities to grow as persons.

Both forms of attentiveness are demanding and difficult to learn, and consequently relate directly to teachers' own development. Intellectual attentiveness draws on teachers' knowledge of subject matter, including knowledge of its logic and structure as well as its relevant facts, and knowledge of psychology, culture, cognition, emotional development, and more. It calls on teachers to be attentive to students' subtle as well as overt responses to subject matter and, more broadly, to the process of learning itself. Moral attentiveness is perhaps even more demanding because it involves pondering and treating students in a larger frame of individuality than the intellectual. Put differently, it calls on teachers to move beyond categories of knowledge bequeathed to them by their education and their formal preparation as teachers. It means attending precisely to what *is* distinctive about individual students, which means that which lies beyond all such categories (although not divorced from them). In this light, moral attentiveness helps contextualize and human-ize teachers' knowledge. It gives teachers a focus for how to make use of their knowledge. Reciprocally, as I have suggested, intellectual atten-tiveness helps orient teachers' moral sensibilities. It helps them move beyond concerns of personal relationship considered in isolation from educational practice.

Teachers at all levels of the system, from preschool through graduate education, cannot help but peg students as thoughtful, unconfident, sprightly, aggressive, well-prepared, unfocused, and so on. Ironically, in light of the argument presented here, this kind of classifying may be necessary as a beginning, provisional way of "seeing" a student. After all, it is impossible for a teacher (or anyone else) to perceive a student's whole character and being and to keep abreast of the often subtle ways they are evolving. No teacher will ever be so observant that he or she can accurately say: Jane became a patient human being today during third period. However, the teacher can say: Today, in third period, marks the first time *I* have recognized patience in Jane. This example underscores the importance of teachers' being open-minded so that they can recognize such growth in the first place. That posture means being willing to pull up the peg, so to speak—to drop an initial impres-sion and to look again. Teachers cannot help but form first impressions, but through the enactment of moral attentiveness they can ensure that these are not final ones. In so doing, they may unknowingly provide stu-dents a moral example, for students are surely as prone as adults are to categorize people.

Open-mindedness, a willingness to change one's views, disciplining oneself to keep focusing on students' learning: these terms describe the teacher's own evolving character as a person. Moral attentiveness de-scribes being observant not just of students' character but also of one's own as teacher. It means being as mindful as possible of how one regards and treats students, both as a group and as individuals. From this point of view, moral attentiveness constitutes a kind of precondition, or dispo-sition, that makes possible giving sustained heed to students' academic learning.

Like its intellectual companion, moral attentiveness also has a tem-poral dimension. It seems to me that both forms of attentiveness are crucial to teaching. Both illuminate what it means to be responsive to ongoing change in students. This is another way of saying that both forms of attentiveness constitute a process, which in this article I have called understanding students. That process has no clear-cut terminus. The end of a school year brings it to a formal close, but even then many teachers continue to ponder some of their students. Moreover, their reflections both during and after the school year fuel their perception and, thereby, their ability to be morally and intellectually attentive with the new students they meet the following year. In short, the more attentive teachers become, the more they end up educating their own perception such that even greater attentiveness becomes possible. What begins as an attempt to understand students becomes, at the same time, a potentially career-long process of the intellectual and moral education of teachers themselves. Understanding students becomes not a means to an end, but an end in its own right, worthy of teachers' very best efforts.

NOTES

1. Jean-Jacques Rousseau, *Émile*, trans. Allan Bloom (New York: Basic Books, 1979 [original work published 1762], 33–34.

2. Immanuel Kant, *Foundations of the Metaphysics of Morals*, trans. Lewis White Beck (Englewood Cliffs, NJ: Prentice Hall, 1990 [original work published in 1785]).

3. Parker Palmer, *To Know as We Are Known* (San Francisco: Harper and Row, 1983), 67.

4. David T. Hansen, *The Call to Teach* (New York: Teachers College Press, 1995).

5. Charles Taylor, *Sources of the Self: The Making of the Modern Identity* (Cambridge, MA: Harvard University Press, 1989), 29, 51.

6. Hugh Sockett, "Education and Will: Aspects of Personal Capability," *American Education* 96 (February 1988): 195–214.

7. For a helpful perspective on this continuum, see Margaret Buchmann and Robert E. Floden, *Detachment and Concern: Conversations in the Philosophy of Teaching and Teacher Education* (New York: Teachers College Press, 1993).

8. Fernando Barcena, Fernando Gil, and Gonzalo Jover, "The Ethical Dimension of Teaching: A Review and a Proposal," *Journal of Moral Education* 22 (Fall 1993): 246.

9. C. J. B. Macmillan and Thomas W. Nelson, eds., *Concepts of Teaching: Philosophical Essays* (Chicago: Rand McNally and Company, 1968); Thomas F. Green, *The Activities of Teaching* (New York: McGraw Hill, 1971).

10. Brent Davis, *Teaching Mathematics: Toward a Sound Alternative* (Hamden, CT: Garland); Magdalene Lampert, "When the Problem Is Not the Question and the Solution Is Not the Answer: Mathematical Knowing and Teaching," *American Educational Research Journal* 27 (Spring 1990): 29–63.

11. Italo Calvino, *Six Memos for the Next Millennium* (Cambridge, MA: Harvard University Press, 1988); Sandra Stotsky, *Connecting Civil Education and Language Education* (New York: Teachers College Press, 1991).

12. R. G. Collingwood, *The Idea of History* (London: Oxford University Press, 1956 [original work published in 1946]); D. Z. Philips, "Is Moral Education Really Necessary?" *British Journal of Educational Studies* 27 (February 1979): 42–56.

13. Anne M. Bussis, Edward A. Chittenden, and Marianne Amarel, *Beyond Surface Curriculum: An Interview Study of Teachers' Understandings* (Boulder, CO: Westview Press, 1976); John I. Goodlad and M. Frances Klein, *Behind the Classroom Door* (Worthington, OH: Charles A. Jones, 1970); Rebecca K. Hawthorne, *Curriculum in the Making: Teacher Choice and the Classroom Experience* (New York: Teachers College Press, 1992); Cynthia Paris, *Teacher Agency and Curriculum Making in Classrooms* (New York: Teachers College Press, 1993); Jon Snyder, Frances Bolin, and Karen Zumwalt, "Curriculum Implementation," in *The Handbook of Research on Curriculum*, ed. Philip W. Jackson (New York: Macmillan, 1992), 402–435.

14. See, for example, Lawrence A. Blum, *Moral Perception and Particularity* (Cambridge, UK: Cambridge University Press, 1994); Iris Murdoch, *The Sovereignty of Good* (London: Ark, 1985 [original work published in 1970]); and Martha Nussbaum, *Love's Knowledge: Essays on Philosophy and Literature* (New York: Oxford University Press, 1990).

15. Margaret Buchmann, "The Careful Vision: How Practical Is Contemplation in Teaching?" *American Journal of Education* 98 (November 1989): 35–61; David C. Bricker, "Character and Moral Reasoning: An Aristolelian Perspective," in *Ethics for Professionals in Education*, ed. Kenneth A. Strike and P. Lance Ternasky (New York: Teachers College Press, 1993), 13–26; James Garrison, *Dewey and Eros: Wisdom and Desire in the Art of Teaching* (New York: Teachers College Press, 1997); Shirley Pendlebury, "Practical Arguments and Situational Appreciation in Teaching," *Educational Theory* 40 (Spring 1990): 171–179.

16. Gary D. Fenstermacher, "The Concepts of Method and Manner in Teaching," in *Effective and Responsible Teaching: The New Synthesis*, ed. Fritz K. Oser, Andreas Dick, and Jean-Luc Patry (San Francisco: Jossey-Bass, 1992), 95–108; Gary D. Fenstermacher and Virginia Richardson, "The Elicitation and Recon-

struction of Practical Arguments in Teaching," *Journal of Curriculum Studies* 25 (March–April 1993): 101–114; Karl D. Hostetler, *Ethical Judgment in Teaching* (Boston: Allyn and Bacon, 1997); Kenneth A. Strike and Jonas F. Soltis, *The Ethics of Teaching* (New York: Teachers College Press, 1985); Kenneth A. Strike and P. Lance Ternasky, eds., *Ethics for Professionals in Education* (New York: Teachers College Press, 1993).

17. Tzvetan Todorov, *Facing the Extreme: Moral Life in the Concentration Camps*, trans. A. Denner and A. Pollak (New York: Henry Holt, 1996 [original work published in 1991]), 161.

18. Compare with Iris Murdoch, *The Sovereignty of Good* (London: Ark, 1985 [original work published in 1970]).

19. Judith N. Shklar, *Ordinary Vices* (Cambridge, MA: Harvard University Press, 1984).

20. Philippa Foot, *Virtues and Vices* (Berkeley: University of California Press, 1978).

21. People can certainly be bullied into doing things, but that is not an "intellectual process" as understood here.

22. See, for example, Deborah L. Ball and Suzanne M. Wilson, "Integrity in Teaching: Recognizing the Fusion of the Moral and the Intellectual," *American Educational Research Journal* 33 (Spring 1996): 155–192; David T. Hansen, "The Emergence of a Shared Morality in a Classroom," *Curriculum Inquiry* 22 (Winter 1992); Philip W. Jackson, Robert E. Boostrom, and David T. Hansen, *The Moral Life of Schools* (San Francisco: Jossey-Bass, 1993); Karne Kozolanka and John Olson, "Life After School: How Science and Technology Teachers Construe Capability," *International Journal of Technology and Design Education* 4 (1994): 209–226; and Magdalene Lampert, "When the Problem Is Not the Question and the Solution Is Not the Answer: Mathematical Knowing and Teaching," *American Educational Research Journal* 27 (Spring 1990): 29–63.

23. John G. Nicholls and Susan P. Hazzard, *Education as Adventure: Lessons from the Second Grade* (New York: Teachers College Press, 1993); Celia Oyler, *Making Room for Students: Sharing Teacher Authority in Room 104* (New York: Teachers College Press, 1996).

MAUREEN: David Hansen, as an educational philosopher, takes a much more theoretical stance than does Patricia Carini in her letter to teachers and parents. He argues for intellectual and moral attentiveness in teaching—moral indicating that which is "good for human beings to do and to be" (p. 24). Central to that endeavor is the need to understand and be close to our students, Hansen reminds us.

In my own teaching, my colleagues and I found it easier to be attentive to students if we cultivated a close personal relationship with the parents as well as the children. We held a meeting for all our parents the first week of school to explain the year's curriculum as well as any procedures or special programs. But we also used that time to talk about ourselves, our goals, our philosophy, our wish to establish a cooperative minicommunity in our upper elementary multiage classroom.

We also asked the parents to help us know their children. A shared perspective of the child at home and at school provides a richer, more accurate, multidimensional portrait. We saw the education of children along a continuum that began in the home and stretched through the school years. We wanted to establish a strong tie to the home and to offer parents a voice in what was occurring at school. We also wanted them to be involved and committed, and we wanted their advice and support. To that end we invited them to actively participate in our program. They taught "minicourses" on writing, sculpture, and foreign language. We had speakers who were firefighters, dental hygienists, and musicians. A pathologist showed us slides of a smoker's lung; a lawyer helped the students put Goldilocks on trial for breaking and entering. The possibilities depended on the parents' expertise. The rewards were a close, personal relationship with all our families. This, in turn, enabled us to embrace our differences as well as our similarities, to share articulated goals, and to celebrate new experiences and understandings.

Hansen's concerns about attentiveness, while directed at teachers with regard to their relationships with students, are equally applicable with regard to teachers' relationships with parents. As adults, we all worry about the same things and we all celebrate the same successes with respect to the children in our lives. We need to share our perspectives.

Vivian Gussin Paley

ON LISTENING TO WHAT THE CHILDREN SAY*

ALEXANDRA: Vivian Paley is a veteran kindergarten teacher from the University of Chicago's Laboratory Schools and a prolific writer of books that bring the classroom to life. She has been a source of inspiration for all educators, not just those in early childhood. Author of over ten books, including White Teacher *(1979) and* Wally's Stories: Conversations in the Kindergarten *(1987), she was awarded a MacArthur Foundation "Genius" award in 1989.*

In this essay from 1986, she explains how a profound change came about in her teaching, a shift from looking for right answers as reassurance she was teaching the children something to listening more carefully to children's ideas and thinking and asking more open-ended questions. What makes Paley's writing resonate with so many is that we can recognize the pitfalls in our inter-actions with children that she so logically explains in her own. It becomes diffi-cult not to agree with her assertion that "real change comes about only through the painful recognition of one's own vulnerability" (p. 38). The tape recorder became her tool of choice for improving her practice because of its "unrelenting fidelity" and the effect it had on revealing her hidden attitudes as well as the children's intriguing world, "containing more vitality, originality, and wide-open potential than could be found in any lesson plan" (p. 40).

Some of Paley's ideas can seem downright radical. For example, she writes of a young boy's confusion about birthdays. After overhearing him say that his mother doesn't have birthdays anymore, she engages in a conversation with him about the topic to uncover his thinking: "Why not just tell Frederick the truth: 'Of course your mother has a birthday; everyone has a birthday.' Tempting as it might be to set the record straight, I have discovered that I can't seem to teach the children that which they don't already know" (p. 42). One might wonder,

*From the *Harvard Educational Review* 56, no. 20 (1986): 122–131.

in light of this statement, if Paley somehow feels the whole enterprise of teaching children that which they don't know is misguided. But I think her intent is rather to look at the way in which the teacher engages in the exchange of ideas. Paley seeks to use the "compelling material" of birthdays to explore Frederick's experiences and perceptions, and to metaphorically weave the threads of his ideas and those of others with her own. She hopes that among the positive consequences will be a building of mutual respect, a sense that everyone has interesting ideas to share, and a curiosity about what those ideas might be. "Children who know others are listening," Paley writes, "may one day become their own critics" (p. 43).

The notion that as educators and parents we must build on, not ignore, our children's ideas, conceptions, and misconceptions reminds me of the countless times I thought my students had grasped a new concept, only to be faced with seemingly mysterious explanations on further probing. If we take Paley's advice to heart, we learn that listening closely moves us in the right direction of deciphering the mystery.

Many of my students describe profound changes in their teaching after reading Paley's writing. One of my graduate students, Margaret Warncke, wrote of Paley's influence on her thinking in her research project, in which she was studying group learning in science. She was interested in connecting words that came out in dialogue to the reality of her students' lives, and sometimes their attitudes tested her patience:

> *I can still hear one of my fifth-grade girls ask me, "Do you have a problem with that?" I returned it with a rather sarcastic response. There is a world waiting to be discovered in a dialogue, no matter how offhand it may seem. I am going to return with her to that moment to ask her what she meant by those words, maybe to discover that world that is hers.*

Maybe Paley can help us all to see that discovery is a participatory act, that confusion is natural and fuels our curiosity, and that connections can lead to meaning making.

———————

Years ago, when I was a young woman in New Orleans, I led a Great Books discussion group that met at the public library. The participants came from many occupations and educational backgrounds, and they were all older and more experienced than I. Whatever advantage I had was contained in the lists of questions provided by the Great Books people, who also sent along the following directive: There are no right or wrong answers. Get everyone talking and then find connections—person-to-person, person-to-book.

The advice was sound: do the required reading, ask most of the questions, and manage to connect a number of the ideas that arise at each meeting. Unfortunately, I did not fare too well; something was missing from my performance—a simple ingredient called *curiosity*. I was not truly interested in the people sitting around the table or curious about what they might think or say. Mainly, I wanted to keep the discussion moving and to avoid awkward silences.

Soon after leading these discussions, I became a kindergarten teacher. In my haste to supply the children with my own bits and pieces of neatly labeled reality, the appearance of a correct answer gave me the surest feeling that I was teaching. Curriculum guides replaced the lists of questions, but I still wanted most of all to keep things moving with a minimum of distraction. It did not occur to me that the distractions might be the sounds of children thinking.

Then one year a high school science teacher asked if he could spend some time with my kindergarteners. His first grandchild was about to enter nursery school, and he wondered what it would be like to teach the youngest students in our school. Once a week he came with paper bags full of show-and-tell, and he and the children talked about a wide range of ordinary phenomena. As I listened, distant memories stirred. "You have a remarkable way with children, Bill," I told him. "They never tire of giving you their ideas, and somehow you manage to use them all, no matter how far off the mark."

"The old Socratic method," he said. "I was a Great Books leader once up in Maine. It seems to work as well with kindergarteners as with my seniors."

Of course. That was exactly what he was doing. He asked a question or made a casual observation, then repeated each child's comment and hung onto it until a link was made to someone else's idea. Together they were constructing a paper chain of magical imaginings mixed with some solid facts, and Bill was providing the glue.

But something else was going on that was essential to Bill's success. He was truly curious. He had few expectations of what five-year-olds might say or think, and he listened to their responses with the anticipation one brings to the theater when a mystery is being revealed. Bill was interested not in what he knew to be an answer, but only in how the children intuitively approached a problem. He would whisper to me after each session, "Incredible! Their notions of cause and effect are incredible!" And I, their teacher, who thought I knew the children so well, was often equally astonished.

I began to copy Bill's style whenever the children and I had formal discussions. I practiced his open-ended questions, the kind that seek no specific answers but rather build a chain of ideas without the need for closure. It was not easy. I felt myself always waiting for the right answer—my answer. The children knew I was waiting and watched my face for clues. Clearly, it was not enough simply to copy someone else's teaching manner; real change comes about only through the painful recognition of one's own vulnerability.

A move to a new school in another city and an orientation speech given by Philip Jackson shook me up sufficiently to allow the first rays of self-awareness to seep in. He described a remarkable study done by two Harvard psychologists, Robert Rosenthal and Lenore Jacobson, who deliberately supplied several teachers with misleading information about their students.[1] In random fashion, children were labeled bright or slow by means of fictitious IQ scores. The teachers, I was shocked to find out, consistently asked more questions, waited longer for answers, and followed up more often with additional comments when they were speaking to a "smart" child.

I was shocked because I knew that one of those unsuspecting teachers could have been me, although certainly I listened more to myself than to *any* of the children in the classroom. Suddenly, I was truly curious about my role in the classroom, but there were no researchers ready to set up an incriminating study to show me when—and perhaps why—I consistently veered away from the child's agenda. Then I discovered the tape recorder and knew, after transcribing the first tape, that I could become my own best witness.

The tape recorder, with its unrelenting fidelity, captured the unheard or unfinished murmur, the misunderstood and mystifying context, the disembodied voices asking for clarification and comfort. It also captured the impatience in *my* voice as children struggled for attention, approval, and Justice. The tape recordings created for me an overwhelming need to know more about the process of teaching and learning and about my own classroom as a unique society to be studied.

The act of teaching became a daily search for the child's point of view accompanied by the sometimes unwelcome disclosure of my hidden attitudes. The search was what mattered—only later did someone tell me it was research—and it provided an open-ended script from which to observe, interpret, and integrate the living drama of the classroom.

I began using the tape recorder to try to figure out why the children were lively and imaginative in certain discussions, yet fidgety and distracted in others ("Are you almost finished now, teacher?"), wanting to return quickly to their interrupted play. As I transcribed the daily tapes, several phenomena emerged. Whenever the discussion touched on fantasy, fairness, or friendship ("the three Fs" I began to call them), participation zoomed upward. If the topic concerned, for example, what to do when all the blocks are used up before you can build something or when your best friend won't let you play in her spaceship, attention would be riveted on this and other related problems: Is it fair that Paul always gets to be Luke Skywalker and Ben has to be the bad guy? And, speaking of bad guys, why should the wolf be allowed to eat up the first two pigs? Can't the three pigs just stay home with their mother?

These were urgent questions, and passion made the children eloquent. They reached to the outer limits of their verbal and mental abilities in order to argue, explain, and persuade. No one moved to end the discussion until Justice and Reason prevailed.

After the discussion, a second, more obvious truth emerged. If the tape recorder was left running, what I replayed later and dutifully transcribed became a source of increasing fascination for me. The subjects that inspired our best discussions were the same ones that occupied most of the free play. The children sounded like groups of actors, rehearsing spontaneous skits on a moving stage, blending into one another's plots, carrying on philosophical debates while borrowing freely from the fragments of dialogue that floated by. Themes from fairy tales and television cartoons mixed easily with social commentary and private fantasies, so that what to me often sounded random and erratic formed a familiar and comfortable world for the children.

In fact, the children were continually making natural connections, adding a structure of rules and traditions according to their own logic. They reinvented and explained the codes of behavior every time they talked and played, each child attempting in some way to answer the question, What is going on in this place called school, and what role do I play?

"Let's pretend" was a stronger glue than any preplanned list of topics, and the need to make friends, assuage jealousy, and gain a sense of one's own destiny provided better reasons for self-control than all my disciplinary devices. A different reality coexisted beside my own, containing more vitality, originality, and wide-open potential than could be found in any lesson plan. How was I to enter this intriguing place, and toward what end would the children's play become my work?

The tape recorder revealed that I had already joined the play. I heard myself always as part of the scene, approving, disapproving, reacting to, being reacted to. The question was not *how* would I enter but, rather, *what* were the effects of my intervention? When did my words lead the children to think and say more about their problems and possibilities, and when did my words circumvent the issue and silence the actors? When did my answers close the subject?

Once again, the decisive factor for me was curiosity. When my intention was limited to announcing my own point of view, communication came to a halt. My voice drowned out the children's. However, when they said things that surprised me, exposing ideas I did not imagine they held, my excitement mounted and I could feel myself transcribing their words even as they spoke. I kept the children talking, savoring the uniqueness of responses so singularly different from mine. The rules of teaching had changed; I now wanted to hear the answers I could not myself invent. IQ scores were irrelevant in the realms of fantasy, friendship, and fairness where every child could reach into a deep wellspring of opinions and images. Indeed, the inventions tumbled out as if they simply had been waiting for me to stop talking and begin listening.

Later, teaching at a nursery school, I found that the unanticipated explanations of younger children bloomed in even greater profusion. The crosscurrents of partially overheard talk lifted my curiosity to new

heights. It was similar to watching the instant replay of an exciting baseball moment. Did the runner really touch second base? Did Frederick
actually say, "My mother doesn't have no more birthdays"? What does a
four-year-old mean by this odd statement made in the doll corner? The
next day I am pressed to find out.

"Frederick, I'm curious about something I heard you say in the doll
corner yesterday. You said your mother doesn't have birthdays anymore."
(Frederick knows my tendency to begin informal conversations in this manner, and he responds immediately.)

"She doesn't. How I know is no one comes to her birthday and she
doesn't make the cake."

"Do you mean she doesn't have a birthday *party*?"

"No. She really doesn't have a *birthday*."

"Does she still get older every year?"

"I think so. You know how much old she is? Twenty-two."

"Maybe you and your dad could make her a birthday party."

"But they never remember her birthday and when it's her birthday
they forget when her birthday comes, and when her birthday comes they
forget how old she is because they never put any candles. So how can we say
how she is old?

"The candles tell you how old someone is?"

"You can't be old if you don't have candles."

"Frederick, I'll tell you a good thing to do. Ask Mother to have a cake
and candles. Then she'll tell you when her birthday is."

"No. Because, see, she doesn't have a mother so she doesn't have a
birthday."

"You think because your grandma died your mother won't have any
more birthdays?"

"Right. Because, see, my grandma borned her once upon a time. Then
she told her about her birthday. Then every time she had a birthday my
grandma told. So she know how many candles to be old."

I turn to Mollie. "Frederick says his mother doesn't have any more
birthdays."

"Why doesn't she?" Mollie wants to know.

"Because," Frederick answers patiently, "because my grandma died
and my mother doesn't know how many candles old she is."

"Oh. Did your grandfather died, too?"

"Yeah. But he came back alive again."

Mollie stares solemnly at Frederick. "Then your grandma told him. If he whispers it to your mother maybe it's already her birthday today."

"Why should he whisper, Mollie?" I ask.

"If it's a secret," she says.

"I think Mollie has a good idea, Frederick. Why don't you ask your grandfather?"

"Okay, I'll tell him if my mommy could have a birthday on that day that they told her it was her birthday."

Why not just tell Frederick the truth: "*Of course* your mother has a birthday; everyone has a birthday." Tempting as it might be to set the record straight, I have discovered that I can't seem to teach the children that which they don't already know.

I had, in fact, made this very statement—that everyone has a birthday—the previous week in another context. I had brought a special snack to school to celebrate my own birthday, and Frederick and Mollie seemed surprised.

"Why?" they asked.

"Why did I bring the cookies?"

"Why is it your birthday?"

"But everyone has a birthday. Today happens to be mine."

"Why *is* it your birthday?" Mollie insisted, attempting to give more meaning to her question by emphasizing another word.

"Well, I was born on this day a long time ago."

The conversation ended and we ate the cookies, but clearly nothing was settled. Their premises and mine did not match. What, for instance, could it possibly mean to be born on *this* day a long time ago?

A week later, Frederick made cause and effect out of the presence of one's own mother and the occasion of a birthday. The matter is not unimportant, because the phenomenon of birthday looms large. It is constantly being turned around and viewed from every angle, as are the acts of going to bed, going to work, cooking meals, shooting bad guys, calling the doctor or the babysitter—to name just a few of the Great Ideas present in the preschool.

Every day someone, somewhere in the room, plays out a version of "birthday." Birthday cakes are made of Play-Doh and sand, and it is Superman's birthday or Care Bear's birthday or Mollie's birthday. "Birthday" is a curriculum in itself. Besides being a study in numbers, age, birth, and death, it provides an ongoing opportunity to explore the three Fs—fantasy, friendship, and fairness.

"You can't come to my birthday if you say that!"

"You *could* come to my birthday, and my daddy will give you a hundred pieces of gum if you let me see your Gobot."

Any serious observation made out of a birthday is worth following up, not in order to give Frederick the facts and close the subject, but to use this compelling material as a vehicle for examining his ideas of how the world works. If I am to know Frederick, I must understand, among many other things, how he perceives his mother's birthday and his grandfather's permanence.

As the year progresses I will pick up the threads of these and other misconceptions and inventions in his play, his conversation, his story-telling, and his responses to books and poems. He will make connections that weave in and out of imagined and real events, and I will let my curiosity accompany his own as he discards old stories and creates new ones.

My samples of dialogue are from the kindergarten and nursery school, the classes I teach. But the goal is the same, no matter what the age of the student; someone must be there to listen, respond, and add a dab of glue to the important words that burst forth.

The key is curiosity, and it is curiosity, not answers, that we model. As we seek to learn more about a child, we demonstrate the acts of observing, listening, questioning, and wondering. When we are curious about a child's words and our responses to those words, the child feels respected. The child *is* respected. "What are these ideas I have that are so interesting to the teacher? I must be somebody with good ideas." Children who know others are listening may begin to listen to themselves, and if the teacher acts as the tape recorder, they may one day become their own critics.

Reading between the lines is both easier and harder when the setting is preschool. It is easier because young children rehearse their lines over and over in social play and private monologues, without self-consciousness; older children have already learned to fear exposing their uncommon ideas. On the other hand, the young child continually operates from unexpected premises. The older student's thinking is closer to an adult's and easier to fathom: the inevitability of birthdays is not an issue in the third grade, and the causal relationship between age and candles has long since been solved. Yet, third graders and high school students struggle with their own set of confusions, fantasies, and opinions that need to be listened to, studied, compared, and connected.

The fact that the thoughts of the teacher and student are furthest apart in preschool makes it a fruitful place for research and practice in the art of listening to what children say and trying to figure out what they mean. My curiosity keeps me there, for I still cannot predict what children of three and four will say and do. One must listen to them over long periods of time. Being their teacher provides me the rare luxury of living with my subjects for two years. Like a slow-motion Polaroid developing its images, piece by piece, over many months, the children's patterns of thought and speech need much time to be revealed.

An early conversation with a group of three-year-olds convinced me that these were the children who would best prove my assumption that the first order of reality in the classroom is the student's point of view, for here the pathways to knowledge lead directly through the doll corner and the building blocks. For me this is where the lessons are to be found.

Carrie has her own version of hide-and-seek, in which she pretends to hide and pretends to seek. She hides a favorite possession, then asks a teacher to help her find it. She pretends to look for it as she takes the teacher directly to the missing item. "Oh, here's my dolly's brush!" she squeals delightedly. All these games resist the unknown and the possibility of loss. They are designed to give the child control in the most direct way.

Sometimes, however, the child has no control; something is really missing. Then the threes are likely to approach the problem as if the question is "What is *not* missing?" This is exactly what happens when I try to direct the children's attention to an empty space in the playground. Over the weekend, an unsafe climbing structure has been removed. The doll corner window overlooks the area that housed the rickety old frame.

"See if you can tell what's missing from our playground?" I ask.

"The sandbox."

"The squirrely tree."

"The slide."

"But I can *see* all those things. They're still in the playground. Something else was there, something very big, and now it's gone."

"The boat."

"Mollie, look. There's the boat. I'm talking about a big, brown wooden thing that was right there where my finger is pointing."

"Because there's too much dirt."

"But what was on top of the place where there's too much dirt?"

"It could be grass. You could plant grass."

Libby and Samantha, four-year-olds, see us crowded around the window and walk over to investigate. "Where's the climbing house?" Libby asks. "Someone stole the climbing house."

"No one stole the house, Libby. We asked some men to take it down for us. Remember how shaky it was? We were afraid somebody would fall."

The threes continue staring, confused. I should have anticipated their response and urged that the structure be dismantled during school hours.[2]

If my words contain more stories than theories, it may be that I have taken on the young child's perspective, which seems to be organized around the imperative of *story*. I am still listening to what the children say, but since the younger children disclose more of themselves as characters in a story than as participants in a discussion, I must now follow the plot as carefully as the dialogue. School begins to make sense to the children when they pretend it is something else. And teaching, in a way, makes sense to me when I pretend the classroom is a stage and we are all actors telling our stories.

We do more than tell our stories; we also act them out. The formal storytelling and acting that often arise out of and run parallel to the children's fantasy play have become a central feature of our day. The children's stories form the perfect middle ground between the children and me, for they enable us to speak to one another in the same language.

Much to my surprise, when I moved from the kindergarten to the nursery school, I found that the storytelling and acting were accepted with equal enthusiasm as the natural order, for nearly everything there takes on more recognizable shape in fantasy.

If, in the world of fantasy play, four- and five-year-olds may be called characters in search of a plot, then the three-year-old is surely a character in search of a character.

Place this three-year-old in a room with other threes, and sooner or later they will become an acting company. Should there happen to be a number of somewhat older peers about to offer stage directions and dialogue, the metamorphosis will come sooner rather than later. The dramatic images that flutter through their minds, as so many unbound stream of consciousness novels, begin to emerge as audible scripts to be performed on demand.[3]

Possibilities for connecting play and outside events are fleeting, but the teacher who listens carefully has many opportunities to apply the glue. In the following episode, Mollie joins the older girls for a pretend valentine party in the doll corner. Here the play is more real to her than the actual event to come. My task is to help Mollie connect the doll corner reality to the classroom celebration—quite different from the usual procedure of connecting *my* reality to a classroom celebration. This is the doll corner version of the holiday.

"Ding-dong. Ring-ring."

"Come in. Who is it?"

"Trick or treat valentine."

"Don't say trick or treat to our house. The baby is sleeping. Don't ring the bell."

"I'm making valentines for the baby. 'I love you.' This spells 'I love you.'"

"Teacher, can you write 'I love you' on my baby valentines? This is my valentine to get married and have a baby. This is Valentine's Day."

"Are you having a valentine party?" I ask Mollie.

"It's the baby's birthday valentine. I'm giving everyone whoever is nice a valentine."

When Valentine's Day arrives Mollie is surprised that her picture valentines are meant to be given away.

"But Mollie, that's why your mother bought them. You're supposed to give one to each child."

"No, it's for me," Mollie insists, starting to cry. "It says M-O-L-L-I-E."

"Mother wrote your name so the children will know they're from you."

She cries vigorously. "I have to bring them home. My mommy said."

"Okay, Mollie. Let's put them back in the box."

Instantly the tears stop. "I'm telling a valentine story and it has a monkey climbed a tree. Then he fell down on a cushion. Then another monkey came."

"Which is the part about Valentine's Day?"

"The part about the monkey climbed a tree." Mollie looks at her box of valentines, then at the table filled with lacy red hearts. Today's event is controlled by others; she can think only of a monkey climbing a tree.

The image of the doll corner valentine party suddenly fills my mind and I gather the children around me. "I have a valentine story for us to act out. Once upon a time there was a valentine family with a mother, father, sister, brother, and baby. They were all busy making valentines because it was Valentine's Day and the baby's birthday also. 'We have to write "I love you" and give them to all the nice animals who ring our bell,' they said. Ring-ring. Who is it? It's the four bears. Good. Here's your valentines. Ring-ring. Who is it? It's the four squirrels. Oh, good. Here's your valentines. Ring-ring. Who is it? It's the four elephants. Oh, very good. Here's your valentines. Ring-ring. Who is it? It's the four rabbits. Oh, very, very good. Here's your valentines. And all you animals must bring your valentines to the baby's birthday valentine party."

Mollie jumps up. "Wait a minute. I'm the sister. I have to get my valentines. I'm supposed to give them to the animals."

Mollie has an entree into the holiday. Moments earlier she was an outsider, just as she was, in fact, to school itself during the first few weeks. She worked her way to an understanding of school through the same doll corner fantasies that now illuminate Valentine's Day. And I, the outsider to three-year-old thinking, am learning to listen at the doll corner doorway for the sounds of reality.[4]

A month later, Mollie tells her own valentine story. "Once a time the valentines came to a little girl that was Fire Star. It was her birthday that day they came. Her real birthday."

"And was it also the real Valentine's Day?" I ask.

"It *was* the real valentine's birthday and also the real Fire Star and also the pretend Fire Star."

Mollie struggles with the idea of a real and pretend Fire Star. She will attempt to explain this enigma to herself and others as she acts it out, and my questions will not always be of help. Often, in fact, my questions fall flat or add to the confusion. At such times, my expectations and those of the children may be too far apart—or the children *think* they are too far apart.

The children cannot always figure out the adults' relation to fantasy play. What powers do we possess that might affect the outcome? Can we, for instance, hear the children's thoughts?

"Why is Leslie doing that?" Mollie asks me. Leslie is her baby sister.

"Doing what?" I ask.

"Crying in my head. Did you listen?"

"Mollie, I can't hear the sounds in your head," I reply.

"Margaret, can you hear Leslie crying in my head?" Mollie asks.

"Yeah, I hear her crying in your house," Margaret says.

"She wants milk from her mama, that's why," Mollie informs her.

"I already knew that," Margaret nods.

I must have misread the question. Did Mollie want me to imagine that Leslie was crying? What do the children think about adults' literal approach to events? . . . Such is the concern, I think, when I unexpectedly appear at the door of the doll corner during a hospital drama.

"Come here, nurse," Libby says impatiently to Mollie. "Come here and undress the baby."

"Are you the mother?" Mollie asks.

"Yes, and Peter is the doctor. I'm sick too. Hurry, put the medicine on me. I cut my knee. Put on the stitches, doctor. Look in my mouth. Say you see bumps. Put us in the x-ray."

"Sh! There's the teacher." Mollie points to me as I pass by. "What if she calls this the doll corner?"

"She can't see us. We're in the hospital. It's far away downtown."

"Sh! She'll think it's the doll corner."

"Get inside the hospital. We're getting far away so she doesn't know where the hospital is."[5]

The vivid image of her sister crying and the equally graphic hospital scene present Mollie with a similar worry. Does the teacher understand the nature of the fantasy and, if not, to what extent do the fantasy and its players exist? When Mollie was two, she did not perceive the boundaries of these internal pictures; by the time she is six, she will know what can be seen and heard by others. But now she may sometimes flounder in doubt between her reality and mine.

So often I drift around on the edge of their knowing without finding a place to land. Here, for example, is a peanut butter and jelly tale that continues to perplex me.

Of the eight children at my snack table, six ask for peanut butter and jelly on their crackers, one wants plain peanut butter, and one, plain jelly. My question: What did I make more of, peanut butter and jelly or plain peanut butter? The children stare at me blankly and no one answers.

"What I mean is, did more people ask for peanut butter and jelly or did more want plain peanut butter?" Silence. "I'll count the children who are eating peanut butter and jelly." I count to six. "And only Barney has peanut butter."

"Because Barney likes peanut butter," Mollie explains.

"Yes, but did I make more sandwiches that have both peanut butter and jelly?"

"Because we like peanut butter *and* jelly," Frederick responds patiently.

My question has misfired again and this time I can imagine several possible reasons. Since everyone is eating peanut butter and/or jelly, the entire group is included in the peanut butter and jelly category. In addition, "more" could refer to those who asked for more than one sandwich. Perhaps the word "plain" is the stumbling block or they may think I want to know why they chose peanut butter with or without jelly.

Another possibility: Peanut butter and jelly may be akin to Peter and the Wolf, in that the words are not easily separated. Thus, "peanut butter and jelly" also represents plain peanut butter or plain jelly.

. . . I anticipate the obvious response, but the children do not follow my thinking. Perhaps at another time they might have accidentally linked their images to mine. Of one thing I am certain: had I put my inquiries into dramatic form and given us roles to play, I would have been understood.[6]

Tomorrow we *will* act it out, but probably not with peanut butter and jelly. Images tend to stay fixed for a long time in the young child's mind. No matter. The proper message has come across: confusion—mine or theirs—is as natural a condition as clarity. The natural response to confusion is to keep trying to connect what you already know to what you don't know.

Next time the children and I may be on the same track, and meanwhile we are getting valuable practice in sending signals. As anyone who attends the theater knows, clues and signals are given all along the way, but the answers are never revealed in the first act. The classroom has all the elements of theater, and the observant, self-examining teacher will not need a drama critic to uncover character, plot, and meaning. We are, all of us, the actors trying to find the meaning of the scenes in which we find ourselves. The scripts are not yet fully written, so we must listen with curiosity and great care to the main characters who are, of course, the children.

NOTES

1. Rosenthal and Jacobson, *Pygmalion in the Classroom: Teacher Expectations and Pupils' Intellectual Development.* (New York: Holt, Rinehart & Winston, 1968).

2. Vivian Gussin Paley, *Mollie is Three* (Chicago: University of Chicago Press, 1986), 69–70. Many of the excerpts from *Mollie is Three* do not conform to the original text. The author has taken the liberty of adding a word or phrase to clarify the extracted passages.

3. Paley, *Mollie is Three*, xvi.

4. Paley, *Mollie is Three*, 92–94.

5. Paley, *Mollie is Three*, 102–103.

6. Paley, *Mollie is Three* 91–92.

———

MAUREEN: *Vivian Gussin Paley investigated her own teaching for a number of years and rewarded us with elegant accounts of her conversations with very young children. She has helped us understand the relationship between research and teaching in a particular classroom context and at a particular time.*

Her work helps us to think about the complicated interactions among parents and teachers and children and to uncover the multiple meanings that are being constructed in many homes and classrooms. At a time when even in preschool and kindergarten children are asked to begin the tedious process of mastering the rudiments of reading, writing, and arithmetic by performing pencil and paper tasks, it is especially refreshing to eavesdrop on a classroom that values the imaginative world of play, where dressing in costumes or examining the wonders of nature provoke engaging discussions.

Paley poses questions about fantasy, fairness, and friendship, three areas of interest to her students that produced conversations involving all the children. Because they were passionate about their opinions, their eloquence soared: "They reached to the outer limits of their verbal and mental abilities in order to argue, explain, and persuade. No one moved to end the discussion until Justice and Reason prevailed" (p. 39).

Taping conversations, as Paley did, gives both parents and teachers the opportunity to uncover children's thinking and the chance to reflect on our own ability to question in such a way as to awaken critical and reflective thinking in the young. Beginning teachers tape lessons that they analyze for the quality of their questioning as well as for the kinds of support and feedback they provide for students during a class discussion. Parents might experiment with the taping of stories, both those they read and those composed by children. Paley has demonstrated the complexities of teaching and learning by sharing her taped transcripts. She enables us as parents and teachers to more effectively analyze and evaluate the problems encountered in the education of young children.

· 4 ·

Loris Malaguzzi

NO WAY. THE HUNDRED IS THERE.*

ALEXANDRA: Loris Malaguzzi was a highly esteemed educational philosopher who founded the network of early childhood schools that the municipality of Reggio Emilia in northern Italy started in 1963. He created a quiet revolution whose influence has slowly spread globally. He helped to develop early childhood practices premised on a relatively simple notion—that children have a hundred languages, a repertoire of expressive outlets and tools. Consequently, the schools he helped found provide inviting opportunities for children to explore their world and to tell others about what they discover in their hundred languages. They talk, play, act, dance, sing, paint, draw, sculpt, construct, observe, and record from the time they are babies (literally!). By the time the children are in preschool, adults visiting the schools are incredulous at their creations and find it hard to believe there has been no adult intervention in creating these works of art. The truth is the adults who teach and learn with these children are some of the most extraordinary educators in the world, who pair up in the classroom to help each other carefully watch, listen, and document what happens when the children are given the freedom to pursue their interests and develop their abilities.

Malaguzzi's poetic prose asks us to ponder ways in which we ask children "to think without hands" and tell them that "work and play . . . do not belong together" (pp. 53, 54). Perhaps then we can begin to imagine schools in which children are not imprisoned all day in desks and chairs, a fifteen-minute recess their only chance for play.

---

*From *The Hundred Languages of Children* (catalog of the exhibition), ed. Reggio Children (Reggio Emilia, Italy: Reggio Children, 1996), 3.

Invece il cento c'é.

ll bambino
è fatto di cento.
ll bambino ha
cento lingue
cento mani
cento pensieri
cento modi di pensare
di giocare e di parlare
cento sempre cento
modi di ascoltare
di stupire di amare
cento allegrie
per cantare e capire
cento mondi
da scoprire
cento mondi
da inventare
cento mondi
 da sognare.
ll bambino ha
 cento lingue
(e poi cento cento
    cento)
ma gliene rubano novantanove.
La scuola e la cultura
gli separano la testa dal corpo.
Gli dicono:
di pensare senza mani
di fare senza testa
di ascoltare e di non parlare
di capire senza allegrie
di amare e di stupirsi
solo a Pasqua e a Natale.

No Way. The Hundred Is There.*

The child
is made of one hundred.
The child has
a hundred languages
a hundred hands
a hundred thoughts
a hundred ways of thinking
of playing, of speaking
A hundred always a hundred
ways of listening
of marveling of loving
a hundred joys
for singing and understanding
a hundred worlds
to discover
a hundred worlds
to invent
a hundred worlds
to dream.
The child has
a hundred languages
(and a hundred hundred hundred
    more)
but they steal ninety-nine.
The school and the culture
separate the head from the body.
They tell the child:
to think without hands
to do without head
to listen and not to speak
to understand without joy
to love and to marvel
only at Easter and Christmas.
They tell the child:

*translated by Lella Gandini

Gli dicono:
di scoprire il mondo che già c'è
e di cento
gliene rubano novantanove.
Gli dicono:
che il gioco e il lavoro
la realtà e la fantasia
la scienza e l'immaginazione
il cielo e la terra
la ragione e il sogno
sono cose
che non stanno insieme.

Gli dicono insomma
che il cento non c'è.
ll bambino dice:
invece il cento c'è.

to discover the world already there
and of the hundred
they steal ninety-nine.
They tell the child:
that work and play
reality and fantasy
science and imagination
sky and earth
reason and dream
are things
that do not belong together.

And thus they tell the child
that the hundred is not there.
The child says:
No way. The hundred is there.

———————

MAUREEN: A hundred languages? Yes, certainly. Perhaps a thousand.

The minute one walks into the Anna Frank School in Reggio Emilia, it is apparent that this school is radically different from those we are accustomed to visiting in the United States. Three things set it apart: the use of space, the availability of materials, and the artistic representations of the children's activity.

There is the immediate impression of openness. Although there are areas sectioned off for various activities, there is no definition of teacher's space versus children's space. Everything is in sight and nothing is out of reach. Immediately the welcoming warmth and the open arrangement of equipment draw visitors in. There is a communal space for social interaction, including a couch for parents with magazines and articles to peruse or just to sit for a chat. There is a huge castle construction for dramatic play and a great wooden ship for long voyages on imaginative seas. There are cartons of caps, canes, and capes for all kinds of dramatic play. There are mirrors to practice characterization or just to try on new faces. There are inviting corners everywhere for smaller groups to gather for more private conversation.

There are bookcases and storage boxes filled with paints, papers, tools, and other raw materials. The students have been taught to use the materials properly and purposefully; everything is carefully sorted, arranged, and immediately available for all. Instead of the standard items manufactured for school use, there are boxes and boxes of acorns, pine cones, dried leaves, stones, sticks, berries—all objects in nature, carefully collected by the children, saved for potential works of art.

And then there are the displays. The products of the workshops are everywhere: large murals of group work, carefully assembled collages of the natural world, imaginative drawings of animals, insightful self-portraits (painted after careful scrutiny in the mirrors), abstract ceramic structures, all carefully exhibited in niches and corners to inspire and amuse both the inhabitants and the visitors. This is an incredible example of an ideal learning environment where children have infinite possibilities, opportunities, and means to express themselves.

What can we learn from this? The flow of plastic toys from super stores for children can diminish, if not deaden, a child's own creativity. Children demand them under the influence of mass media advertising, and adults buy them only to watch with disappointment as their appeal fades rapidly. Instead we can introduce our children to nature and the joy of collecting interesting and beautiful examples of found treasures. We can urge and participate in spontaneous dramatic play that mimics daily life or dramatizes the favorite tales and myths we have read aloud as a family. We can fill the kitchen sink almost to overflowing to permit water explorations as young children reenact familiar family cleaning chores. We can awaken the dormant imagination of children and provide aesthetic experiences to open windows into the realm of the imagination. Then we most certainly will begin to hear, see, and touch the hundred languages of children.

SUGGESTED RESOURCES AND FURTHER READING

For more information on the Descriptive Review, Prospect, and the school's archives, see http://www.prospectcenter.org.

For information about the municipal schools of Reggio Emilia, see Reggio Children at http://zerosei.comune.re.it and the North American Reggio Emilia Alliance (NAREA) at http://www.reggioalliance.org. A noteworthy collaboration between researchers at Harvard's Project Zero and educators from Reggio Emilia resulted in the book *Making Learning Visible: Children as Individual and Group Learners* (Reggio Emilia, Italy: Reggio Children and Project Zero, 2001).

■ PART II ■

WHAT'S WORTH LEARNING?

In this next section we have assembled essays that take a very different approach to the problems of subject matter and content than prescribing what knowledge should be pursued at different grade levels. Rather than attempting to be comprehensive, we chose writers who help show how difficult it is to separate the issues of the disciplines and the pursuit of knowledge from issues of students and teaching. Often they also show how trying to neatly compartmentalize subjects so that they can be learned one at a time creates artificial boundaries that can be shattered by children's questions and inquiries. The authenticity of students' sense making comes when experiences in the world outside the classroom are brought to bear on lessons pursued inside the classroom. The inverse is also true, for parents and friends can help children further inquiries begun at school.

5

Maxine Greene

ART AND IMAGINATION:
RECLAIMING THE SENSE OF POSSIBILITY*

MAUREEN: Maxine Greene, the William F. Russell Professor Emerita in the Foundations of Education at Teachers College, Columbia University, may be the most influential American philosopher of the century. She has written many wonderful books, including Teacher as Stranger *(1973) and* Releasing the Imagination: Essays on Education, the Arts, and Social Change *(1995), and she continues to write and teach in her New York apartment, where scholars from around the world come to visit and exchange ideas with her. In this sense, she embodies her work, for as she so perceptively reminds us, she is not yet what she is becoming. She is also Philosopher in Residence at the Lincoln Center Institute for the Arts in Education. The philosophical descendant of John Dewey, whose work appears in part 5 of this book, she has far exceeded his influence. Like Dewey, she is not a philosopher in an ivy-covered tower. She cares passionately about teachers, our students, our classrooms. She cares too about the spaces we inhabit and challenges us to enliven and enrich them by a constant search for new possibilities. Greene has helped thousands of teachers to appreciate the aesthetic dimensions of their lives and the lives of their students. Her emphasis on awakening the imagination, dismantling barriers to creative thinking, and freeing children to make intelligent choices has had a profound impact on American education.*

During a visit to my school many years ago, we asked her what she considered the essential characteristics of a teacher. Without a moment's hesitation she enumerated seven: integrity, courage, critical and creative thinking, solicitude, autonomy, a capacity for indignation, and a tolerance for ambiguity. I quickly made note of them on a scrap of paper as she spoke, and after thirtysome years I still carry that yellowing list in my wallet.

*From *Phi Delta Kappan* 76, no. 1 (1995): 378–382.

Maxine, as she is known, is a brilliant teacher. When I studied with her at Columbia University, I marveled at her ability to make all her students feel as if their contributions to the discussion were of great moment. In addition to her compelling lectures and her activism in the schools, she is a role model in other ways. She is a voracious reader, has a passion for the arts—concerts, theater, movies, museums, and dance. To listen to her speak is a magnificent journey through the labyrinth of her thought, a splendid voyage of discovery and redis- covery of what we know, what we think we might know, and connections and re- lationships of which we never dreamed. She is a founder of the Lincoln Center Institute, and a special New York City school for the arts. Her books, articles, and papers fill my bookshelves, and though I've read almost all she has written, I keep rereading her work because she is so inspirational. She has been my best friend and my beloved teacher for over forty years. Each time we talk, whether at a class, at a conference, over dinner, or on the telephone, I am left with new ques- tions, new possibilities, new areas of discovery, and most especially, with new in- sights into the human experience. It was hard to decide what to include in this volume that might best represent the breadth of her thinking, the voracity of her reading, and the magnitude of her understanding of the human heart.

In these times, more than a decade after this article was written, it seems es- pecially pertinent to ponder her thoughts on standards and norms and the role of the arts in helping young people to find multiple meanings and alternative possibilities. Are we helplessly at the mercy of administrators who establish meaningless norms because they are uneasy with their inability to control? Can encounters with the arts "move the young to imagine, to extend, and to renew," as Maxine urges?

The existential contexts of education reach far beyond what is conceived of in Goals 2000.* They have to do with the human condition in these often desolate days, and in some ways they make the notions of world- class achievement, benchmarks, and the rest seem superficial and lim- ited, if not absurd. They extend beyond the appalling actualities of family breakdown, homelessness, violence, and the "savage inequalities" de-

---

*The Goals 2000: Educate America Act was signed into law on March 31, 1994, by President Clinton. Many believe it to be the predecessor of the No Child Left Behind Act, which was signed into law on January 8, 2002.

scribed by Jonathan Kozol, although social injustice has an existential dimension.

Like their elders, children and young persons inhabit a world of fearful moral uncertainty—a world in which it appears that almost nothing can be done to reduce suffering, contain massacres, and protect human rights. The faces of refugee children in search of their mothers, of teenage girls repeatedly raped by soldiers, of rootless people staring at the charred remains of churches and libraries may strike some of us as little more than a "virtual reality." Those who persist in looking feel numbed and, reminded over and over of helplessness, are persuaded to look away.

It has been said that Pablo Picasso's paintings of "weeping women" have become the icons of our time.[1] They have replaced the statues of men on horseback and men in battle; they overshadow the emblems of what once seemed worth fighting for, perhaps dying for. When even the young confront images of loss and death, as most of us are bound to do today, "it is important that everything we love be summed up into something unforgettably beautiful."[2] This suggests one of the roles of the arts. To see sketch after sketch of women holding dead babies, as Picasso has forced us to do, is to become aware of a tragic deficiency in the fabric of life. If we know enough to make those paintings the objects of our experience, to encounter them against the background of our lives, we are likely to strain toward conceptions of a better order of things, in which there will be no more wars that make women weep like that, no more bombs to murder innocent children. We are likely, in rebelling against such horror, to summon up images of smiling mothers and lovely children, metaphors for what ought to be.

Clearly, this is not the only role of the arts, although encounters with them frequently do move us to want to restore some kind of order, to repair, and to heal. Participatory involvement with the many forms of art does enable us, at the very least, to see more in our experience, to hear more on normally unheard frequencies, to become conscious of what daily routines, habits, and conventions have obscured.

We might think of what Pecola Breedlove in *The Bluest Eye* has made us realize about the meta-narrative implicit in the Dick and Jane basal readers or in the cultural artifact called Shirley Temple, who made so many invisible children yearn desperately to have blue eyes.[3] We might recall the revelations discovered by so many through an involvement with *Schindler's List*. We might try to retrieve the physical consciousness of unutterable grief aroused in us by Martha Graham's dance "Lamentation," with only feet and hands visible outside draped fabric—and agony expressed through stress lines on the cloth. To see more, to hear more. By such experiences we are not only lurched out of the familiar and taken-for-granted, but we may also discover new avenues for action. We may experience a sudden sense of new possibilities and thus new beginnings.

The prevailing cynicism with regard to values and the feelings of resignation it breeds cannot help but create an atmosphere in the schools that is at odds with the unpredictability associated with the experience of art. The neglect of the arts by those who identified the goals of Goals 2000 was consistent with the focus on the manageable, the predictable, and the measurable. There have been efforts to include the arts in the official statements of goals, but the arguments mustered in their favor are of a piece with the arguments for education geared toward economic competitiveness, technological mastery, and the rest. They have also helped support the dominant arguments for the development of "higher-level skills," academic achievement, standards, and preparation for the workplace.

The danger afflicting both teachers and students because of such emphases is, in part, the danger of feeling locked into existing circumstances defined by others. Young people find themselves described as "human resources" rather than as persons who are centers of choice and evaluation. It is suggested that young people are to be molded in the service of technology and the market, no matter who they are. Yet, as many are now realizing, great numbers of our young people will find themselves unable to locate satisfying jobs, and the very notion of "all the children" and even of human resources carries with it deceptions of all kinds. Perhaps it is no wonder that the dominant mood in many classrooms is one of passive reception.

Umberto Eco, the Italian critic of popular culture, writes about the desperate need to introduce a critical dimension into such reception. Where media and messages are concerned, it is far more important, he says, to focus on the point of reception than on the point of transmis-

sion. Finding a threat in "the universal of technological communication" and in situations where "the medium is the message," he calls seriously for a return to individual resistance. "To the anonymous divinity
of Technological Communication, our answer could be: 'Not thy, but
our will be done.'"[4]

The kind of resistance Eco has in mind can best be evoked when
imagination is released. But, as we well know, the bombardment of images identified with "Technological Communication" frequently has the
effect of freezing imaginative thinking. Instead of freeing audiences to
look at things as if they could be otherwise, present-day media impose
predigested frameworks on their audiences. Dreams are caught in the
meshes of the salable; the alternative to gloom or feelings of pointless-
ness is consumerist acquisition. For Mary Warnock, imagination is
identified with the belief that "there is more in our experience of the
world than can possibly meet the unreflecting eye."[5] It tells us that experience always holds more than we can predict. But Warnock knows
that acknowledging the existence of undiscovered vistas and perspectives requires reflectiveness. The passive, apathetic person is all too
likely to be unresponsive to ideas of the unreal, the as if, the merely possible. He or she becomes the one who bars the arts as frivolous, mere
frills, irrelevant to learning in the postindustrial world.

It is my conviction that informed engagements with the several arts
would be the most likely way to release the imaginative capacity and
give it play. However, this does not happen automatically or "naturally."
We have all witnessed the surface contacts with paintings when groups
of tourists hasten through museums. Without time spent, without tu-
toring, and without dialogue regarding the arts, people merely seek the
right labels. They look for the artists' names. There are those who
watch a ballet for the story, not for the movement or the music; they
wait for Giselle to go mad or for the Sleeping Beauty to be awakened or
for the white swan to return.

Mere exposure to a work of art is not sufficient to occasion an aesthetic experience. There must be conscious participation in a work, a
going out of energy, an ability to notice what is there to be noticed in
the play, the poem, the quartet. "Knowing about," even in the most formal academic manner, is entirely different from creating an unreal world

imaginatively and entering it perceptually, affectively, and cognitively. To introduce people to such engagement is to strike a delicate balance between helping learners to pay heed—to attend to shapes, patterns, sounds, rhythms, figures of speech, contours, lines, and so on—and freeing them to perceive particular works as meaningful. Indeed, the inability to control what is discovered as meaningful makes many traditional educators uneasy and strikes them as being at odds with conceptions of a norm, even with notions of appropriate "cultural literacy." This uneasiness may well be at the root of certain administrators' current preoccupation with national standards.

However, if we are to provide occasions for significant encounters with works of art, we have to combat standardization and what Hannah Arendt called "thoughtlessness" on the part of all of those involved. What she meant by thoughtlessness was "the heedless recklessness or hopeless confusion or complacent repetition of 'truths' which have become trivial and empty."[6] There is something in that statement that recalls what John Dewey described as a "social pathology"—a condition that still seems to afflict us today. Dewey wrote that it manifests itself "in querulousness, in impotent drifting, in uneasy snatching at distractions, in idealization of the long established, in a facile optimism assumed as a cloak."[7] Concerned about "sloppiness, superficiality, and recourse to sensations as a substitute for ideas," Dewey made the point that "thinking deprived of its normal course takes refuge in academic specialism."[8]

For Arendt, the remedy for this condition is "to think what we are doing." She had in mind developing a self-reflectiveness that originates in situated life, the life of persons open to one another in their distinctive locations and engaging one another in dialogue. Provoked by the spectacle of the Nazi Adolf Eichmann, Arendt warned against "clichés, stock phrases, adherence to conventional, standardized codes of expression and conduct, which have, she said, "the socially recognized function of protecting us against reality, that is, against the claim on our thinking attention that all events and facts make by virtue of their existence."[9] She was not calling for a new intellectualism or for a new concentration on "higher-order skills." She was asking for a way of seeking clarity and authenticity in the face of thoughtlessness, and it seems to me that we might ask much the same thing if we are committed to the release of the imagination and truly wish to open the young to the arts.

Thoughtfulness in this sense is necessary if we are to resist the messages of the media in the fashion Eco suggests, and it is difficult to think of young imaginations being freed without learners finding out how to take a critical and thoughtful approach to the illusory or fabricated "realities" presented to them by the media. To be thoughtful about what we are doing is to be conscious of ourselves struggling to make meanings, to make critical sense of what authoritative others are offering as objectively "real."

I find a metaphor for the reification of experience in the plague as it is confronted in Albert Camus' novel. The pestilence that struck the town of Oran (submerged as it was in habit and "doing business") thrust most of the inhabitants into resignation, isolation, or despair. Gradually revealing itself as inexorable and incurable, the plague froze people in place; it was simply there. At first Dr. Rieux fights the plague for the most abstract of reasons: because it is his job. Only later, when the unspeakable tragedies he witnesses make him actually think about what he is doing, does he reconceive his practice and his struggle and talk about not wanting to be complicit with the pestilence. By then he has met Tarrou, who is trying to be a "saint without God" and who has the wit and, yes, the imagination to organize people into sanitary squads to fight the plague and make it the moral concern of all.

Tarrou has the imagination too to find in the plague a metaphor for indifference or distancing or (we might say) thoughtlessness. Everyone carries the microbe, he tells his friend; it is only natural. He means what Hannah Arendt meant—and Dewey and Eco and all the others who resist a lack of concern. He has in mind evasions of complex problems, the embrace of facile formulations of the human predicament, the reliance on conventional solutions—all those factors I would say stand in the way of imaginative thinking and engagement with the arts. "All the rest," says Tarrou, "health, integrity, purity (if you like)—is a product of the human will, of a vigilance that must never falter." He means, of course, that we (and those who are our students) must be given opportunities to choose to be persons of integrity, persons who care.

Tarrou has a deep suspicion of turgid language that obscures the actualities of things, that too often substitutes abstract constructions for concrete particulars. This is one of the modes of the thoughtlessness Arendt was urging us to fight. She, too, wanted to use "plain, clear-cut language." She wanted to urge people, as does Tarrou, to attend to what is around them, "to stop and think." I am trying to affirm that this kind of awareness, this openness to the world, is what allows for the consciousness of alternative possibilities and thus for a willingness to risk encounters with the "weeping women," with Euripides' Medea, with *Moby-Dick*, with Balanchine's (and, yes, the Scripture's) *Prodigal Son*, with Mahler's *Songs of the Earth*.

Another novel that enables its readers to envisage what stands in the way of imagination is Christa Wolf's *Accident: A Day's News*. It moves me to clarify my own response to the technical and the abstract. I turn to it not in order to add to my knowledge or to find some buried truth, but because it makes me see, over the course of time, what I might never have seen in my own lived world.

The power the book holds for me may be because it has to do with the accident at Chernobyl, as experienced by a woman writer, who is also a mother and grandmother. She is preoccupied by her brother's brain surgery, taking place on the same day, and by the consequences of the nuclear accident for her grandchildren and for children around the world. She spends no time wondering about her own response to such a crisis; her preoccupation is with others—those she loves and the unknown ones whom she cannot for a moment forget. It is particularly interesting, within the context of an ethic of care, to contain for a moment within our own experience the thoughts of a frightened young mother, the narrator's daughter, picturing what it means to pour away thousands of liters of milk for fear of poisoning children while "children on the other side of the earth are perishing for lack of those foods."

The narrator wants to change the conversation and asks her daughter to "tell me something else, preferably about the children." Whereupon she hears that "the little one had pranced about the kitchen, a wing nut on his thumb, his hand held high. Me Punch. Me Punch. I was thrilled by the image."[10] Only a moment before, another sequence of pictures had come into her mind and caused her to

> admire the way in which everything fits together with a sleepwalker's precision: the desire of most people for a comfortable life, their tendency to believe the speakers on raised platforms and the men in white coats; the addiction to harmony and the fear of contradiction of the many seemed to

correspond to the arrogance and hunger for power, the dedication to profit, unscrupulous inquisitiveness, and self-infatuation of the few. So what was it that didn't add up in this equation?[11]

This passage seems to me to suggest the kind of questioning and, yes, the kind of picturing that may well be barred by the preoccupation with "world-class achievement" and by the focus on human resources that permeate Goals 2000.

But it does not have to be so. Cognitive adventuring and inquiry are much more likely to be provoked by the narrator's question about "this equation" than by the best of curriculum frameworks or by the most responsible and "authentic" assessment. To set the imagination moving in response to a text such as Wolf's may well be to confront learners with a demand to choose in a fundamental way between a desire for harmony with its easy answers and a commitment to the risky search for alternative possibilities.

Wolf's narrator, almost as if she were one of Picasso's weeping women, looks at the blue sky and, quoting some nameless source, says, "Aghast, the mothers search the sky for the inventions of learned men."[12] Like others to whom I have referred, she begins pondering the language and the difficulty of breaking through such terms as "half-life," "cesium," and "cloud" when "polluted rain" is so much more direct. Once again, the experience of the literary work may help us to feel the need to break through the mystification of technology and the language to which it has given rise.

The narrator feels the need to battle the disengagement that often goes with knowing and speaking. When she ponders the motives of those who thought up the procedures for the "peaceful utilization of nuclear energy," she recalls a youthful protest against a power plant and the rebukes and reprimands directed at the protesters for their skepticism with regard to a scientific utopia. And then she lists the activities that the men of science and technology presumably do not pursue and would probably consider a waste of time if they were forced to:

Changing a baby's diapers. Cooking, shopping with a child on one's arm or in the baby carriage. Doing the laundry, hanging it up to dry, taking it down, folding it, ironing it, darning it. Sweeping the floor, mopping it, polishing it, vacuuming it. Dusting. Sewing. Knitting. Crocheting. Embroidering. Doing the dishes. Doing the dishes. Taking care of a sick child. Thinking up stories to tell. Singing songs. And how many of these activities do I myself consider a waste of time?[13]

Reading this passage and posing a new set of questions, we cannot but consider the role of such concrete images in classroom conversation and in our efforts to awaken persons to talk about what ought to be. The narrator believes that the "expanding monstrous technological creation" may be a substitute for life for many people. She is quite aware of the benevolent aspects of technology: her brother, after all, is having advanced neurosurgery (which he does survive). But she is thinking, as we might well do in the schools, about the consequences of technological expansion for the ones we love. Her thinking may remind us of how important it is to keep alive images of "everything we love." I want to believe that by doing so we may be able to create classroom atmospheres that once again encourage individuals to have hope.

This brings me back to my argument for the arts, so unconscionably neglected in the talk swirling around Goals 2000. It is important to make the point that the events that make up aesthetic experiences are events that occur within and by means of the transactions with our environment that situate us in time and space. Some say that participatory encounters with paintings, dances, stories, and the rest enable us to recapture a lost spontaneity. By breaking through the frames of presuppositions and conventions, we may be enabled to reconnect ourselves with the processes of becoming who we are. By reflecting on our life histories, we may be able to gain some perspective on the men in white coats, even on our own desires to withdraw from complexity and to embrace a predictable harmony. By becoming aware of ourselves as questioners, as makers of meaning, as persons engaged in constructing and reconstructing realities with those around us, we may be able to communicate to students the notion that reality depends on perspective, that its construction is never complete, and that there is always more. I am reminded of Paul Cézanne's several renderings of Mont St. Victoire and of his way of suggesting that it must be viewed from several angles if its reality is to be apprehended.

Cézanne made much of the insertion of the body into his landscapes, and that itself may suggest a dimension of experience with which to ground out thinking and the thinking of those we teach. There are some who suggest that, of all the arts, dance confronts most directly the question of what it means to be human. Arnold Berleant writes that

> in establishing a human realm through movement, the dancer, with the participating audience, engages in the basic act out of which arise both all experience and our human constructions of the world. . . . [That basic act] stands as the direct denial of that most pernicious of all dualisms, the division of body and consciousness. In dance, thought is primed at the point of action. This is not the reflection of the contemplative mind but rather intellect poised in the body, not the deliberate consideration of alternative courses but thought in process, intimately responding to and guiding the actively engaged body.[14]

The focus is on process and practice; the skill in the making is embodied in the object made. In addition, dance provides occasions for the emergence of the integrated self. Surely, this ought to be taken into account in our peculiarly technical and academic time.

Some of what Berleant says relates as well to painting, if painting is viewed as an orientation in time and space of the physical body—of both perceiver and creator. If we take a participatory stance, we may enter a landscape or a room or an open street. Different modes of perception are asked of us, of course, by different artists, but that ought to mean a widening of sensitivity with regard to perceived form, color, and space. Jean-Paul Sartre, writing about painting, made a point that is significant for anyone concerned about the role of art and the awakening of imagination:

> The work is never limited to the painted, sculpted or narrated object. Just as one perceives things only against the background of the world, so the objects represented by art appear against the background of the universe. . . . [T]he creative act aims at a total renewal of the world. Each painting, each book, is a recovery of the totality of being. Each of them presents this totality to the freedom of the spectator. For this is quite the final goal of art: to recover this world by giving it to be seen as it is, but as if it had its source in human freedom.[15]

In this passage Sartre suggests the many ways in which classroom encounters with the arts can move the young to imagine, to extend, and to renew. And surely nothing can be more important than finding the source of learning not in extrinsic demands, but in human freedom.

All of this is directly related to developing what is today described as the active learner, here conceived as one awakened to pursue meaning. There are, of course, two contradictory tendencies in education today: one has to do with shaping malleable young people to serve the needs of technology in a postindustrial society; the other has to do with educating young people to grow and to become different, to find their individual voices, and to participate in a community in the making. Encounters with the arts nurture and sometimes provoke the growth of individuals who reach out to one another as they seek clearings in their experience and try to live more ardently in the world. If the significance of the arts for growth, inventiveness, and problem solving is recognized at last, a desperate stasis may be overcome, and people may come to recognize the need for new raids on what T. S. Eliot called the "inarticulate."

I choose to end this extended reflection on art and imagination with some words from "Elegy in Joy," by Muriel Rukeyser:

> Out of our life the living eyes
> See peace in our own image made,
> Able to give only what we can give:
> Bearing two days like midnight. "Live,"
> The moment offers: the night requires
> Promise effort love and praise.
>
> Now there are no maps and no magicians.
>
> No prophets but the young prophet, the sense of the world.
>
> The gift of our time, the world to be discovered.
>
> All the continents giving off their several lights,
> the one sea, and the air. And all things glow.[16]

These words offer life; they offer hope; they offer the prospect of discovery; they offer light. By resisting the tyranny of the technical, we may yet make them our pedagogic creed.

NOTES

1. Judi Freeman, *Picasso and the Weeping Women* (Los Angeles: Los Angeles Museum of Art, 1994).

2. Michel Leiris, "Faire-part," in E. C. Oppler, ed., *Picasso's Guernica* (New York: Norton, 1988), 201.

3. Toni Morrison, *The Bluest Eye* (New York: Washington Square Press, 1970), 19.

4. Richard Kearney, *The Wake of Imagination* (Minneapolis: University of Minnesota Press, 1988), 382.

5. Mary Warnock, *Imagination* (Berkeley: University of California Press, 1978), 202.

6. Hannah Arendt, *The Human Condition* (Chicago: University of Chicago Press, 1958), 5.

7. John Dewey, *The Public and Its Problems* (Athens, OH: Swallow Press, 1954), 170.

8. Ibid., 168.

9. Hannah Arendt, *Thinking*: vol. 2, *The Life of the Mind* (New York: Harcourt Brace Jovanovich, 1978), 4.

10. Christa Wolf, *Accident: A Day's News* (New York: Farrar, Straus & Giroux, 1989), 17.

11. Ibid.

12. Ibid., 27.

13. Ibid., 31.

14. Arnold Berleant, *Art and Engagement* (Philadelphia: Temple University Press, 1991), 167.

15. Jean-Paul Sartre, *Literature and Existentialism* (New York: Citadel Press, 1949), 57.

16. Muriel Rukeyser, "Tenth Elegy: An Elegy in Joy," in idem., *Out in Silence: Selected Poems* (Evanston, IL: TriQuarterly Books, 1992), 104.

ALEXANDRA: One thing teacher education programs generally do not prepare teachers for is handling local, national, even global tragedies in the class-

room. While horrifying images—such as those that took over the media during the Columbine school shooting or during the tragic events of September 11th—are seen by children in television and in print, their parents and teachers are largely left to their own ingenuity when it comes to helping children process the meaning of those images. Certainly a primary concern is reassuring a frightened child, but what if multiple exposure to senseless violence in television, movies, and video games leaves a child indifferent to these horrors? I was shocked to discover this pattern in my class of sixth graders in Seattle the day after the Oklahoma City bombing in April of 1995. This article by Maxine Greene helped me overcome feelings of despair and moved me to action.

Experiences in the arts, particularly in drama and visual art, enabled my students to, as she says, see more, hear more, to be wide awake. In addition to their own creative experiences, students benefited from reflecting on the meanings they derived from works of art. For example, we went on a field trip to see an art installation entitled Witness *by contemporary artist Beliz Brother in the Seattle Art Museum. A greenhouselike glass and steel structure curving from the floor to the ceiling was filled with glass panes, some painted white, others painted with a photographic transfer technique to show pictures and fragments of pictures from the Civil War. Lining the back wall in a single row were other medical record photographs of wounded soldiers, calmly displaying their injuries to the camera. After viewing the piece, students sat in focused concentration around the floor to write about feelings evoked by the piece, and by the artist's use of photographs from the Civil War, which they had been studying at the time. Julia wrote, "This touches me in my heart, seeing everybody lying dead from the war. This is a piece of Americans fighting Americans, thinking they were enemies."*

More than a decade later, some would say that things are bleaker than ever. The uncontrollable spread of AIDS, war and genocide, unending chaos in the Middle East, and closer to home, the unforgettable devastation of Hurricane Katrina all conspire to overwhelm us, and so, it seems to me, we seek refuge in the mind-numbing dramas of "reality television" and the sugary pop star dreams of American Idol. *In a recent visit to the Smithsonian American Art Museum, I encountered the powerful work of Alabama artist William Christenberry. A quote from the artist was displayed above a sculpture evoking figures from the Ku Klux Klan. "My work is who I am, what I am about, and what I feel deeply about. This is my way, meager as it might be, to deal with evil." With funding cuts for the arts and for arts education threatening to endanger the cultural future of our society, we should all heed Maxine's call to "confront learners with a demand to choose in a fundamental way between a desire for harmony with its easy answers and a commitment to the risky search for alternative possibilities" (p. 67).*

6

Caroline Pratt

TRIAL FLIGHT*

ALEXANDRA: I stumbled upon Caroline Pratt's book I Learn from Chil-dren *in my mother's collection of old education books in the basement one sum-mer. I was so startled by the wisdom contained in those pages that I had to double-check the publication date. Caroline Pratt founded City and Country School in 1914 in New York City's Greenwich Village. The school, known for its progressive approach, is still in existence today, and Pratt is also well known for designing the wooden unit blocks used in classrooms and day-care centers. Educators are often so eager to embrace the next new thing that they tend to overlook important history. But there is much to be learned from Pratt's early progressive experimentation and observation of young children. Convinced that the "children learn to work harmoniously with each other . . . if there is little or no adult interference" (p. 80), Pratt had faith in allowing children's innate methods of learning by playing to freely evolve when given space and adaptable materials.*

Children have a natural need to invent stories and see them come to life, but nowadays when they are bombarded with multimedia storytelling and are asked to use their imaginations less and less, the adult's role in supporting and encouraging their curiosity has never been more important. Dolls, blocks, dress-up clothes, and plastic dinosaurs are being replaced with video shooting games and superhero cartoons that neglect an essential of human development— wondering what if? Children's natural desire to learn through experimenta-tion and creative play can be thwarted by an overdose of passively taking in information. Pratt reminds us to resist the urge to answer children's questions, and instead to find ways to "let the child find the answers himself" (p. 79).

*From I Learn from Children: An Adventure in Progressive Education (New York: Simon & Schuster, 1948).

I had thought so much about what I wanted to do that I had to take whatever opportunity was offered to see it in action.

So, with whatever restrictions, I had my floor space. Next was the crucial point in my plan, the materials. Crayons and paper, scissors and paste were obvious. What I sought was something so flexible, so *adaptable*, that children could use it without guidance or control. I wanted to see them build a world; I wanted to see them re-create on their own level the life about them, in which they were too little to be participants, in which they were always spectators.

I knew children yearned to do this, and did it whenever they were allowed, with whatever materials they could lay their hands on. They moved dining-room chairs together to make trains; they set up housekeeping on the beach and baked pies out of sand; they towed coal barges of shingles laden with pebbles. And I had seen children playing with blocks at Teachers College, when the gifted Patty Hill had charge of the Kindergarten there.

She had designed the blocks herself, for the children in her classes to use during their free periods. They were not a part of her teaching program, but I had watched what the children had done with them during those short play periods when they could do what they liked. To me those play periods seemed the most important part of the school day.

Of all the materials which I had seen offered to children ("thrust upon" would better fit the situation), these blocks of Patty Hill's seemed to me best suited to children's purposes. A simple geometrical shape could become any number of things to a child. It could be a truck or a boat or the car of a train. He could build buildings with it from barns to skyscrapers. I could see the children of my as yet unborn school constructing a complete community with blocks.

But would they? There was something more they needed, a body of information. The little railroader on the nursery floor had evidently picked up information about railroads from observation and experience, and his wise parents had left him free to digest what he had seen, to take it into himself, and then to translate it into physical terms which he could handle. He had been allowed the freedom to gather together whatever he needed to reproduce in his own way what he knew. He was reconstructing a part of his world in which he was most interested.

Just as he had learned to walk and to talk by experiment, he was now carrying his method on to new fields of learning. He was learning about the world, thinking about it, reasoning about it, accepting this, rejecting that, putting it together and making it work.

Children have quite a body of information, more than adults generally guess. I am not talking about information which has been told them or read to them and which, parrotlike, they repeat, to the admiration of the same misguided adults. I mean the information which they have gained by their own efforts, firsthand, often unconsciously. What the groceryman and the milkman bring, what goes on inside the home, in the street or, for country children, on the farm—all this is most exciting knowledge, unless they have been sidetracked by having read to them stories of such sensational content that everything they are familiar with seems tame.

The child is already possessed of a method of learning, which served him well in babyhood. And he has gathered for himself a small body of related information. He needs only opportunity to go on with his education.

That "the proper study of mankind is man" he does not need to be told. He has been studying it since the day he was born. But he studies it in his own way, by experiencing it with his own eyes and ears and muscles. He makes a train of dining-room chairs so that he can be a locomotive engineer; like his grown-up counterpart, he watches signals and curves, toots the whistle, rings the bell, stops for water, for coal, for passengers. He is himself the train as well as the man who runs it, as well as the whistle and the chuffing steam and the bell, and his performance is accurate and realistic in proportion to his knowledge and experience of trains. He could not make these sounds and movements, he could not feel the imaginary motion of his chair-train in his own body, if he had merely been told about trains and shown pictures of them. But if he has ridden in trains, watched the locomotive come into the station, seen the engineer leaning out of his cab—then, in his play, he can create a train for himself to run. In his play he is no longer an onlooker merely; he is a part of the busy world of adults. He is practicing to take his place in that world when he is grown. He is getting his education.

With this faith in children and what they would do if freed to do it, I went forth into the neighborhood of Hartley House to look for pupils for my trial school. I knew the neighborhood and had no trouble finding half a dozen likely five-year-olds. My choice was carefully made; I had been given only two months for my experiment, too little time to prove anything except with responsive youngsters. Those who already looked at the world will dulled eyes would take a little longer than the time I had to spend with them.

I invited my chosen six to come and play at Hartley House, and when they came on the first Monday morning I was ready for them. There were the blocks I had had made, and toys I had designed and made myself; there were crayons and paper, and there was clay. I had laid them out carefully so the children would not only see them, but could go and take what they wanted without asking. Nothing was out of their reach; everything was visible, accessible, and theirs for the taking. I had planned my display like a salesman, thinking of everything I knew about my small customers: anticipating the short reach of little arms, the tendency of piled-up objects to fall down and frighten a shy child away, the reluctance of a small child to hunt for something he needs. I made it all as easy and inviting as I knew how, and then I stood aside and let them forage for themselves.

The preliminary shufflings and scufflings were suspenseful minutes for me. So anxious was I, waiting for Marjory, finger in mouth, to cry; for Alice and Joseph to come to terms over a box of bright crayons, that I did not see what Michael was doing until he was well started.

Michael had apparently made straight for the blocks, recognizing them at once as just the thing he needed, for when I caught up with him he had already begun to lay out a city street. He built houses, horse-stables (this was, remember, more than thirty years ago!), and brought into his scheme all sorts of things which he had already stored up in his own brief experience.

I couldn't have asked for a more appropriate demonstration of my belief in the serious value of children's play. Michael was so deeply absorbed, so purposeful in his construction, that he might have been a scientist

working out an experiment in a laboratory. The likeness was no accident. He was precisely that, on his own level. He was not merely pushing
blocks around; he was not even merely learning what could be done with
blocks. With blocks to help him, he was using all his mental powers, reasoning out relationships—the relation of the delivery wagon to the store,
the coal cart loaded from the barge in the river and carrying its load to
the home—and he was drawing conclusions. He was learning to think.

In time several of the other children caught on to what Michael was
doing. Although the trial period was too short for all of them to develop
such freedom as his, his very concentration made him the focal point of
the room. Joseph began to build a house on Michael's street; he who had
fought Alice for a box of crayons one day voluntarily handed over a
wooden man to drive Michael's coal wagon; eventually they were planning a firehouse together. Marjory gave up crying and got herself a toy.
Constructions of one sort or another began to spring up at various
places on the floor. Some of the children took more readily to crayons
and clay, but all of them were busy at something. Quarrels flared and
died, rarely needing arbitration. The work in hand was too absorbing to
brook interruption for long.

When the busy minds slowed down and the work stalled for lack of
information, we had ways of getting started again. We might sit around
on the floor—what part of it was left clear—and discuss, and out of the
children's storehouses of memory would come more facts and more relationships. Or we could go out into the street and make our own discoveries about the interesting everyday life around us.

How much those five-year-olds taught me in two short months!
With my heart filled with gratitude to them for justifying my faith, I was
kept busy checking theory against practice. It was so clearly right that
play was learning, that this voluntary, spontaneous play-work was far
too valuable to be ignored as our schools ignored it, or relegated to
spare "free periods" in the school day, or to the home where a child
could work out such play schemes when parents were too busy or too
wise to interfere.

Other basic and precious truths became clear. Secondhand knowledge was of little or no use to these children. Words are too recent an
acquisition to a five-year-old; his tools of learning, the ones with which

he is most capable, are still his own senses. When we thrust verbal information upon him, stories and talk, we are actually coming between him and the things he is trying to learn.

Devoted mothers who spend much of their time with their children in the early years should especially take this lesson to heart. Eager to give of themselves, they make the mistake of telling a young child too much, even in answering questions. Much later in my work with children I learned the truth of the discovery Lucy Sprague Mitchell made: a young child's question is not always meant to be answered. It may be a way to open a conversation; it may be a question to which he himself wants to supply the answer, to verify a recently acquired bit of knowledge. That all children's questions must be answered is a rule with too many exceptions. A better rule is to let the child find the answers himself.

My six little teachers soon showed me I could do better than read stories to them about the things they needed to know. I could take them where they could see for themselves. Later, when the school became established, these journeys in search of firsthand knowledge became a most important part of the work. They became actual field trips, comparable to the field trip of any adult scientist. A question arises in the seven-year-old group: where does the garbage truck take the garbage? A trip to the Sanitation Department's disposal plant is the miraculously simple answer!

During this two-month trial there was no time to go far afield, nor for five-year-olds was it necessary. Their horizon was still quite close to home. But the principle came through clearly. If the child's own playwork was to be his learning method, as I insisted it should, then he must get his inspiration for it in his own way, by knowledge gained with his own eyes and ears, questions asked by him about things *he* wants to know, answers found by him within the limits of his own ability to find and understand them. A teacher or parent or sympathetic adult can help and encourage him in his researches, but the original impulse comes from him.

A really understanding mother understands not merely that the baby wants his ball. She understands also that she must let him get it himself. So with the less tangible things for which the child reaches as he grows older. Encourage him when he needs encouragement, comfort him mildly when he fails the first few times—but let him try, let him do, let him think for himself. He learned to walk and talk that way; it is his own true way of learning.

Just as I could not do the experiencing for the children—they had to do it for themselves—in the same way I saw that I could not meet their social situations for them. For my six little teachers were teaching me not only that children can and do learn by play. They were also showing me that children learn to work harmoniously with each other the more quickly and effectively if there is little or no adult interference.

MAUREEN: My first year of teaching, at the Brearley School in New York City, was formative. I was an assistant to an experienced, lively, and imaginative woman named Margaret Young, who shared not only her responsibilities and curriculum decisions but also the thought processes she used to define her teaching. She was a devoted follower of Caroline Pratt.

I remember clearly the conversations we had about the importance of block building. I hadn't played with blocks as a child, so watching second-graders construct buildings and bridges as well as castles and imaginary structures was a new experience for me. I often participated in the building so I could become part of the constant conversation that engaged these young architects.

Pratt was one of the first of many pioneering educators who designed building blocks for young children. She reminds us that, as parents of young children, we instinctively know that we have to encourage children to work hard to complete, on their own, certain tasks, including catching a ball or walking and talking. We provide the supportive environment and the necessary tools, the tangibles. Older children need these things, too, but they also need the encouragement to think and accomplish tasks without interference from parents or teachers.

Experiences with blocks afford children an opportunity to learn independently and stretch their imaginations. They learn about balance, gravity, geometric relationships, and mathematical concepts such as the relationship of parts to wholes. Less obvious are the social skills they develop working in collaboration with others.

The blocks most schools use are heavy maple and well polished so splinters are never a problem. Because half the fun of building an edifice is knocking it down, the blocks are built to last a lifetime. There are different sizes of squares, rectangles, and triangles in addition to arches, ramps, and other special pieces so that young architects can design housing, roads, bridges, or whole cities. I remember students building a model of the Fulton Street Fish Market after we went on a field trip, solidifying all that they had observed during their visit. Learning is always enhanced by imaginative reconstruction of an event.

Contrast these experiences with what is happening today in many kindergartens, where the desire to accelerate learning by beginning to teach the basics earlier has replaced the exploration of the environment. Even four-year-olds are pressured to acquire reading and writing skills, which, after testing and scoring, are used to group them for instruction in kindergarten and first grade. Recess time has all but disappeared and little value is placed on the kind of creative play blocks inspire. Instead, our children are at the mercy of normative, programmed material sequenced by a publisher, or by inadequate and often inappropriate media offerings.

Pratt's contributions to early childhood education are important for parents to understand because we often panic if we think our children are "falling behind" or not "ready" when all the other children are "ready" for "the basics." Blocks have endured because they represent what is most basic in learning. They are the tools children use to make sense of their world. It is playthings such as blocks, which are really tools, which open up the world to children. If you are skeptical, watch and listen as I did over fifty years ago. You will hear the most amazing conversations in the block corner.

7

Brian Cambourne

AN ALTERNATE VIEW OF LEARNING*

MAUREEN: If I had to recommend one modern theorist for today's schooling to parents, I'd choose Brian Cambourne. He is one of Australia's most eminent scholars and researchers of literacy learning and is currently an associate professor in the Faculty of Education at the University of Wollongong. In 2001 he was awarded the Outstanding English Language Arts Educator Award by the National Council of Teachers of English. His work is easily understood and incredibly important for both parenting and teaching. The principles he developed came as a consequence of observing how children acquire oral language and are especially pertinent to the acquisition of literacy skills in general.

Whenever parents are discouraged about their children's reading and writing skills, I give them a copy of this chapter and urge them to examine the opportunities that might exist for their implementation at home. We forget that our own lived lives act as demonstrations about living for our children. Parents and teachers are always models for the young. All too often, they are not conscious of that fact, but to become aware of it is to begin to make our influence explicit and structured. If we present reading and writing as enjoyable and authentic, we are teaching the importance of learning and helping to develop confidence and independence in our youngsters.

I think the single most important thing for teachers to emphasize when speaking with parents is the importance of reading aloud to their children throughout their elementary schooling. Reading aloud provides opportunities to discuss shared family values, to explore diverse cultures, to demonstrate the efficacy as well as the joy of literature, and, often, to open the possibility of deal-

*From Whole Story: Natural Learning and the Acquisition of Literacy and Responsive Evaluation (New York: Scholastic Press, 1988).

ing with issues that are initially painful to discuss. Most important, it re-
mains one of the oldest and most efficient ways of teaching children to read.
Reading aloud is sometimes called the "lap method," because if children are cud-
dled up next to the reader they begin to follow the words being read. When
beloved stories are read again and again, the repetition alone creates an incen-
tive to learn the story. Even after children are proficient readers themselves,
they still enjoy being read to. Even my graduate students often ask me to read
children's books aloud.

---

1. THE ORAL AND WRITTEN FORMS OF THE LANGUAGE ARE ONLY SUPERFICIALLY DIFFERENT

By "superficially different" I do not mean "trivially different." I'm using superficial in the sense of "on the surface" not in the sense of "unimportant." Of course the two modes of language differ in many complex and interesting ways. Of course the two require different kinds of knowledge which learners must acquire in order to operate with and on them. Of course there are certain aspects of the use of the written mode which require specific knowledge which can't be carried over from the oral mode and vice versa.

However, in terms of how the brain processes them, at the deep levels of production and comprehension, there are no differences of great moment. Reading, writing, speaking and listening, while different in many respects, are but parallel manifestations of the same vital human function—the mind's effort to create meaning. The fact that speaking and listening are tied to the production and/or comprehension of patterned sequences of sound, while reading and writing are tied to the reception/production of graphic marks, is not of such great importance at the level of how the brain goes about creating meaning with them.

In terms of reception, i.e. listening in the oral mode and reading in the written mode, once past the eye or ear, the sound waves (oral mode) or light waves (written mode) which set the processes of meaning construction in action are reduced to the same basic sets of neural impulses. The same neural processes are involved, using the same neural machinery. With respect to the production of meaning (speaking/writing) the texts which are created for others to hear or read originate in the same parts of the cerebral cortex, traverse much the same kinds of neural pathways, using much the same kinds of neural processing, before the organs of production (tongue/hand) go into action. While the ease with which the organs of production can be brought under control may differ—speaking is easier than writing—this difference is also a superficial one.

So What? What Does This Mean for Literacy Learning?

These are important assumptions. If they are valid (and I'm not the only one who thinks they are: see *Smith 1979*; the work on sentence understanding by *Wanner 1973*; much of the work of the psycholinguists of the '60s, *Fodor, Bever & Garrett 1966*; and many others), it's not such a huge, intellectual leap to accept that the brain can also **learn** to process oral and written forms of the language in much the same way, **provided the conditions under which each is learned are also much the same**. (Please keep this notion in mind, for I intend to return to it later.)

2. LEARNING TO TALK IS A STUNNING INTELLECTUAL ACHIEVEMENT

Learning to use and control the oral version of the language of the culture into which we're born is a successful, easy and painless task. It occurs with such monotonous regularity and success that we take it for granted, overlooking the enormity of the task which is regularly achieved by each normal infant which is, or ever has been, born.

It is important to ask just what is involved in learning to talk. What is it that has to be learned in order to learn one's language? At the general level the answer to this question is quite straightforward. When one has learned to control the oral version of one's language, one has learned literally countless thousands of conventions. Each language spoken on Earth today (some three or four thousand) comprises a unique, arbitrary set of signs, and rules for combining those signs to create meaning.

These conventions have no inherent "rightness" or "logic" to them, just as driving on the right or left side of the road has no intrinsic rightness or logic to it. Yet each language is an amazingly complex, cultural artifact, comprising incredibly complex sets of sounds, words and rules for combining them, with equally numerous and complex systems for using them for different social, personal and cognitive purposes. All of this complexity must be learned by the individual members of each language community.

One gets an inkling of just how complex a system a language is, when one tried to map the grammatical rules that a native speaker of English must know implicitly when he can use, for example, the reflexive system of English. Imagine you have the task of programming a computer to produce and/or comprehend simple sentences involving a reflexive transformation. That is, the computer has to produce and/or comprehend only acceptable reflexives such as *I wash myself, you wash yourself, he/she washes him/herself, we wash ourselves, etc.* and reject aberrations such as *I wash himselves*. I can assure you that it would involve you in a most demanding form of cognitive effort—I had to do it for an undergraduate assignment once! On the other hand, while they may not be able to state the rules, most four-year-olds have learned to use and understand reflexives without much obvious effort on their part.

The rules which describe how reflexives are used represent one tiny segment of all the knowledge that speakers of English come to learn to control. Imagine that complexity and that quantity multiplied perhaps a millionfold and you'll get some idea of how incredibly complex and detailed is the oral form of the language. Yet little children with extremely immature brains have been learning it successfully for thousands of years. What is even more impressive is that they seem to have most of it under control by the time they are about five or six years of age. *How could learning to control the written form of the language be considered any more difficult, complex or demanding than learning to control the oral form?*

How do they do it? Most of those who work in the field of language acquisition/development will argue that they do it because they're human. They will state quite simply that the Director of the Universe (whomsoever she might be) has designed us with a nervous system that has been specially programmed to learn language. And this is true. There is no other species on Earth which is capable of learning a language to the same degree. However, I believe that there is more to it than merely being neurologically designed or genetically pre-programmed to learn language. There is, for example, evidence that humans who are born with that amazing piece of neural equipment we call a nervous system sometimes do **not** learn to talk, or have great difficulty in learning to do so. Inevitably the cause for such a failure can be traced to the environmental conditions in which the potential language learner is placed.

> As recently as 1970, a child, called Genie in the scientific reports, was discovered who had been confined to a small room under conditions of physical restraint, and who had received only minimal human contact from the age of eighteen months until almost fourteen years. She knew no language and was not able to talk, although she subsequently learned some language (Curtiss, 1977).

It seems that this amazing potential for language learning, which is part of all human equipment, needs certain conditions to prevail before it can be realised. If we were able to identify these conditions we could ask two important questions about learning to control the written mode:

(i) Are the conditions which prevail when the oral form of the language is being acquired, typically present when the time comes for formal literacy instruction?

(ii) Can they in fact be applied to the learning of literacy?

In what follows I intend to explore what these conditions might be and then to assess their relevance and applicability to the teaching and learning of literacy.

Learning to Talk: Conditions Which Made It Successful

Newly-born members of any society have no foreknowledge of the language culture into which they're born. If they are to become full members of that culture they are faced with the task of working out how to make meaning using the same language conventions that the rest of the community uses. As stated above, there are literally thousands of items of knowledge about the sound system, the vocabulary, the grammar and the social uses of language which must be learned. This is a daunting task but fortunately, over the millennia, a pedagogy has been developed which maximises the probability that the task will be successfully completed by the overwhelming majority of the community. This pedagogy is one which perfectly matches the contours of the contexts in which the learning takes place, i.e. it fits in with the social, physical and emotional parameters of what could be called the "family unit." Although the family unit differs from culture to culture and has differed from age to age, there are certain core features which seem to be constant across time and cultures.

For example, the young learners are always in close proximity to proficient users of the language. Furthermore, among these proficient users (the "experts") there is usually at least one with whom the learner forms a significant bond. Most probably there is a range of "experts" of different degrees of language proficiency with whom bonds can be formed. There is a community of "user experts." Within this framework there are certain conditions present which contribute to the learning processes which take place. Figure 1 is an attempt to capture these conditions in flow chart form.

My intention is to elaborate briefly on each of these concepts.

Immersion

From the moment they are born, young language learners are saturated in the medium they are expected to learn. The older members of the culture, the language "experts," make available to the new members of the society thousands upon thousands of examples of the medium. For most of their waking time infants are within hearing distance of others using what it is that they are expected to learn. Other members of the community either talk at them or are talking around them. Before the new arrivals are probably aware of what is going on around them, they

A Schematic Representation of Brian Cambournes Model of Learning As It Applies to Literacy Learning

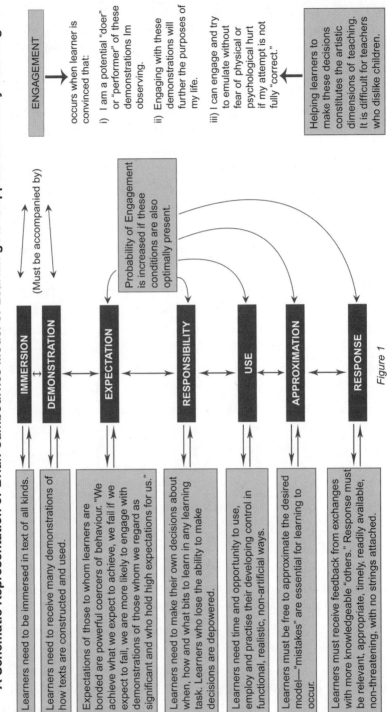

ENGAGEMENT

occurs when learner is convinced that:

i) I am a potential "doer" or "performer" of these demonstrations Im observing.

ii) Engaging with these demonstrations will further the purposes of my life.

iii) I can engage and try to emulate without fear of physical or psychological hurt if my attempt is not fully "correct."

Helping learners to make these decisions constitutes the artistic dimensions of teaching. It is difficult for teachers who dislike children.

(Must be accompanied by)

Probability of Engagement is increased if these conditions are also optimally present.

IMMERSION

DEMONSTRATION

EXPECTATION

RESPONSIBILITY

USE

APPROXIMATION

RESPONSE

Learners need to be immersed in text of all kinds.

Learners need to receive many demonstrations of how texts are constructed and used.

Expectations of those to whom learners are bonded are powerful coercers of behaviour. "We achieve what we expect to achieve, we fail if we expect to fail, we are more likely to engage with demonstrations of those whom we regard as significant and who hold high expectations for us."

Learners need to make their own decisions about when, how and what bits to learn in any learning task. Learners who lose the ability to make decisions are depowered.

Learners need time and opportunity to use, employ and practise their developing control in functional, realistic, non-artificial ways.

Learners must be free to approximate the desired model—"mistakes" are essential for learning to occur.

Learners must receive feedback from exchanges with more knowledgeable "others." "Response must be relevant, appropriate, timely, readily available, non-threatening, with no strings attached.

Figure 1

are being exposed to the sounds, rhythms and cadences of what it is that they must ultimately learn. It is important to appreciate that what does saturate them, that which is available and in which they are immersed, is always whole, usually meaningful and in a context which makes sense or from which sense can be construed.

Demonstration

Demonstrations can take two forms. They can be actions or they can be artifacts. Father asking at the breakfast table, "Will you pass the sugar, please?" and the subsequent passing of the sugar is not only a demonstration of what that particular sequence of sound means but also a demonstration of what language can be used for, how it functions, how it can be tied to action and so on. Young learners receive literally millions of demonstrations of what the spoken form of language means, does, sounds like, can be used for and so on. These demonstrations are the raw data that young learners must use in order to tease out how the language which they must learn is structured. I've come to believe that demonstrations are the raw material of nearly all learning, not only language learning. Potential bike riders need demonstrations of how a bike is ridden before they can begin bike riding. The same applies to shoelace tying, singing, reading, writing and spelling. Demonstrations can also be provided through artifacts. A book is an artifact. It is also a demonstration of what a book is, what print is and does, how words are spelled and how texts are structured. Demonstrations are necessary conditions for learning to occur. Without them learning will not occur. However, while necessary, demonstrations are not in themselves sufficient. Before learning can occur, a process which Smith (1981) labels "engagement" must occur.

Engagement

Learners are exposed to thousands of demonstrations each waking moment of their lives. However, a high proportion of these demonstrations merely wash over them and are ignored. Accordingly, learning will not occur. Learners will only engage with demonstrations under certain conditions. Among other things, before engagement will begin, learners need to be convinced of the following:

(i) That any demonstration which is witnessed must be perceived as "do-able" or "owner-able" by them. In other words, potential learners must see themselves as potential talkers, readers, bike riders, writers and so on.

(ii) That emulating the demonstrations they've witnessed will somehow further the purposes of their lives.

(iii) That attempting to emulate the demonstration will not lead to any un-pleasant consequences if they fail.

What leads learners to be convinced of the wisdom of engaging with any particular demonstration or set of demonstrations? I believe that the notion of **expectation** has something to do with it.

Expectation

Expectations can be talked about from a number of different perspectives. In one sense, the term can refer to the expectations that the learner holds about himself as a learner. As hinted at above, learners must believe that what they are setting out to learn is actually learnable **by them**. Smith has argued that young learners actually believe that they are capable of learning **anything** until they're convinced otherwise (Smith, 1981).

In another sense, expectations can refer to what "significant others" communicate to learners. If those to whom the learner is bonded behave in ways that communicate the message that certain kinds of learning are expected, then that learning usually takes place. Try asking the parents of a very young child whether they expect their pride and joy to learn to talk. Pay attention to the kind of response that you get!

Expectations are subtle and powerful coercers of behaviour. The re-search literature is replete with examples of the ways in which expec-tations of significant others can influence learner behaviour. Young learner talkers receive very clear indications that they are expected to learn to talk and that they are capable of doing it. Never are they given any expectations that it is too difficult a task or that it is beyond their capabilities. Expectations can also work against learning. For example, in our culture there is an expectation that swimming is dangerous, difficult and beyond young children's capabilities. Consequently, at the annual state-sponsored swimming lessons that are offered to young children each summer, about half of those who are enrolled do not learn to swim.

Responsibility

When learning to talk, learner talkers are left to decide (take responsibility for) which particular convention or set of conventions they will attend to and subsequently internalise in their repertoires. Their "tutors" don't try to sequence what the learner should learn. Instead they give off very strong expectations that the task will ultimately be completed. They also continue to provide high saturation and to give meaningful demonstrations. However, the learner himself or herself is left to decide just what part of the total task will be internalised at any one time.

In order to understand this notion, one must view language in a particular way—namely, as a network of interlocking systems, all of which operate simultaneously. Atwell (1983) describes this network with an effective visual metaphor.

Atwell's Visual Metaphor

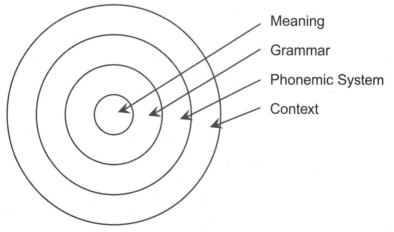

Figure 2

Oral language has an inner core of meaning which is wrapped in outer layers of grammatical, phonemic, pragmatic systems. It's a little like a transverse section of a coaxial cable. Any natural language act cuts across all these systems. For example, the demonstration referred to earlier ("Pass the sugar, please"), could be represented using the same metaphor.

Extension of Atwell's Visual Metaphor

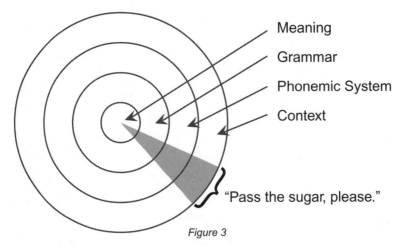

Meaning

Grammar

Phonemic System

Context

"Pass the sugar, please."

Figure 3

All the linguistic and sociolinguistic systems are present. Ultimately, the learner must come to know them all. The significant others in his environment give off very strong expectations that full learning will occur eventually. Usually, the vast majority of learners respond and full learning does occur. When a learner engages with a demonstration such as this hypothetical one, the tutor has no way of knowing which layers will be attended to, engaged with and ultimately learned. Will the learner "hook into" the phonemic rules from this demonstration or perhaps the grammatical conventions? Then again, there are the sociolinguistic rules of breakfast behaviour. All the tutor is certain of is that, ultimately, all of it will be learned. What is important is that which is demonstrated and that which is available to be immersed in, is always a whole slice of the "language pie" with all of the systems present.

While the tutor has the responsibility for supplying the demonstrations and for providing the climate of expectation, the learner has two levels of responsibility. Firstly, he is expected to become proficient in the total act; this is not negotiable—he **must** eventually learn to talk.

Secondly, he is expected to make decisions about the most useful aspect with which to engage from the demonstration which he is currently experiencing. It's my belief that once we take this responsibility away from the child by predetermining which layer he should or can learn, and then isolate it from the others, we begin to complicate the process of learning by decontextualising and fragmenting the language act. We also begin to trivialise language.

Approximation

When learning to talk, learner talkers are **not** expected to wait until they have all the systems and sub-systems fully intact before they're allowed to talk. If this were the case they would not begin to produce audible speech until they were nine or ten years of age at the earliest. Carol Chomsky found some linguistic structures which are typically not under control until about this age (Chomsky, 1968). Young learner talkers are expected to have a go, i.e. to attempt to emulate what is being demonstrated, and their childish attempts are enthusiastically, warmly and often joyously received. There is no expectation that fully developed, "correct" (fully conventional) adult forms will be produced. In short, "baby talk" is expected, is warmly received and treated as a legitimate, relevant, meaningful and useful contribution to the context. Nor is anxiety displayed about the unconventional forms which proliferate in baby talk. If any direct intervention is given, it is given only when the teacher adult (parent) thinks the "truth value" of what the learner talker is trying to say is compromised. The learner points to a truck and says, "Dat car." When the truth value is **not** compromised, direct instruction on a particular error is not given, e.g. "You omitted the verb to be (is) and the indefinite article (a). Say after me, Dat is a car."

Furthermore, there is no anxiety that the immature attempts of the adult form will become permanent fixtures of the learner's repertoire. On the contrary. Those who are responsible for the learner's language development know and expect that the immature forms will drop out and be replaced by conventional ones. And they do. What is more, they have been doing so for as long as children have been allowed to produce language.

This willingness to accept approximations is absolutely essential to the processes which accompany language learning. In fact it sets in motion the "hypothesise, test, modify hypothesis, test again" cycle which characterises all natural learning. Modification of hypothesis can only occur, if as a consequence of testing the hypothesis, some "unrest" sets in train the reformulation of the hypothesis and so on. Without the condition of ready acceptance of the approximations, the whole hypothesis/test/modification cycle would not occur. Neither would learning. The processes shown in figure 4 would simply not occur if error-free perfection was demanded prior to employment.

Use

Young learner talkers need both time and opportunity to use their immature, developing language skills. They appear to need both time and opportunity to use their language with others, as well as time alone, away from others to practise and use what they've been learning. Ruth Weir's classic study of the pre-sleep monologues in which young children run through portions of their ever-increasing linguistic repertoires is an example of this form of use (Weir, 1962).

Response

I used to refer to this as **feedback**. I've switches to **response** because the term feedback has mechanistic and behaviourist overtones. It also implies a predetermined purpose on the part of the feedback giver. My data (Cambourne, 1972) convince me that parents are not consciously aware of the "giving feedback" function which their exchanges with children serve. Rather, these exchanges appear to serve the function of the "sharing of information" about both the language and the degree of control that the learner has over it at any one time. When the learner talker says, as he points to a cup on the table, "Dat cup," the response from the parent, if indeed it is a cup, typically goes something like this, "Yes, that's a cup."

How Learning to Mean "Proceeds"

(The "Processes" Involved)

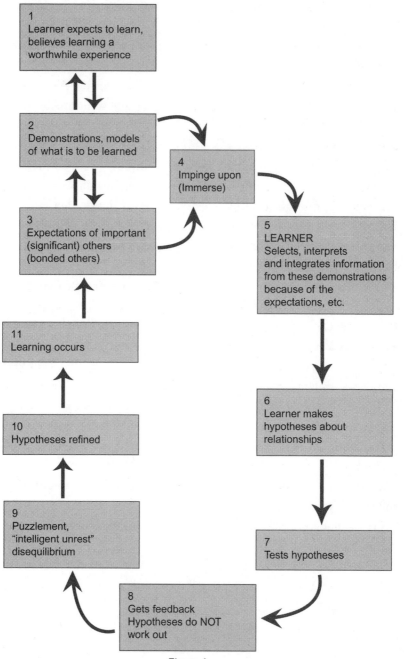

Figure 4

What is being exchanged here? The parent is supplying the missing bits of the child's approximation. The child is supplying the parent with an example of what he is currently capable of doing. It is interesting to look back through a "bugging" study of mine and note what the parents did **not** do in these mutual exchanges. For example, the child who says to the parent "Dat cup," or something similar, was never given any specific information about the errors which had been made. No parent in my data ever made specific reference to the nature of the auxiliaries, indefinite articles or the pronunciation of "th." The information which is shared by the "expert" in this kind of situation is a **full** (as opposed to fragmented) version of what the learner attempted. It is as if the expert intuitively understands the importance of responsibility and says to himself, "I've no right to decide which aspect of this learner's approximation should be attended to right now. Therefore I'll give him the conventional version of what I think he wanted to say and leave him to decide which aspect he'll attend to and adjust."

While exchanges may vary in detail and richness from parent to parent and sub-culture to sub-culture, they have certain things in common: a) they are readily available, frequently given, non-threatening and **with no strings attached**; b) there is no penalty for not getting the conventional form correct the next time it is produced. There is no limit to the number of exchanges which are offered and given.

Quite often the expert in these exchanges provides a scaffold for further language learning to occur, "Yes, that's Daddy's blue cup, isn't it?," thus keeping the conversational game going and providing more opportunities to employ, practise, hypothesise, specify, elaborate, generalise and so on. This does not mean that there's not an implicit contract involved (remember expectations), or that it's merely potluck learning. It's a very specific form of contextually specific learning which aims at maximum impact.

The thesis presented in this chapter is not new. In fact, as long ago as 1898 a Miss Harriet Iredell argued thus in an article she wrote for the magazine *Education*.

> When we have command of a language both in its spoken and written form we pass impartially from one to the other. Whether we hear a thing or

see it; whether we speak or write, there is to the mind no sense of difference in the fact. Since the two forms of the one mode of expression are so alike in themselves and in their psychological and practical use and effect, it would seem that the principles and rules which govern the acquirement of the one, must govern the acquirement of the other, and in the natural order of things they would be learned alike. So much depends upon the truth or falsity of this, that the question claims earnest and immediate consideration (pp. 233–238).

I can understand how learning to talk is natural, but learning to read and write . . . how can that be natural?

While learning to talk (that is, learning to control the spoken form of language) is seen as a "natural" form of behaviour by most people, there is not the same agreement that learning to read and write (that is, learning to control the written form) is as "natural." There are even some who would argue that learning to read and write **cannot** be described as a natural form of behaviour at all.

The reasons for this are obvious. Talking is a universal medium of communication. Every culture has an oral form of language which every member of that culture strives to learn, sometimes against overwhelming disabilities and handicaps, e.g. blind, deaf, or mentally deficient children. The stream of everyday, ongoing behaviour keeps providing opportunities for all new members of a culture, i.e. recently born children, to use their developing language for purposes other than learning it. As a consequence they seem to learn to control it as a by-product of using it.

The same cannot be said for the written form of the language. The real world does not naturally provide the same kinds of opportunities for the written form of the language. Of course, in our print-saturated society it is possible to argue that demonstrations of how the written form of the language can be read might, under ideal circumstances, be naturally provided by the environment. For example, adults reading stories to young learners who can see the print, mothers reading the supermarket print while their infants watch and so on. But there are very few contexts in the real world where writing is the major medium of communication, where young learners can engage with it in much the same way that they can engage with demonstrations of the spoken form. The very strong need in our society to be error-free—to meet all the conventions of written language before producing a text for public consumption—means that before one really engages in acts of writing, one must know how to do it first, otherwise it cannot possibly be error-free. This is a paradox which I haven't quite explained satisfactorily for myself. Furthermore, writing is perceived mainly as a medium of communication. It is usually performed in special settings, (offices, classrooms, libraries) in isolation. All of these factors must militate against the skills of writing being learned as a by-product of using it. The real world simply does not provide the conditions for learning to write that it provides for learning to talk.

But surely this is not a valid reason for not attempting to simulate, for the written form of language, those conditions which made learning the oral form possible?

The only reason for **not** trying to simulate for the written form what we know happened when young learners set out to learn the oral form, would be to assume somehow, that the written form of the language **cannot** be learned under the same conditions even if they are provided. I find this argument difficult to sustain, for it assumes that learning is either a topic-based or process-based phenomenon. It assumes, in other words, that while one can learn to talk under the conditions of learning described above, a completely different set of conditions is needed for learning writing or maths or singing or art or playing the piano or science . . .

I find it much more satisfying to believe that there is a single, unitary, very effective process of learning which is exemplified by learning to talk and, that over the long period of human evolution, the brain has evolved so that it prefers to learn this way and that most learning, especially language-related learning, proceeds most effectively under these conditions.

What we need to realise is that while the "natural" world provides the opportunities for oral language learning processes to go into action, it does not provide them for other kinds of learning, especially learning to read and write. Herein lies the function of schools. Schools are settings in which we need to create those opportunities for learning to read and write that the real, everyday world does not provide, at least to the degree that it provides them for learning to talk. Thus, when I use the phrase "learning to read and write naturally," I'm really talking about simulating the natural conditions that we know work for learning to talk, so that they're available for the learning of reading and writing. On the surface it might seem to be a kind of paradox. I'm arguing that teachers need to simulate nature (the real world) because nature will not provide the opportunities for these other types of learning to proceed naturally.

However, there is no paradox. Just because the world does not provide the same kinds of natural conditions for learning to control the written forms of language, this is not a valid reason for trying to teach literacy by imposing conditions which interfere with the processes for which evolution has obviously prepared the brain.

REFERENCES

Atwell, N. (1983). Reading, writing, speaking, listening: Language is response to context in Hardt, V. (Ed.) Teaching reading with the other language arts, Delaware: International Reading Association.

Cambourne, B. (1972). A naturalistic study of the language performance of grade 1 rural and urban schoolchildren. Unpublished doctoral thesis, James Cook University of North Queensland.

Chomsky, N. (1968). Language and mind. New York: Harcourt Brace & Jovanovich.

Curtiss, S. (1977). Genie: A psycholinguistic study of a modern day wild child. New York: Academic Press.

Fodor, J.D., Berer, T. & Garrett, M. (1966). The active use of grammar in speech perception. Journal of Perception and Psychophysics 1, 30–32.

Iredell, H. (1898). Eleanor learns to read. Education 19, 233–238.

Smith, F. (1979). *Reading without nonsense*. New York: Teachers College Press.

Smith, F. (1981). Demonstrations, engagement, and sensitivity: The choice between people and programs. *Language Arts* 58, 634–642.

Warner, E. (1973). Do we understand sentences from the outside in or the inside out? *Daedalus*, 185–194.

Weir, R. (1962). Language in the crib. The Hague, Netherlands: Mouton and Co.

———————

ALEXANDRA: There is a beautiful logic to Cambourne's theory that the conditions that make it possible for young children to learn to talk are also important for learning to read and write. The excitement shown in an adult's facial expression, voice tone, and oral response when a baby communicates, even when it's more babble than recognizable words, are contagious signals to the child to keep at it. Sadly, when they arrive in preschool and kindergarten and have difficulty distinguishing among b, d, p, q, *and* g *(and who wouldn't?), we tend to stop with the smiles and enthusiasm, and all of our bad habits of correction and oversimplification kick in, perhaps from our own early schooling experiences. As early as kindergarten, we begin to give spelling tests, expecting that studying* bat, rat, fat, cat, *and* mat *at the same time will make things easier rather than harder for the child. Most children would much rather recite, "I do not like green eggs and ham!" than memorize a list of rhyming monosyllabic words. That's because context matters to them, and they are astute enough to recognize when we are, in Cambourne's words, trivializing language.*

The importance of immersing children in and demonstrating language in its whole-pie form cannot be overstated. Before children have learned to formally read text in a book, they have learned to read environmental print, from the boxes of cereal to the brands of cars on the road, and this knowledge can be exploited in the classroom and at home to build bridges to more challenging texts. If only reading aloud were as familiar a family ritual as watching favorite TV shows, literacy learning would surely skyrocket. In my sixth-grade classroom, I saved my most cherished novels for read aloud. Students would spread out comfortably around the room and settle in for the most relaxing and pleasurable part of the day. Sometimes even after thirty minutes they would beg me not to stop. I know that the shared experience of those books is what enticed the reluctant readers to read more, encouraging readers stuck on one genre to branch out in their choices. I also know that the demonstration of the excellent writing in those novels inspired their own creative stories and gave them courage to read them aloud to their classmates.

8

Christopher Clark

WHAT YOU CAN LEARN FROM APPLESAUCE: A CASE OF QUALITATIVE INQUIRY IN USE*

ALEXANDRA: Apples and education just seem to go together: A is for apple; an apple for the teacher; apple-picking field trips. In this piece, Christopher Clark revisits a write-up of his experience watching first-graders make applesauce to explore its usefulness as an example of qualitative research in education. Unlike some other fields of research in the social sciences, most educational research is driven by the quest for answers to problems, for solutions that work, and by a never-ending desire for improvement. Something as quaint and old-fashioned as six-year-olds learning to make applesauce together may seem an unlikely candidate for reflecting on the lofty goals of educational improvement. But Clark illuminates layers of learning in this example in clear prose that makes you think hard about the limitations of research that is only based on test scores. Formerly a professor at Michigan State University from 1976 to 2000, he is now Professor Emeritus and the former director of the School of Education at the University of Delaware. He is the author of Thoughtful Teaching *(1995) and more recently edited* Talking Shop: Authentic Conversation and Teacher Learning *(2001).*

In the original text, "What You Can Learn from Applesauce," Clark names features of the day's activities that are educationally sound for any curriculum: continuity of experience and links to prior knowledge; equity of outcome and cooperation among participants; patience; and everyone's delight in the ownership of the task and their active, multisensory participation in the activities. He also suggests interdisciplinary connections and helps us to see the many potential learning outcomes of a seemingly ordinary curriculum about apples. Next he shows how the teacher's reflection, and the fact that the event

---

*From Qualitative Inquiry in Education: The Continuing Debate, ed. E. W. Eisner and A. Peshkin (New York: Teachers College Press, 1990), 327–357.

was written up by a researcher, lead to the use of the case story by the teacher, her principal, other teachers, and many teacher educators for multiple purposes. What the purposes share in common is that the case study served to fill the need for a compelling example. Large-scale educational research studies that rely on test results lack the immediacy and tangible evidence found in studies that use qualitative classroom data, because the latter kind of research is often full of rich examples that bring the teachers and students to life in ways that test scores cannot. As Clark points out, "Reports of qualitative inquiry can help people to imagine themselves in the place of the teacher" (p. 114) and can serve purposes of informing a lay audience about the complexities and rewards of teaching so that the profession and the work it entails are better understood by the public at large.

I want to share with you the short history of a little report called "What You Can Learn from Applesauce." I wrote it in October 1987 to describe an afternoon in an elementary school where I had been working as a "professor in residence" for the whole school year. The short version of the story goes like this:

1. I was a participant-observer in a fascinating classroom experience.
2. I wrote a description and analysis of my experience.
3. I gave copies of that text to twenty-five or thirty friends and acquaintances.
4. I have heard from ten or fifteen of these individuals about how they have responded to or used the paper.
5. Now, I want to come to an understanding of how qualitative inquiry *can* be used by describing how this case *has* been used.

Before I get into responses and categories, let me show you what my friends were responding to. Here is the text of "What You Can Learn from Applesauce." As you read it, think about how you might make use of this example of qualitative inquiry.

WHAT YOU CAN LEARN FROM APPLESAUCE

In mid-October I spent a couple of fall afternoon hours helping twenty-one first- and second-graders make a pot of applesauce. The day climaxed with the great moment of tasting, when the contents of the pot, spiced with cinnamon and divided into twenty-two portions, was consumed with delight. Children and teacher alike declared that this was a fine and magical afternoon—one of those memorable high points that we cherish as examples of the way education should be all of the time.

At the risk of spoiling the magic by too much analysis I would like to reflect on what was learned (or could have been learned) in this classroom on an October afternoon. What can you learn from applesauce? This question applies not only to the learning of the six- and seven-year-olds, but also to the teacher and to me.

I've decided the list of what was learned from applesauce into those learnings intended or anticipated by the teacher, followed by surprises and subtle side effects of the activity. Since I did not interview the teacher in advance about her plans and expectations, the line between intentions and surprises is not definitive, but rather suggestive. This would remain true even after a post hoc interview, since her direct experience of the afternoon powerfully influences recollection and reconstruction of her plans and expectations. Hopes and fears about what might happen in the future (the stuff of planning) disappear like smoke in hindsight.

Anticipated Learnings and Conditions Supportive of Them

Simply put, the two most obvious academic learning goals of applesauce making were for the children to learn about the concept of orderly sequencing of steps in a moderately complex process and to practice expressing (through writing and drawing) an understandable description of their own activities. The former is a specific objective of the first-grade mathematics curriculum; the latter is a general aim of the language arts curricula for both grades. They were jointly pursued through teacher-led instruction about the sequence of steps to be followed and through the children's alternately acting out steps in the sequence and creating individual booklets describing and depicting the process. Seven children at a time peeled and cut apples with the help and supervision of two adult volunteers, while the remaining fourteen children drew pictures and wrote captions describing five steps in the applesauce-making process. After each child finished operating on one apple, he or she washed hands and returned to recipe-booklet making, being replaced at one of the seven cutting boards by a classmate. During the hour or so of apple cutting and peeling, the teacher was involved in helping children (especially first-graders) spell words for their booklet captions and in directing the flow of children between their writing desks and the cutting-and-peeling stations. The first hour and a quarter ended with slices and chunks of twenty-one apples simmering in a cinnamon-spiced pot, twenty-one recipe booklets nearing completion, and a great wad of newspaper, peelings, and apple seeds in the wastebasket. This might have been enough learning to satisfy most educators, but there was much, much more learned from applesauce.

Part of what else was anticipated and learned from applesauce falls under the heading "continuity of experience." First, the experience of food preparation constituted a link between home and school. Young children daily see, smell, and sometimes participate in food preparation in their own kitchens. Their prior out-of-school knowledge and experiences were drawn upon in this in-school project. More proximately, the applesauce-making activity drew on two recent school activities. The most immediate and direct connection was to a field trip to Uncle John's Cider Mill, where the children saw recently harvested apples by the bushel, saw and smelled the process of large-scale cider making in action, and obtained apples to bring back to school. The teacher saw an opportunity for children to mentally connect their visit to orchard and cider mill with their own transformation of apples into applesauce.

The second connection was to a prior field trip to a farmers' market, where the children purchased a variety of vegetables, brought them back to school, and made "stone soup." The applesauce-making project was structurally quite similar to the stone-soup project (with the important difference that there was no children's literature story or folk tale around which to organize the applesauce making, as there was with stone soup).

In sum, this second set of intended learnings had to do with the idea (and experience) that life outside school is (or can be) connected to life in school; that school learning activities need not be segregated from one's taken-for-granted everyday knowledge and learning; and that transformations of a grand scale (bushels of apples transformed into gallons of cider) can be effectively modeled on a manageably small scale. But this was not the whole story.

The probably anticipated but secondary student learnings from the applesauce project had to do with safety, sanitation, and satisfaction of two kinds. Learning to use a paring knife safely was intended, taught directly by modeling, tried empirically, and then backed away from when, in the judgment of the teacher, the risk of self-inflicted wounds appeared too high. (We switched to using plastic knives after the first few exciting minutes.) Nonetheless, the points were made: Safety is important, sharp knives must be handled with care, and relatively mature fine-motor coordination is required to peel an apple safely with a sharp knife. The role of sanitation in food preparation was emphasized by having the children wash their hands before and after food handling. Satisfaction as an outcome of this learning activity was intended to come both from the delicious and immediate tasting of the fruits of one's own labors and from having a booklet to take home that would serve as a prop and support for a "show-and-tell" conversation with parents. A subtle characteristic of these satisfactions is that they do not depend on competitiveness for success. Rather, there was "equity of outcome," in that everyone got to contribute, everyone got to taste from the pot, and everyone got to take home a booklet. The underlying message here is that learning can be fun, delicious, and communicable to an absent audience through the magic of writing. Again, for most of us, this would have been enough. But there was more to this applesauce than is usually the case.

Applesauce, unsurprisingly, is not all academic. The teacher intended (at least implicitly) that this set of activities would serve some social-learning functions as well. First among these was the idea that *co-operation* within the classroom social group could produce a delightful product that no one individual or small group could have produced. *Patience* in letting the project take as long as it needed to and the twin pleasures of *task ownership* by the children ("I'll cut *my* apple *my* way") and *active, multisensory participation* in a learning activity ("This is messy." "That smells good." "Look, I cut a seed in half!") were required, or at least encouraged, by the structure of the tasks and also hoped for as enduring, transferable, long-term outcomes of the process. Making applesauce may have served to make this classroom social group happier, more cohesive, more patient, and more confident. ("If we can make applesauce together, perhaps we can make a newspaper in the spring.")

Perhaps more could have been made of the math and science learning potential of applesauce. We could have weighed the apples, weighed what went into the pot, and weighed the contents of the pot after an hour of simmering, then hypothesized about how to account for the differences. We could have carefully emphasized how halves, quarters, eighths, and sixteenths are related to the whole. We could have counted seeds, dissected seeds, planted seeds, talked about nature's "intended" role for seed and fruit. We could have demonstrated bilateral and cross-sectional symmetry. (Have you ever cut an apple in half the "wrong" way? Try it: there is a delightful surprise within.) We could have taught juggling or given examples of the role of the apple in religion, myth, literature, and the economy of Michigan. We did none of these things, although I would not be surprised if the apple example arises again when large fractions are studied in math.

Surprises and Side Effects

What did the teacher learn more generally about herself and about teaching from applesauce? From her response to seeing the apparent danger of sharp knives in little hands, she learned something about her own tolerance for risk in the name of learning. In this case, the risk of injury appeared substantial, the particular learning aim of successful use of paring knives was marginal, and a safer alternative (plastic knives) was at hand. But it is interesting that the need for revision of this important detail of the applesauce-making plan did not arise during preactive planning, but only in the vividness of action. Perhaps this was a case of overgeneralization from the accident-free stone soup project, in which various vegetables were sliced and diced using the same sharp set of par-ing knives. What became clear as the first seven children began to work on their apples was that it is considerably easier to slice a celery stalk or a carrot than it is to peel an apple.

The teacher and I also learned something about the necessity of de-tailed planning of a complex activity. In this case, the planning challenge was to design a pair of activities that were substantively connected, academically defensible, and robust enough to be sustained in the face of internal interruptions (i.e., the children's continually shifting from drawing and writing to apple peeling and then back again to drawing and writing). It was also crucial to carrying out this plan that the teacher have one or two adult helpers, and the manifest success of the activity confirmed (for the teacher) the wisdom of seeking help in this kind of teaching. A final lesson learned (or reconfirmed) by the teacher was that, especially with young children, resolution of a cause-and-effect process during a single afternoon is quite satisfying. Beginning the afternoon with a bag of apples and ending the day with one's own recipe booklet and the taste of warm applesauce fits the attention span of six- and seven-year-olds quite nicely. Multiday projects may make sense later in the year.

Two subtle but important lessons about individual student differences and about gender roles were learned from applesauce. Some children who had various difficulties with reading or with verbal participation in group activities positively shone at apple cutting and peeling. They acted confidently and competently, even helping classmates learn how to cut and peel. The activity structure made it possible for them to thrive in the same classroom and group in which they typically struggle. Teacher, adult volunteers, and children noticed these individual differ-ences to different degrees, and the consequences of this consciousness raising will take time to manifest themselves. But for now, it is worth noting that these insights would not have arisen in the context of more verbally loaded classroom activities. The issue of gender roles was sub-tle in that the question of whether it was appropriate for boys to be so involved in food preparation never came up. Boys and girls together pitched in and got the job done. One can only hope that this egalitarian approach will continue throughout the children's school experiences.

Conclusion

In conclusion, more was learned from applesauce than at first meets the eye. The planning, acting, revising, and happy resolution of the applesauce-making activity affected everyone involved. Academic, social, and professional-development learning potentials were realized in subtle and obvious ways. Reflection on the experience suggested additional curriculum potential that may be realized next year by this teacher and her students, or at any time by other teachers and students. And learnings about teaching, activity structures, and individual students may continue to influence this teacher's planning for the remainder of the school year. General abstract principles—such as continuity of experience, equity of outcome, multiability task demands, comprehensive planning, flexible revision of plans, and sensitivity to developmental capabilities of school children—take on vividness and new meaning when depicted in the garb of a concrete, visualizable classroom activity. And I, for one, will never be able to see a Macintosh in quite the same simple light as I did in the days before learning from applesauce.

RESPONSES

So what do you think? How did this account connect with your background experiences? What uses might *you* make of it? I do want to hear your answers, but first, let me share with you some answers that I have already heard from others: the teacher and the principal, teacher-educators, researchers, and civilians.

Teachers and Teacher-Educators

I want to begin by describing how the teacher of the applesauce episode, Ms. Anderson, responded to the case description. Emotionally, she was flattered and pleased. She also expressed delight that so much could be made of what was, for her, a relatively ordinary set of events. She was eager to show the draft document to the school principal. Most significant, I think, was her wish to keep a copy on file in the school office as a preemptive response to parents who might question the academic value of enjoyable and practical activities such as applesauce making. That is, Ms. Anderson held an intuitive conviction that such activities are of value but did not feel confident that she alone could defend applesauce making on academic grounds. Now she had both the language and the authority of a professor to support her belief in the good of the work she was doing. Interestingly, the challenge never came—no parent lodged a complaint to which the applesauce case served as a response. But the support and affirmation that Ms. Anderson felt as a result of reading this description and analysis of her own teaching seemed to be important to her confidence and morale. To be known and to be appreciated are two of the psychic rewards of teacher participation in qualitative inquiry.

The school principal, Ms. McClintock, made use of the applesauce case with several different audiences. First, with the teachers and instructional aides she used the case study at a staff meeting to demonstrate that valuable learning can take place as a result of activities that fall outside the scope of published curriculum materials. The principal reported that this was received as an important message of encouragement to the staff, who were feeling a bit overwhelmed by central office expectations that they should literally implement a new science curriculum and a new spelling program. The principal also reported that having a professor's endorsement of the importance of such activities made the case more credible to teachers.

A second way in which Ms. McClintock made use of the case study was to add to the local language of practice. She now uses the expression *an applesauce event* to refer to school activities that combine elements of fun, teamwork, practical activity, and many social and academic learning opportunities. She had used (and explained) this language in conversations with teachers, individual parents, and members of the school parents' council to make a case for how teachers at Whitehills School sometimes go beyond the published curriculum to promote a wide range of valued kinds of learning and development. She also plans to begin the next school year, when several new teachers will join the staff, with a challenge to teachers to develop and share "applesauce activities" of their own.

Finally, Ms. McClintock sent a copy of the applesauce case to the superintendent, curriculum director, and each member of the school board at the end of the school year. Her cover letter introduced the case as an example of the good things that had happened at Whitehills School during the year. A more subtle, implied message was that educationally rich and exciting things have been taking place at this school, outside the limits of published and mandated curricula. The underlying theme here is promoting and defending teachers' autonomy in deciding the "what" and the "how" of classroom teaching.

Let me now move 700 miles east from Ms. Anderson's classroom to the world of another teacher who is also a teacher-educator in a small church college. Ms. Potter, a veteran of twenty years of teaching multi-grade classes in church schools, has been education department chair at a church college for about five years. Her personal response to reading "Applesauce" was nostalgic: "It took me right back to my own elementary teaching days; to the kinds of projects I loved to do with my kids. But while I was *doing* all that, it wasn't possible to sit back and *see* all the learning, all the complexity." One way, then, that Ms. Potter used this example of qualitative inquiry was to remind herself of the difficulty, perhaps impossibility, of acting and reflecting simultaneously. And in teaching, the demands of action often crowd out reflection.

In her role as teacher-educator, Ms. Potter used this case to show her students how many of the skills and dimensions of teaching and school learning fit together. Her students had been chafing at the reductionistic way in which their texts treat teaching and learning. Reading "Applesauce" aloud in class gave her students hope and optimism that all the pieces of teaching studied separately can come together again. This case study provides a visualizable context for novices to see how abstract ideas from educational psychology, curriculum theory, and methods courses look and feel and interact.

At another college of education, another teacher-educator read "Applesauce" aloud to his section of twenty prospective math teachers. In this instance, the intended purpose of so doing was to provide an example, if not a model, of how the undergraduate listeners could write about their own field observations of teaching and learning. These students, who had visited classrooms twice earlier in the term, were working on an assignment that called for describing an episode of teaching and learning by using concepts and ideas from their university coursework. Hearing the applesauce text helped them see one way in which literal description of teacher and student behavior could be interwoven with hypotheses, analysis, speculation, and interpretation. And, as important, the case supported the professor's claim that there is much more to teaching and school learning than meets the eye; that the extraordinary and complex lurk just below the surface of the ordinary and commonplace.

A teacher of elementary school mathematics who is also a teacher-educator read the applesauce paper and immediately mailed it to her stepdaughter. The stepdaughter was a first-year elementary school teacher and had intended to keep a written record of her experiences as a novice teacher. Her stepmother thought that the voice and form of the applesauce paper made it helpful as a model or example of how to write about one's own practice.

A final example of use by teacher-educators took place at a small college in North Carolina. The department chair in education was eager to encourage her faculty to do more research while at the same time maintaining the high quality of a labor-intensive teacher-preparation program. The applesauce paper was offered to faculty as one example of how qualitative or interpretive research could be done on a small scale while pursuing other ends and practical activities (e.g., supervision of student teaching). Beyond serving as a possible model for research in practice, the circulation of the applesauce paper also stimulated faculty deliberation about what counts as "real" research. That discussion, in turn, broadened the way in which this faculty thought about qualitative research in education.

The teachers and teacher-educators who made use of "What You Can Learn from Applesauce" used it primarily as an *example*: an example of a way of describing teaching, an example of how a practical activity can promote academic learning, an example of how the elements of teaching can all fit together again, an example of how the extraordinary and complex underlie the commonplace, an example of small-scale research on teaching. Each teacher and teacher-educator seized on this example to fill a practical pedagogical need—to teach or show something to an audience of parents, faculty colleagues, a stepdaughter, or prospective teachers. The need, the audience, and the principles to be taught were all in place before "Applesauce" came along. Teachers are always on the lookout for fresh, compelling examples, and qualitative research is a rich source of such examples. But as researchers, we cannot predict or control just how our cases will be used, for that is the task of the teacher.

Researchers

How did my colleagues and friends who are researchers make use of this example of qualitative research? Their responses ranged from the romantic to the revolutionary, and, as with teachers, it seemed that at least some of the researchers' goals, intentions, and audience were already in place before "Applesauce" came along.

Three researchers were moved to nostalgia by reading this case. They wrote me that they were reminded of times when they themselves had pursued fieldwork of the kind that I have been doing, and they took the occasion to thank me for reminding them of those days and to encourage and assure me that this is a good thing for me to be doing. Two other researchers responded by sharing with me their current work in progress and making a case that what they were doing had much in common with the spirit and direction of the work from which "Applesauce" developed. In all five of these instances the primary uses of the case study were to come to know me (as author) better and to come to be known better by me. These are personal and social functions that strengthen the community of educational research.

One researcher responded somewhat like a teacher—she used "Applesauce" as an example of a practical case in which "higher-order learning" could be pursued with young children. The research group that she leads had been discussing abstract theoretical ideas about higher-order learning for some time, and she felt a need to ground those ideas in a real, visualizable classroom situation. Reading "Applesauce" provided a way to put their theorizing to a small test and to bring a kind of practical balance to their decisions about research design, instrumentation, and methods of inquiry.

Still another researcher got an idea for a paper that he might write from reading the applesauce case. He is an instructional designer, and he saw in this case a starting point for a piece tentatively titled "Experience in Search of Objectives." The depth of curriculum potential revealed by the case study moved him out of the familiar ends-means paradigm for teacher planning and instruction. For a time, at least, he saw and appreciated how and why teachers do not always begin their plans by specifying measurable learning outcomes. Practice confronted theoretical prescription, and theory blinked first. My own habitual ways of seeing teaching and learning have been challenged and stretched by the direct experience of working in classrooms. Apparently, reading a case description can also raise fundamental questions in a thoughtful researcher's mind about his teleological orientation and perceptual framework.

This leads to my final example of researchers' responses to the applesauce case. A newly met friend, himself a leader in the qualitative tradition, encouraged me to use this case as the basis for a fundamental epistemological challenge to the field of educational research. He saw in this case an opportunity to show that researchers of every tradition systematically undercomplicate the educational settings under study. To fit the constraints of research design, time, language, theory, expectations, convenience, and preordained forms for reporting our work, we find ourselves studying cleaned-up, stripped-down caricatures of reality. Small wonder, then, that practicing educators rarely find realistically helpful support, enlightenment, or guidance from the research community. This is not the time or place to pursue this line of thought to conclusion. Rather, it serves as one example of how a specific case of qualitative research can connect with the philosophical project of a scholar and encourage him to enlist another in the cause.

Civilians

I have two responses to "Applesauce" to share from people who are neither teachers nor researchers. One of these readers did teach for two years in the early 1970s and is the mother of two school-aged children. The other is a nineteen-year-old college sophomore who is also my daughter. I think it is significant to note that the particular example of qualitative research under consideration here was understood and responded to by this lay audience. *Some forms of qualitative inquiry can be used to open communication about education with the public.* In this instance, the young student reported that reading this piece showed her that elementary school teaching demands a kind of sustained attention and "thinking on your feet" that she was not aware of. The former teacher told me that she was reminded of and reexperienced the intensity of her days teaching second grade, years ago. My daughter has since decided to become an elementary school teacher, and the former teacher has since taken steps to renew her teaching credential and seek a position teaching French to elementary school children. I am not claiming that reading "What You Can Learn from Applesauce" was the major influence in these two career decisions, but I do claim that picturing oneself in a new professional role is an important element in the personal decision-making process. Reports of qualitative inquiry can help people to imagine themselves in the place of the teacher; to simulate how that would feel and be; to take account of such a vicarious experience in deciding on a career in teaching.

CONCLUSION

What have we learned about qualitative inquiry in use? First, that reports of qualitative inquiry *can* be used and *are* being used by teachers and principals, teacher-educators, researchers, and civilians. This is encouraging to me, and I hope it is encouraging to others who pursue this form of scholarship. Second, the accounts of how people responded to the applesauce case remind us that people make sense of text in relation to their own past experiences, their beliefs and expectations, and their present needs and aspirations. While most reports of qualitative inquiry steer clear of making prescriptions for specific action, people can and have been moved to take specific action, advocate change, and make consequential decisions inspired or influenced by reports of qualitative inquiry. Like art, literature, poetry, and music, qualitative accounts of the drama of teaching and learning can have profound and unpredictable effects on human thought and action.

Third, several of the accounts of response to the applesauce case suggest that qualitative inquiry can fill a felt need to understand how teaching and learning fit together in context. The narrative-analytic form of this case helped readers see the flexible and uncertain yet real ways in which teaching skills, strategies and style, practical experience, knowledge of children, and more played parts in support of learning. Yes, teaching is complicated; no, teaching is not impossible.

Finally, qualitative inquiry can be used to explore the boundaries, limits, and possibilities of our own learning from experience. I have been surprised and delighted by what I have learned from "Applesauce." And I suspect that I am not finished learning from "Applesauce," as I look forward to the response of those who read these words and join the conversation.

MAUREEN: In my fiftysome years of teaching I think I must have made gallons and gallons of applesauce. It's a classic endeavor in American primary grades during the month of September. I could sense the trepidation of Ms. Anderson when she realized the knives were too sharp to be trusted in the hands of the children, and I could almost smell the apples and cinnamon cooking on the hot plate. I remember reading a poem about discovering the star in the apple and challenging the children to find it. (You must cut the apple in the midsection.)

I'm also reminded again of John Dewey, who urged teachers to bring the school closer to home and neighborhood life and to make the studies in the curriculum closer to a child's everyday experience. He felt the basic "occupations" provided continuity for children, and that cooking, sewing, and carpentry were made the center of school studies not for purely utilitarian purposes but rather because they were purposeful activities. They were the kinds of action that required long-range planning, knowledge of underlying principles, patience, perseverance, and a host of other qualities. Thus, discipline could be internalized and satisfaction was gained by creativity and cooperation.

Ms. Anderson wisely connected the activity with the home by involving parents in the production of the applesauce. When I team-taught in the Interage Program in the Great Neck Public Schools with upper elementary children, we always asked the parents to come in and help us teach. They almost never refused. Thus they were not mere observers, but participants in the teaching, and they became huge supporters of the Interage Program. For example, we taught two brothers three years apart in age; and because this was a three-year program, we had the parents with us for a total of six years. Every year their mother came into the class for a period of weeks to teach units on China. They were among our most popular studies. Because of parent involvement, we were once able to offer a choice of five languages for study: French, Italian, Hebrew, Farsi, and Spanish. I taught Italian and parents taught the other languages. Children had a taste of what it would be like when they moved on to the upper grades and would have the opportunity to formally study a language. I say "taste" because we learned a lot about customs and a lot of vocabulary as we made spaghetti and pizza in those classes.

Clark makes us fully aware of how many lessons were learned in the making of applesauce and helped Ms. Anderson herself realize the full potential of the study. She certainly had an intuitive conviction that such activities are of value but, alas, she did not feel confident that she alone could defend them. That is the function of theory in education. Teachers must be aware of the underlying purposes and outcomes of their curricula and be able to articulate them for both students and parents. As Clark points out, the article supports the claim made by a professor who shared "Applesauce" with his students "that there is much more to teaching and school learning than meets the eye; that the extraordinary and complex lurk just below the surface of the ordinary and commonplace" (p. 111).

SUGGESTED RESOURCES AND FURTHER READING

For information on the City and Country School founded by Caroline Pratt, see http://www.cityandcountry.org.

For information on the work of the Lincoln Center Institute for the Arts in Education, see http://www.lcinstitute.org.

The following professional organizations are noteworthy for their educational contributions to the subjects of language arts, mathematics, science, and the social studies:

National Council of Teachers of English: http://www.ncte.org

National Council of Teachers of Mathematics: http://www.nctm.org

National Science Teachers Association: http://www.nsta.org

National Council for the Social Studies: http://www.ncss.org

PART III

THE WORK OF TEACHING

The next three essays provide a nuanced focus on important aspects of teaching that are touched on in other selections as well. These include conceiving of the work of instructing students as being as much about listening, reflecting, and observing as about generating conversation and talk to achieve clarity or to pose new questions to consider. Such a view often means starting from the learner, rather than focusing on a desired outcome, and questioning the dominant paradigm of teaching as telling or merely transmitting information. While learning certainly can occur as students listen to a fascinating lecture, they also need a well-balanced diet that includes explaining, creating, imagining, playing, and conjecturing.

9

Eleanor Duckworth

TEACHING AS RESEARCH*

ALEXANDRA: Teaching is a profession that involves continuous learning. Each day, in even the smallest of interactions, teachers are learning about children, their families and communities, and about subject matter. They are also asked to learn in formal ways, by attending professional development seminars or taking university courses, but it's rare that they have both time and permission to investigate deeply what Eleanor Duckworth describes in this piece as "the nature of the teaching and learning phenomena they experience as they learn" (p. 124). A professor of education at the Harvard Graduate School of Education, and a former student and translator for the internationally renowned scholar Jean Piaget, she recently published "Tell Me More": Listening to Learners Explain *(2001). In her course, Duckworth cleverly absorbs her teacher education students in studying the moon each night and asks them to record their observations in a journal. Soon they are describing the changes not just in the moon, but in their thinking, as in the student who wrote, "My observations formed my questions, which caused the focus of my observations to change" (p. 124).*

Lest we believe that the sharing of their thinking in class serves mostly as evidence for Duckworth's beliefs about what constitutes "good" teaching, she is clear about the fact that "it is the students *who make sense of all of this," not the professor. While she does occasionally take the floor to say what she thinks on the topic, she knows that "students are likely to have convictions that they are comparing with what they understand me to be saying," (pp. 132–133) which she believes can only be helpful for their learning. She also seems to know intuitively that memorable learning experiences are contagious—you can't wait to*

*From "The Having of Wonderful Ideas" and Other Essays on Teaching and Learning (New York: Teachers College Press, 1987).

share your latest discovery and try out a new idea—and that holds true for learning about subject matter content as well as learning about "teaching and learning phenomena." All learning should inspire the sharing of ideas.

Although she doesn't say so explicitly, it is clear from this piece that Duckworth finds moon watching fascinating. Bringing your passions to bear on your teaching makes for more meaningful interactions with children. As a parent, you don't necessarily teach your children how to cook, paint, rock climb, or ski because you want them to be just like you, but because those are things you are excited about and want to share. Children, and even adult learners, can tell when the teacher is genuinely interested in the subject at hand, and is learning along with everyone else, and that often generates an infectious curiosity to find out more.

An important implication of Duckworth's approach is that students are learning more deeply and gaining greater clarity of their ideas when they explain their thinking to others, whether they are siblings, relatives, or classmates. Techniques such as having students turn and talk to the person next to them when it seems everyone is eager to share their thinking on a particular topic, or pairing up younger and older students for shared reading experiences are but two examples of ways in which teachers can step back and let the students do the explaining and questioning. Cynthia Ballenger once said in a public address that she tries to live by the credo that "the child is always making some kind of sense." Duckworth advises us to "keep trying to find out what sense the students are making" (p. 133) and to share the responsibility of ensuring they understand one another.

What I love to do is to teach teachers. I love to stir up their thoughts about how they learn; about how on earth anyone can help anyone else learn; and about what it means to know something. I love to help them feel that any aspect of human endeavor is accessible to them and that they can make it accessible to any person they teach. I love to try to find ways into a subject that will catch everybody's interest; to find out what people think about things and to find ways to get them talking about what they think; to shake up things they thought they knew; to get people wrapped up in figuring something out together without needing anything from me; to help build their fascination with what everybody else thinks, and with the light that other people's thinking might shed on their own. I love to see the most productive of questions be born out of laughter, and the most frustrating of brick walls give way to an idea that has been there all along.

But there are two main reasons that I love to teach teachers in particular. One is that teachers are as interested as I am in how people learn, so the dialogue is deeply felt. The second is that I always learn from them in return, when I see the endless variations on how they use what they learn in their own teaching. This chapter is about how I teach, how teachers respond to it, and what one can learn through teaching in such a way.

It was a conviction about learning that got me started teaching the way that I do. As a student of Piaget, I was convinced that people must construct their own knowledge and must assimilate new experiences in ways that make sense to them. I knew that, more often than not, simply telling students what we want them to know leaves them cold.

So what is the role of teaching, if knowledge must be constructed by each individual? In my view, there are two aspects to teaching. The first is to put students into contact with phenomena related to the area to be studied—the real thing, not books or lectures about it—and to help them notice what is interesting; to engage them so they will continue to think and wonder about it. The second is to have the students try to explain the sense they are making, and, instead of explaining things to students, to try to understand their sense. These two aspects are, of course, interdependent: When people are engaged in the matter, they try to explain it and in order to explain it they seek out more phenomena that will shed light on it.

ENGAGING WITH PHENOMENA:
THE FIRST ASPECT OF TEACHING

Since I am teaching about teaching and learning, the phenomena with which I must engage my students must entail teaching and learning.*

---

*In the course referred to in this chapter, I usually have about 45 students in a class, including experienced classroom teachers, undergraduates seeking teacher certification, and professionals from other careers who have chosen to switch into teaching. Their teaching interests cover all subject matters, dramatic arts through geography, and all ages, preschool through adult. I have done similar work with groups of urban public school teachers, and with undergraduates in a teachers' college.

Rather than reading and hearing lectures, the students must learn and teach or watch people learn and teach, and somehow I must make these phenomena interesting and different enough to intrigue them and raise questions they had not thought of before.

There are three major kinds of teaching and learning phenomena with which I try to engage the students. This account is complicated, though, by the fact that within each of these three—circles within circles— we find both of the aspects of teaching mentioned above: Since I am teaching about teaching, the phenomena I present are themselves composed of the two aspects.

The first kind of phenomenon in which I try to engage these students is demonstrations with one or two children or adolescents. In these demonstrations, I attempt to engage the children with some problem or activity (first aspect), and to understand their explanations (second aspect). I try to capture the students' interest in the children's ideas and their enjoyment of this intellectual work. I also try to show that the children have reasons for thinking what they think, and that it is possible to find out what these reasons are.

The second kind of phenomenon consists of the students' own attempts to carry out a similar inquiry with one or two people at a time, outside class. They are instructed to present some phenomenon (for example, a particular reflection in a mirror) in a manner that engages people, and to try to understand their explanations of it. This is quite a new and difficult experience for people whose idea of teaching is to do the explaining.

The third kind of phenomenon for the students in this course is to learn as a group about a particular subject other than teaching and learning, for example, about pendulums, or floating and sinking, or mathematical permutations. Again we find the two aspects. I try to engage the students in the subject and encourage them to explain how they are thinking about it. My challenge is to engage the students in such a way that they are intrigued not only by the subject we are studying—which I shall call the secondary subject—but by the nature of the teaching and learning phenomena they experience as they learn (and I teach) this secondary subject. We proceed on both these levels at once. It is this third activity, learning a secondary subject together as a group, that I would like to discuss at greater length in this chapter.

Both of the levels present the difficulty, in my classes, of a great range

in what people know, or think they know. As far as teaching and learning are concerned, I can at least count on the fact that they are interested in the topic, and everybody is prepared to think that they can learn
more. The secondary subject, by contrast, is something they have not
bargained for and do not particularly care to learn about. Furthermore,
a number of them believe they know all about it already, while many
think that they are incapable ever of learning about it. Engaging students in the secondary subject is a considerable challenge.

I go about engaging the students in the secondary topic in about the
same way as I go about engaging them in the topic of teaching and
learning. I look for some phenomenon to draw their attention to, counting on it to do the work of engaging them. I make sure there is always
something to do or to watch and make sense of so that everybody can have
something to say, even if it is only to say what they saw. My focus on
what they themselves *see* and how they make sense of it goes a long way
toward providing a common ground. Part of what I have learned to do
is to find phenomena that, familiar as they are and simple as they seem,
do not lend themselves to satisfactory explanations by distant theories.

Of the many different secondary subjects I have used to engage
teachers, the example I will use here is the study of the habits of the
moon.* Before we start, I usually ask them when they last saw the moon,
what it looked like, when they think they'll see it next, and what it will
look like then. Sometimes this preliminary discussion gives rise to conflicting ideas, so some students find themselves immediately engaged.
Once, for example, one person said that the previous night she had seen
the moon as illustrated in Figure 1 and another said she saw it as shown
in Figure 2. The class was about evenly divided among those who thought

Figure 1   Figure 2

<hr />

*Engaging students in moon watching as a way into astronomy is an approach I learned from Donald Ford, a fellow
staff member at the Elementary Science Study, in 1965, when he was preparing a moon-watching teacher's guide
(Elementary Science Study, 1968).

they both could have seen what they said they saw, those who thought at least one person must be mistaken, and those who had no idea whether it was possible or not.

More often, there is no discord at the start, nothing particular to talk about. Some people accept this as a rather flaky assignment that they will do because it does not seem too complicated, and why not seize the chance to be flaky in the midst of graduate school. Some accept it solemnly because they have been asked to do it. Some resist it as an imposition and a waste of time. Some like the idea right from the start.

I ask the students to keep and bring to each class a separate notebook in which they make an entry every time they see the moon—when and where they see it and what it looks like. By the first week's reporting time, at least some people have something specific they want to look for in the following week. Little by little, the assignment changes from one that is flaky, arbitrary, or easy to one that is absorbing and serious.

The following excerpts from retrospective accounts that students wrote late in the term exemplify this range of responses. Some of the writers include quotes from their daily moon notebooks.

Student One

I guess the major question I had going into this experiment was, "Is she serious?" In fact the requirement almost stopped me from taking this class—I really thought it was silly. I also thought it would be a lot of tedious work. I was wrong.

I keep [my notebook] on my bedside table and every night it's there to remind me to look out the window. . . . It only takes 2 or 3 minutes to write down my observations and draw my pictures, but later, when I sit down and read several weeks' notes all together, I can spend 15 to 20 minutes just generating questions and checking answers. I get excited when the moon moves across the sky just the way I thought it would, and I'm so disbelieving when it does something unexpected that I check my notes again and again. . . .

My observations formed my questions, which caused the focus of my observations to change. I'm now concentrating on the path of the moon each night, not on its color or shape, although I'm still shaky enough to always note those, too. . . . Everything . . . is expanding—my questions and observations are getting broader. . . .

My biggest problem in this class [is] forgetting about being a teacher and relearning how to be a learner. This [notebook] is a big help. I can make hypotheses, and they can be *wrong*—that's OK. . . . I can share observations and theories and be proud when someone says, "Ah, that's good. Tell me how it turns out." I can move at my own pace and ask my own questions. I like it.

Student Two

My knowledge of the moon has become internalized. It is not what someone is trying to "teach" me. Rather, it is an area of interest I choose to explore. . . . As such . . . moon knowledge represents the way in which I have come to understand learning.

I have come to see the unknown as available and optional areas of exploration rather than as required and restrictive areas of study. I am not bound by my lack of knowledge. I am free to explore in my own time, at my own pace. That change has not occurred suddenly. The following excerpts from my journal may help to illustrate the transformation.

9/25   Moon watching is proving difficult. I am never in the same place at the same time and in any event, I can't see it from my house. Irritating.

9/29   I'm finally succeeding at my moon watching. I was looking too early in the evening and in the wrong direction. . . . Now that I've found it, I can watch it. [Little did I realize that once found is not always found!]

10/7   Even though being able to watch the moon is the most difficult part, I know I've already learned some things. (1) It isn't always the same color. (2) It goes from A to B [see Figure 3]. (3) It rises and sets at different times. (4) It comes up in different places.

Figure 3

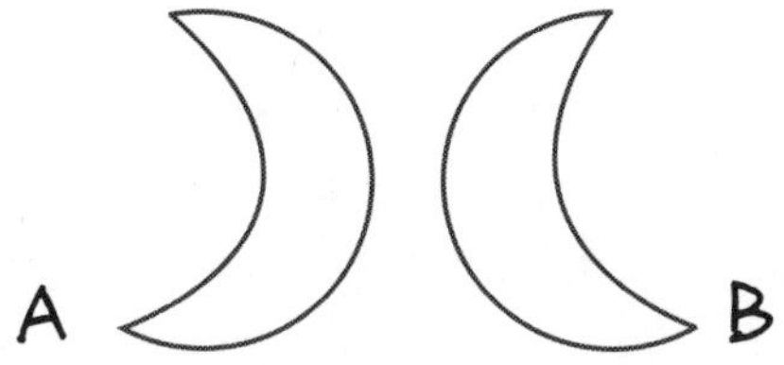

10/8   Learning about the moon is . . . like I have a bunch of uncon-
nected facts—a puzzle. It's fun to think about it without being punished.

10/20   I have found the moon again. Yea!! It shines mostly during the
day right now. Before this, even though I saw it sometimes during the day, I
really thought it only shone at night.

10/22   I thought the moon had changed tilt and now I know it
does. . . .

10/26   I am having a wonderful time learning about the moon. I can't
believe how much it changes in just two days. . . .

The evolution from student to learner occurred over time as a change
of perspective. In September, I saw the moon and its habits as external
pieces of knowledge which were somehow requirements of the course. I
now see them as orienting devices, a way of looking at learning.

Student Three

At the beginning I didn't want to watch the moon. I felt that being required to do so was an imposition without any sense. Why did I have to
watch the moon? Why did I have to write about it? I felt that in doing so
I was being conducted to a new relationship with nature, that I was being
told to relate with nature in a predetermined way. . . . During the first
weeks of classes, I looked at the moon without allowing myself to get
too much involved. I was trying to understand the course, trying to grasp
what was really happening. Little by little things were getting clarified.
But there was still one piece missing: The moon . . . I was still resisting
to watch it. I wanted to understand, but I couldn't. I hadn't yet realized
that in order to really learn about the moon . . . I had to watch it.

I must say that during this period, I did look at the moon more frequently than before. The discussions in class, my thoughts about the
course, and mirrors [another secondary subject] led me to an increasing
curiosity: "There must be something in this moon watching." And then
I began to catch myself looking at it, thinking about it. . . .

Then, questions began to arise from this "casual watching." . . . The
questions led to new questions, to new curiosities and, also, to new sur-

prises. I'm still a beginner as a moon-watcher and I have thousands of questions: How do changes in shape occur? Why do I see it sometimes "here" and sometimes "there"? Does it move always at the same pace? Where does it go when I don't see it?

Student Four

During my first observations of the moon was when I realized that my understanding of the moon had nothing to do with the theory, and that in fact I am very ignorant about the movement of it. I thought that the moon was sufficiently high and for that reason you could see it from every angle. I also thought that the moon was at the same place every night. This was my first discovery (to understand that my understanding of the moon was wrong).

Student Five

October 10: *The Morning Moon*

6:00 A.M. What! The moon is where it was at 7:30 P.M. last time I saw it. It's early morning. What time did it rise? Why? Is there a connection between its waning and its rising time?

October 11–16: *The Moon Turns Around (or seems to)*

During this five-day period, I am intent upon systematically measuring the angle of the moon in the sky. I am also checking whether or not I can see it well into the morning. I record the moon on the 11th as shaped like this . . . [See Figure 4.] Then, between the 13th and 15th I lose it, don't see it at all.

7:00 A.M.

Figure 4

6:15 P.M.   Figure 5

One evening coming out of Longfellow Hall, 6:15 P.M., I see it right up Appian Way toward the Charles. As if that's not astonishing enough, I notice and record (thank goodness) that the *direction of the horns has changed*. [See Figure 5.] I commented on it in my diary, but had thought little more of it until right now.

Student Six

I like a lot of things about the moon watching. I seem to connect with other things in the sky. I look up and observe the stars. I also watch the sun—especially when it sets.

I also like the idea that friends of mine are getting interested in the moon-watching idea and discuss things with me. One friend called me up two weeks ago at 4:15 A.M. and told me to look at the huge moon in the western sky!

Student Seven

I felt that I knew a great deal about the moon (I'd thought about the moon as part of a unit in astronomy with six graders [I thought I had]). I knew things about orbits and distance and reflected light and was very comfortable that my familiarity with my friend the moon was an intimate one. . . . The first class discussion . . . clued me in to the fact that my knowledge of the moon falls far short of an understanding. My knowledge was one from a perspective way out in space looking in. It was always easy to think about these three objects in space and their interactions (sun, moon, earth). With this new perspective I had many questions without answers. . . .

Not knowing can be so much more fun than knowing. It's opened my eyes to look for understanding. I curse whatever it was that led me to believe this puzzle was solved.

THE STUDENTS EXPLAIN:
THE SECOND ASPECT OF TEACHING

Having the students watch the moon corresponds to the first of the two aspects of teaching that I mentioned: It engages them with phenomena. It serves this purpose at two levels. With regard to engaging with the solar system, it puts them in touch with the motions of the moon (and, it always turns out, of other heavenly bodies). With regard to engaging with teaching and learning, it puts them in touch with themselves and each other as learners, and with what I am doing as a teacher.

Similarly, the second aspect is brought into play at both of these levels. With regard to the motions of the moon, I continually ask them what they notice and what they make of it, and I encourage them to do the same with each other. The questions that we ask over and over again in class are: "What do you mean?" "Why do you think that?" "I don't quite get it." "Is that the same as what (someone else) thought they saw?" We also talk about what sense they are making of the primary subject of teaching and learning—what do they notice about this experience as learners and what do they make of that?

At both levels, although much more often in the secondary subject, more knowledgeable class members sometimes get impatient. I invite them then to put their efforts into trying to elicit and understand someone else's explanation—to join me in practicing teaching by listening rather than by explaining. I also point out that it serves nobody's purpose to declare something if you are sure of it. It does serve a purpose to propose a tentative idea—because then people can help you think it through.

The students also keep journals of their thoughts, their reactions, and the sense they are making of the discussions.

In some ways, it is easier to understand how this works with respect to teaching and learning than with respect to the solar system. After all, what one believes about teaching and learning is complicated, large-scale, hard to define, and close to the soul. If one stops to think about it, it is hard to imagine students learning about teaching and learning *other than* by working out for themselves what they think. Of course, when I say "working out for themselves" I do not rule out presenting people with material for them to make sense of, as I try to describe here—experience in which they learn, try to explain what they are learning, watch others learn, try to help other people explain, and hear other people's ideas. But it is the *students* who make sense of all of this. It could not be otherwise. And they make sense by trying out their own ideas, by explaining what they think and why, and seeing how this holds up in other people's eyes, in their own eyes, and in the light of the phenomena they are trying to understand.

In other matters less close to the soul I believe that it works the same way. Whatever it is that a person believes and understands, it is *that person* who believes and understands it. Paley (1986), engaged in a very similar exercise in her teaching of 3-year-olds, observed, "Why not just tell Frederick the truth: '*Of course* your mother has a birthday; everybody has a birthday.' Tempting as it might be to set the record straight, I have discovered that I can't seem to teach the children that which they don't already know" (p. 126). The best Paley can do is to accept the children's perspectives and to draw attention to some aspects they might think about at the same time. When older children or adults are struggling to make sense, they might be more inclined than Frederick to repeat what I have told them, but I have found that they are no more likely to have integrated it; I have not "set the record straight." Evidence to this effect comes up time and time again, whether the subject is the habits of the moon, a foreign language, fractions, photosynthesis, reading, or poetry.

Instead of explaining to the students, then, I ask them to explain what they think and why. I find the following results. First, in trying to make their thoughts clear for other people, students achieve greater clarity for themselves. Much of the learning is in the explaining. (Why should the teacher monopolize occasions for trying to make herself clear?) Second, the students themselves determine what it is they want to understand. It is not only the explanations that come from them, but also the questions. Third, people come to depend on themselves: They are the judges of what they know and believe. They know why they believe it, what questions they still have about it, their degree of uncertainty about it, what they want to know next about it, how it relates to what other people think. Any other "explanation" they encounter must establish its place within what they know. Fourth, students recognize the powerful experience of having their ideas taken seriously, rather than simply screened for correspondence to what the teacher wanted. One student, an elementary school principal, speaks to these third and fourth points:

> Moon watching has been a profound experience for me. From the beginning, I was thoroughly engaged by the activity. . . . I wrote in my journal, "One of the things I love about moon watching is this—as a nonscientific person, I have finally been afforded the opportunity to learn about a 'scientific' phenomenon without feeling dumb and unscientific because I don't know the scientific answers. Hurray . . . !"
>
> Here was a profound difference from my previous experience with science. Why? In this case, no premium was placed on "quick right answers." Instead, totally mistaken notions were not only accepted, but honored. . . . How could I feel dumb when whatever I was thinking was accepted with respect?
>
> Do I understand the moon now? I understand a great deal more than I did four months ago, but I feel fairly certain that some of what I "know" is probably wrong, and there's still a lot I don't begin to understand. Why doesn't that bother me? I no longer think I'm dumb if I don't know the "quick right answer." . . . What I do know about the moon is mine forever.

Fifth, students learn an enormous amount from each other:

> Class discussions have helped out a lot. Often people see the moon at different times than I do, and they can tentatively fill in some of my gaps in knowledge (the gaps won't really be filled in until *I* see things for myself). I also like to hear other people's hypotheses, because they give me other avenues and ideas to check out. I especially like it when I can't believe what someone else has seen—it makes me slow down and reevaluate my own notes and theories.

Finally, learners come to recognize knowledge as a human construction, since they have constructed their own knowledge and they know that they have. What is written in a book is viewed as somebody else's creation, a creation produced just as they produced their own. Its origin is not of another order. (By contrast, most students—adults and children—believe "knowledge" to be an absolute, which some people have caught on to, and which they, if they are smart enough, will be able to learn from someone who has caught on.) The following excerpt speaks to this point.

> I had seen the moon changing shape in regular ways, but I never thought of trying to make sense of this, to see it in connection to how the moon and sun and earth work. It's this connection that's been so exciting, this realizing that the moon that we see in our visible world can tell us about a larger world which I thought before was only to be found in classrooms and libraries, that we can watch the world and begin to understand how it works. . . .
>
> There's so much I don't understand, and trying to understand means giving things up, at least partially trading part of a familiar way of seeing for the beginnings of another. But I also have this terrific feeling of an *opening* of things—that's the word that goes around inside my head when I think about moon watching. It's exciting! It's opened up a way of thinking and learning about the world, a potential to slowly make sense of what I see and know and for this visible, familiar world to reach me about things I don't see or understand.

While the major burden is on the students to explain what they think, I actually do try to say much of what I myself believe on the subject of teaching and learning. I often remark on what I see in our work together and I try to say what I think about issues that students raise. (After all, I too am grateful for the occasion to learn from trying to say clearly what I think.) I do not take much air time, though. And I have no illusions that what I say will mean the same thing to others as it does to me, nor that the students will, in general, give credence to what I say. But what I say does add to the assortment of things they have to think about. It is partly because of the complicated nature of teaching and learning, where people cannot possibly understand everything that anyone else means by what they say, and partly because these students are likely to have convictions that they are comparing with what they understand me to be saying, rather than taking what I say at face value, that I feel it may be helpful rather than harmful to say what I think.

However, in the case of the secondary subject in which they have as yet little interest and about which they have few ideas of their own (the moon, in this instance), I do not usually say what I think. My efforts are centered on enabling people to see that their own ideas are perfectly reasonable and, in fact, are the best starting points. It would be all too easy, if I were to give my account, for people to sit back, stop thinking, and assume that they understand what I am saying and that what I say is right—not to mention the likelihood that the topic will cease to hold any interest for them if they are simply listening to what I think. I do, though, offer ideas for consideration if I can see a different point of view that no one else has mentioned. Sometimes such an idea is one I believe in, and sometimes it is not. In either case, I do not present it as a "right" idea, but simply as another one that should be considered. (I usually introduce it by saying, "Some people say . . .") If the discussion gets to a point where I am not at all sure what I think, then I might enter with my own tentative thoughts, acknowledged as mine.

The essential element of having the students do the explaining is not the withholding of all the teacher's own thoughts. It is, rather, that the teacher not consider herself or himself the final arbiter of what the learner should think, nor the creator of what that learner does think. The important job for the teacher is to keep trying to find out what sense the students are making. This sometimes involves what has come to be called in my classes "monkey wrenches"—some idea or evidence that raises a question about what a learner has just said, even if that might be something I agree with. "Throwing a monkey wrench," instead of "reinforcing the right answer" (as the common wisdom of the trade goes), at first seems a perverse teaching practice. Yet it is *because* of the basic concerns of a teacher—*because* of wanting to be sure that students understand—that one remains noncommittal, resists early acceptance of a student's understanding, and searches for any soft spots that require more thinking.

There is one other important aspect to having students do the explaining. I try to have all the students share with me the responsibility of making sure they understand each other. This is tough for many people.

For one thing, it is often hard to admit to oneself that one does not understand. Second, many (in fact, most) of the adults I have taught assume that if they have not understood what has been said, the shortcoming is their own. Few think that the speaker said it unclearly, and even fewer that the speaker might not have been clear in his or her own mind.

The following excerpt indicates how significant it is even for competent adults to take this step.

> [We paid] careful attention . . . to the understanding of each other's understanding, as well as our own. . . . For the first time in my life, I heard myself say to a fellow classmate, in front of approximately 50 others, "I don't think I understand what you mean. Could you please say that again?" Never before had I experienced the self-confidence, the freedom and, perhaps, the comfort necessary to do such a thing. What is significant, however, is that such an honest statement on my part was able to lead to further explanation and exploration of the other's thoughts, thereby raising issues in his own mind to be shared with the others as he experienced them, himself. In a journal entry . . . I wrote the following:
>
>> For the first time, I was able to examine another's thoughts at work. Simultaneously, it seemed, I could examine my own. Excitement! I feel like a supercharged machine, discovering realms of my own capacities which I'd never known were there! What other worlds within worlds within me exist?
>
>> Such euphoria was certainly not the norm, but what joy to experience! I felt as though my eyes and ears were operating at heights never before reached—certainly not within a classroom.

TEACHING-RESEARCH

My view of teaching suggests an analogy to the work of a psychotherapist with a research interest. She is both a practitioner and a researcher. She could not possibly learn anything significant about psychodynamics if she were not genuinely engaged in the therapeutic process. It is only because she knows how to do her job as a practitioner that she is in a position to pursue her questions as researcher. I would like to propose that, similarly, one is in a position through teaching to pursue questions about the development of understanding that one could not pursue in any other way. If as a researcher one is interested in how people build their understanding, then the way to gain insight is to watch them do it, and try to make sense of it as it happens (to paraphrase Armstrong, in Engel, 1984).

When I speak of "teaching," I do not necessarily mean schoolteaching. I am not, myself, a school teacher, for example. By "teacher" I mean someone who engages learners, who seeks to involve each person wholly—mind, sense of self, sense of humor, range of interests, interactions with other people—in learning. And, having engaged the learners, a teacher finds his questions to be the same as those that a researcher into the nature of human learning wants to ask: What do you think and why? While the students learn, the teacher learns, too. And it helps if, like Paley (1986), he is *curious* about the students' thoughts. How do other people really think about these matters? Which ideas build on which others and how? Which interests build on other interests? Which ideas get in the way of other ideas? What seems to be, in Hawkins's (1978) phrase, the "critical barriers" in this field? How is an idea modified? How does a firmly held conviction influence how a person reads an experience? What is the range of conceptions covered by a "right-sounding" word or phrase? In what circumstances is a person confused by/deaf to/helped by another person's thoughts? What factors keep interest high? How does a specific representation of one's thoughts influence how the thoughts develop further? How does a new idea lead to a new question, and vice versa?[*]

This kind of research, which I am calling teaching-research, need not take place in a classroom. But it does require, as researcher, someone who knows ways into a subject matter well enough to engage a great variety of learners, and to keep them going as they ask and answer further questions—that is, it requires someone who is a good teacher.[†]

After her experience in the course just described, Delaney (1986a), a

---

[*]Besides my own work, already referred to, see the following sources, listed in the References, for a variety of approaches to such work: Apelman, 1982; Armstrong, 1980; Bamberger, 1979; Bussis et al., 1985; diSessa, 1985; Duckworth et al., 1985; Hart, 1979; Hawkins, 1986; Julyan, in preparation; Kamii et al., 1980; Lampert, 1986; Lawler, 1985; Paley, 1986; Rowe, 1987; Tierney, in preparation.

[†]For a related view of teachers as researchers, see Cobb and Steffe, 1983.

high school teacher of government on leave from her classroom, did some pilot research of this kind. As she stated in the project proposal,

> I am attempting to understand how two high school students [Mark and Tim] . . . make sense of the presidency. In so doing, I would like to be able to identify questions and problems that interest people and prompts them to take notice of their own understanding and to elaborate on it. I am especially interested in . . . four aspects of the presidency: the powers of the president, the restrictions on these powers, the relationship between the president and other government institutions (particularly Congress), and the relationship between the president and the electorate. These four aspects of the presidency seem to be sufficiently broad so that I might be able to glimpse how the national government is understood. Yet they are sufficiently focused so that we have specific problems and issues to explore. (p. 1)

Each of her students kept a notebook in which they recorded each day at least one observation of the president, taken from news broadcasts, papers, or magazines.

Even though she was "attempting to understand," her primary interest in the project was in being a teacher. "The most important goal of this project for me was that [they] learn to think about some aspect of the president in some new way" (Delaney, 1986a, p. 4). She did succeed in "engaging" the students, the first aspect of teaching described above. At the end of the study, she wrote, "The most amazing aspect of this project . . . has been how engaged both Mark and Tim stayed. Every time I called them [to confirm the meetings], they wanted to tell me what they thought of some event and ask what I thought." The following excerpts from one of her field reports further show how the two, research and teaching, are one. Tim was sick this day, and the session took place with Mark alone.

> Mark rarely hesitates in stating his opinions or thoughts. If his statements seem contradictory to me and I ask him to explain, he calmly states each statement again, not bothering to reconcile the contradiction (Delaney, 1986a, p. 20).

In our last session, when I asked Mark if a person is disloyal to the country when he or she disagrees with the president, he replied: "No. You have to distinguish between two things. A president is gonna base his decision on two things: either on what the majority of the people like *or* on what he knows best. . . . If he decides to rule by his feelings on a subject on which he knows more than the public then you can't say those people are un-American. Not every American knows in-depth."

Because I did not understand this explanation, I asked Mark about it again [in this session]. I read to him what he had said. He said, "Yeah, I know you didn't really understand all that. . . ." He explained: "People that do [know] as much as Reagan, they still disagree. Because on a particular subject, if they didn't agree . . . Now you got me stuck." "Good. . . ." Mark was truly stuck. He was hesitant from "particular subject" on. He does not like being stuck. When I replied "good," we both laughed. I could see him relax. (Delaney, 1986b, pp. 1–2)

Delaney chose to back off from that question for the time being, in order to put him at ease. Later she returned to it. This passage is particularly interesting in enabling us to see the kinds of decisions Delaney is making throughout this work.

I asked him to explain once again his notions of the two ways presidents can make decisions. He said, "Well, first of all, it's not just the president. All politicians have that choice. . . . It would be good if politicians in order to get into office tell people what they want to hear, but once they're in just do what they think is best. . . . [I]f what they're doing is right that's OK."

My mind went in two different but related directions: (1) What if what the politicians do is wrong? and (2) who determines what is right and wrong, and how . . . ? For some time I had suspected that Mark's view of decision making rested on an assumption that decisions could be classified into either right or wrong decisions. . . . [I asked him:]

"How do you determine if a decision is right?"

"What would benefit overall the people."

"How do you decide what would benefit the people overall?"

"I'm not sure."

"Let's look at an example that we've talked about. . . ."

"Okay."

"Contra aid. In the public opinion polls, the majority of the American people seem to oppose aid to the contras. Yet the president supports it. How does he decide that the majority is wrong and he is right?"

". . . You don't know that. The majority could be people who just don't like it. Some people know. Some don't."

From this statement I realized that Mark probably thought of the "majority" as one huge chunk—a monolithic entity holding the same views for the same reasons. . . . I suggested that we make up a poll. . . . I asked: "This 52% represents 624 individuals and this 48% represents 576 individuals. Had you thought of that?"

"Yes."

"Okay, how do you know if these 624 individuals know or do not know about the contra aid issue?"

He responded: "I could say the majority don't know or I could say the minority don't know. You would have to do a very in-depth study."

"Knowing" to Mark seems to be directly linked to "right" and "not knowing" to wrong. In this session and the last . . . he uses "right" and "knowing" interchangeably. To know is to be right. . . . I asked if it might be possible that some people in the majority be misinformed and some be informed? "It's hard to say . . . because some people just base it on what they saw in the news and not on what's real."

In this last statement we have plenty of questions for another [session]. . . . What's the difference between the news and "what's real"? Bypassing this for a moment, I decided to rephrase my question using his terminology. "Is it possible that some people in the majority base their decisions on the news and others on what's real?" Silence. Mark was thinking— *hard*. I could practically hear his brain working when he said, "Wow, I never thought of that before."

"What?"

"That a majority could have different reasons why they're on that side." (Delaney, 1986b, pp. 4–6)

Here was confirmation of her hunch about how Mark was thinking (Delaney as researcher) and, at the same time, a great new idea on his part (Delaney as teacher). The session had to come to an end shortly after this. Delaney asked Mark to watch the news "for examples of how people on the same side of an issue . . . may agree for different reasons," and for "more data on how the president decides."

Among her several comments on the session is this one, where she uses the insight gained into Mark's thinking to help her understand something that had puzzled her since the first session:

> From our last session, I had suspected that Mark's notion of decision-making tested on a belief that absolutely right and absolutely wrong decisions were possible, and that part of the president's job was to identify *the* right decision. He said in our first session, "It's wrong to change your opinion. You can't just change it like that." This seems a curious statement at first glance, and the juxtaposition of the statements seems even more curious. However, if you believe that your opinion is right then both statements and their relationship begin to make sense: If you *are* right then changing your opinion *is* wrong (Delaney, 1986b, p. 9)

What, then, has Delaney learned as a researcher? On the face of it, it might look as if what she learned was particulars about Tim and Mark. Of course that *is* what she learned, and at one level we could say that what she learned helped her make specific decisions about how to go further with them. In this, she is being a "reflective practitioner," in Schön's (1983) sense. But there are other levels where her learning goes far beyond her work with Tim and Mark. She contributes to our knowledge of what is involved in an understanding of how the American government works, and how such understanding can evolve. For readers with no interactions at all with Tim and Mark, her field reports are fascinating. So that's what you have to think about as you try to help someone understand the workings of government!

In her final report, she uses Hawkins's (1978) notion of "critical barriers" in discussing two factors she found to characterize Tim and Mark's ideas about the workings of the government. One factor was what she called "single-group nouns"—"majority," "public," and also "White House" (in referring vaguely to the president and/or his staff)— which the boys used, as she put it, to "communicate a single entity and obscure the diversity inherent in them" (Delaney, 1986a, p. 31). The second factor is their tendency to view the presidency in what she called "bipolar terms"—characterized by making "right" and "wrong" decisions. She points out that the first of these barriers makes it difficult, for example, to appreciate the central importance of diversity in a democracy. The second makes it difficult, for example, to appreciate why a democracy limits the powers of its leaders.

Even from this exceedingly small-scale study there seem to be countless questions for further teaching-research into what is involved in order for people to come to understand the workings of a democratic government. That is one kind of contribution this approach to research makes.

Furthermore, in shedding light on the growth of understanding about a democratic government, such research also sheds light on the growth of understanding in general. Oversimplifying single-group nouns and viewing situations as bipolar are both widespread characteristics of human thinking and a lively concern of psychologists (see Basseches, 1984). Just as specifics can be understood only through generalities, so generalities can be understood only through specifics: It is helpful to think of bipolar thinking as a critical barrier; at the same time, it is only possible to understand what critical barriers are when we see instances of them.

I believe there is yet another kind of knowledge to which this research contributes—namely, knowledge of curriculum possibilities. Delaney's attempts to learn how these youngsters understand government seem to me to indicate ways to *teach* youngsters about government. This almost seems like a tautology—the procedures that result in people's getting involved enough to want to talk about what they think are the very procedures that result in people's getting involved enough to learn. But if it is a tautology, it certainly has not been much recognized. In any event, Delaney has also learned and written about how to approach the teaching of government in a way that I think would certainly be helpful to other classroom teachers. If we take "curriculum" to be ways of engaging students in giving thought to those matters we think important, then she has started to develop curriculum.

SCHOOLTEACHING

Delaney did not carry out this research while working as a school teacher. She used her capacities as a teacher, but in a less pressured situation. It is a rare school teacher who has either the freedom or the time to think of her teaching as research, since much of her autonomy has been withdrawn in favor of the policies set by anonymous standard setters and test givers.

But even given the terrible constraints, and even if no resources are available to make known what they learn, there is some opportunity—and I think great need—for teachers to listen to their students explain what they think (for another perspective on this point, see Nussbaum & Novich, 1982).

Another student in this course, who was at the same time teaching science in a middle school, did a project with small groups of students from her class (Young, 1986). The following are some of her comments about this work and her regular teaching job.

> I chose to center my field work around the topic of pulse as an avenue to understanding the . . . circulatory system (a curriculum which I was supposed to "cover"). Initially, I was doubtful about how far we could get with our investigation. I had never given pulse much thought and imagined that it offered a few tactile experiences but might not turn out leading the students on to more questions. . . . I was amazed to discover how much investigation was generated from the pulse work.
>
> My research on students' understanding of pulse is entwined with my . . . teaching. . . . The teacher is researching the student and his understanding and then trying to help that student move on to more unknown territory. My bent is to apply my small group work to my classes . . . ! This is the ultimate challenge. The task appears so immense and fragile with one or two people, that the prospect of applying the same concentration to a large group is overwhelming. I do think that it is possible though with some modifications.
>
> If nothing else . . . the teacher would be more sensitive to listening, observing and then talking with her students rather than at them. Although I did not initially link my research with what I do in room 126 at the Middle School, I now see a crucial relationship. . . . My research has become and hopefully will remain a vital element in my teaching. I realize that my understanding of myself as a learner weighs heavily on how I perceive the understanding of other learners. So, we in room 126 are all learners.

CONCLUSION

I am not proposing that school teachers single-handedly become published researchers in the development of human learning. Rather, I am proposing that teaching, understood as engaging learners in phenomena and working to understand the sense they are making, might be the sine qua non of such research.

This kind of researcher would be a teacher in the sense of caring about some part of the world and how it works enough to want to make it accessible to others; he or she would be fascinated by the questions of how to engage people in it and how people make sense of it; would have time and resources to pursue these questions to the depth of his or her interest, to write what he or she learned, and to contribute to the theoretical and pedagogical discussions on the nature and development of human learning.

And then, I wonder—why should this be a separate research profession? There is no reason I can think of not to rearrange the resources available for education so that this description defines the job of a public school teacher.

So this essay ends with a romance. But then, it began with passion.

REFERENCES

Apelman, M. (1982). On Size and Scale: Learning with David Hawkins. *Outlook*, 45, 18–51.

Armstrong, M. (1980). *Closely observed children.* London: Writers and Readers Publishing.

Bamberger, J. (1979). *Music and cognitive research: Where do our questions come from; where do our answers go?* (Working Paper No. 2). Cambridge: Massachusetts Institute of Technology, Division for Study and Research in Education.

Bussis, A., Chittenden, E., Amarel, M., & Klausner, E. (1985). *Inquiry into meaning.* Hillsdale, NJ: Erlbaum.

Delaney, M. K. (1986a). *Understanding the presidency: Final report.* Unpublished manuscript, Harvard University, Graduate School of Education.

Delaney, M. K. (1986b). *Protocol 5, 4/28/86.* Unpublished manuscript, Harvard University, Graduate School of Education.

DiSessa, A. (1985). Learning about knowing. In E. L. Klein (Ed.), *Children and computers* (New Directions for Child Development, No. 28). San Francisco: Jossey-Bass.

Duckworth, E., Julyan, C., & Rowe, T. (1985). *Understanding equilibrium: The study of complex systems* (Final Project Report). Cambridge: Harvard University, Educational Technology Center.

Engel, B. (1984). Interview with Michael Armstrong. *Elementary School Journal, 84*, 350–356.

Hart, R. (1979). *Children's experience of place.* New York: Irvington Publishers.

Hawkins, D. (1978). Critical barriers to science learning. *Outlook, 29*, 3–23.

Hawkins, F. (1986). *The logic of action.* Boulder, CO: Colorado Associated Universities Press.

Julyan, C. (in preparation). *Understanding trees: Four case studies.* Unpublished doctoral dissertation, Harvard University.

Kamii, C., & DeVries, R. (1980). *Group games in early education.* Washington, DC: National Association for the Education of Young Children.

Lampert, M. (1986). Teaching multiplication. *The Journal of Mathematical Behavior, 5*, 241–280.

Lawler, R. W. (1985). *Computer experience and cognitive development: A child's learning in a computer culture.* New York: Halsted Press.

Nussbaum, J., & Novich, S. (1982). Alternative frameworks, conceptual conflict and accommodations: Toward a principled teaching strategy. *Instructional Science, 11*, 183–200.

Paley, V. (1986). On listening to what the children say. *Harvard Educational Review, 56*, 122–131.

Rowe, T. (1987). *Using introspective methods to investigate the learning strategies of adult foreign-language learners: Four case studies.* Unpublished doctoral thesis, Harvard University.

Schön, D. (1983). *The reflective practitioner.* New York: Basic Books.

Tierney, C. (in preparation). *Construction of fraction knowledge: Two case studies.* Unpublished doctoral dissertation, Harvard University.

Young, L. (1986). *Teacher as learner in research and the classroom.* Unpublished manuscript, Harvard University, Graduate School of Education.

MAUREEN: In this essay, Eleanor Duckworth explores the meaning of teaching and the dynamics of learning. This piece is especially important for parents and for beginning teachers because it offers a kind of blueprint for work with children. Duckworth argues that teaching, as opposed to preaching (something we teachers are prone to do), means engaging students with phenomena and asking them to explain what they are discovering, thus requiring them to continue the process of seeking more information on what they need to know. What a great approach to both parenting and teaching! She actually defines our work as "practicing teaching by listening rather than explaining" (p. 129).

The moon journals Duckworth describes have become a standard requirement in many elementary and secondary classrooms as well as in teacher education programs. They become recollections of thought, sense, and reaction, which then become the basis of class discussions as students explain their own thinking. Duckworth says, "Much of the learning is in the explaining" (p. 130). What a model for turning teaching into something more than showing and telling, and as she explains in the conclusion, what a resource for the study of education. Why not define the job of a public school teacher as one of researcher? Why not ask parents to join in such a project?

· 10 ·

Sylvia Ashton Warner

LIFE IN A MAORI SCHOOL*

ALEXANDRA: Sylvia Ashton Warner was a New Zealand educator and writer best known for her innovative methods and multicultural approach with Maori students and white students of European descent described in her book Teacher, *which brought her international recognition. In this excerpt, her diary entry begins with a casual exchange between two teachers, one a veteran (the writer), the other a visitor who sees the Maori children's energy as "trouble" that is best contained by keeping a "foot on their neck." I am reminded of countless conversations I have had with teachers and administrators who complained about energetic students who must be properly disciplined and taught to behave through elaborate systems of reward and punishment. Sadly, corporal punishment actually still occurs in American public schools today. There are also countless other less physically harmful examples of "madnesses and spiritual deaths" inflicted on those children who don't or won't conform, and whose exuberance is crushed by a traditional model of schooling that values, above all else, quiet and passive compliance.*

Ashton Warner chooses instead to harness bravely the very things most teachers try to suppress—children's desire to socialize and communicate with each other, and their desire to make things—and bases her teaching methods on them. She also describes cultivating in students an inner and outer discipline. "For the spirit to live its freest, the mind must acknowledge discipline" she writes (p. 147). What a fantastic quote to hang on classroom walls! She doesn't sugarcoat the process by which students' "volcanic energy" is given direction, or try to suggest that learning to teach in these conditions of freedom is by any means easy. She invites us to see that teaching is greatly rewarding, for the

*From Teacher (New York: Simon & Schuster, 1963).

funny and wild things that happen, and the "wide and happy fields" that open up when children are taught to see themselves as resources for each other's learning.

———————

And how are you getting on with the Maoris? I ask a visiting teacher to the school.

"Oh, it's the energy that's the trouble. They're always on the go. But once you've got your foot on their neck they're all right.

I understand . . . I understand. . . .

I do. But I don't talk about it. I don't try to describe to others the force of the energy in our New Race. Indeed, when I speak of it as "force of energy" I'm grossly understating it. It's more like a volcano in continuous eruption. To stand on it, in my Maori infant room anyway, to stand on it with both feet and teach it in quiet orthodoxy would be a matter of murders and madnesses and spiritual deaths, while to teach it without standing on it is an utter impossibility. The only way I know of dealing with it is to let it teach itself. And that's what I've been forced to do.

And that's exactly what I do. I stand back, something like a chairman, and let it teach itself. The only thing I step forward to teach is style. And believe me, I teach that. I teach it all the time in everything, because the rest follows. I teach style, and only style.

You've got to be either brave or desperate to take this road, even though in the end it leads to wide and happy fields. And I'm not brave. But I've got to the wide and happy fields. I'm all too aware that they are noisy fields, since my teacher's mind has been set by the past into the tradition of silence. But they're the only fields that I can understand and believe in, I being so simple—and even though the price is professional isolation and ineradicable, inescapable and corrosive guilt, here we stay.

From long sitting, watching and pondering (all so unprofessional) I have found out the worst enemies to what we call teaching. There are two.

The first is the children's interest in each other. It plays the very devil with orthodox method. If only they'd stop talking to each other, playing with each other, fighting with each other and loving each other. This unseemly and unlawful communication! In self-defence I've got to use the damn thing. So I harness the communication, since I can't control it, and base my method on it. They read in pairs, sentence and sentence about. There's no time for either to get bored. Each checks the other's mistakes and hurries him up if he's too slow, since after all his own turn depends on it. They teach each other all their work in pairs, sitting cross-legged knee to knee on the mat, or on their tables, arguing with, correcting, abusing or smiling at each other. And between them all the time is this togetherness, so that learning is so mixed up with relationship that it becomes part of it. What an unsung creative medium is relationship!

The other trouble with this New Race is their desire to make things. If only they'd sit like the white children with their hands still and wait until they're told to do something and told how to do it. The way they draw bombers and make them with anything and roar around the room with them.

Noise, noise, noise, yes. But if you don't like noise, don't be a teacher. Because children are noisy animals and these in particular, the young of a New Race, the noisiest I have ever known. But it's a natural noise and therefore bearable. True, there is an occasional howl of rage, a shout of accusation, soprano crying and the sound of something falling, but there is also a voice raised in joy, someone singing and the break, break, break of laughter. In any case it's all expulsion of energy and as such, a help. I let anything come . . . within safety; but *I use it*.

I use everything. They write their own books every morning for a start, to read when reading time comes. And the reading time . . . ah well, this is getting into the matter of method again and I'll get myself led miles away from what I'm talking about: the foot on the neck.

The spirit is so wild with the lid off. I'm still learning how to let it fly and yet to discipline it. It's got to be disciplined in a way that's hard to say. It still must have its range and its wing . . . it must still be free to dare the gale and sing, but it's got to come home at the right time and nest in the right place. For the spirit to live its freest, the mind must acknowledge discipline. In this room anyway. In this room there is an outer discipline as well as an inner. They've got to listen to me when I speak and obey what I speak. I can only say that I don't often speak. And that I carefully weigh what I do speak. But the track between these two conditions, the spiritual freedom and the outer discipline, is narrower than any tightrope, and seldom can I say that I have walked it.

The volcanic energy, precipitated from the combustion of the old race and the young, the volcanic energy of the New Race blows—but is directed. It was exhausting at first, this controlling of the direction of the blasts; and not without risks, this changing of the vents, for the young Maori warriors are full of "take, break, fight, and be first" when they come; but it is not as exhausting or as dangerous as standing in the way of it. Sometimes when a tribal excitement surges through the school, the tidal emotion rises up to the level of our eyes and over our signposts so that we think as we drown, "the foot on the neck." But I know that there is too much material and too much drive in the wake of these floods, so we hold our breath and rely on the inner disciplines. At least it's life. For both them and me. And the creative work that comes from it, especially the books, is something I'd pay anything for.

Yet I'm a disciplinarian. It's just that I like the lid off. I like seeing what's there. I like unpredictability and gaiety and interesting people, however small, and funny things happening and wild things happening and sweet, and everything that life is, uncovered. I hate covers of any kind. I like the true form of living, even in school. I'm in love with the organic shape.

"They're all right once you've got your foot on their neck."

I understand. I understand. But communication and creativity are abler teachers than a foot.

But I'm still no nearer to describing this energy. It has to be seen to be understood; the energy when the lid's off, I mean. And I don't talk about it either; so insignificant a thing as an infant room of the young of a minority race, in a small country, on a paltry planet, in a comparatively junior universe. It's too mere. It's enough for myself that "The least thing stirs me; the greatest cannot make me quake."

———————

MAUREEN: Sylvia Aston Warner's view of teaching and learning is extraordinary in that it both challenges our conventional notions of how children learn and sustains those of us wanting to experiment with new approaches. To have the courage to have our students freely express themselves in an invigorating climate of support and understanding can be daunting, but in the last analysis is one of life's most rewarding experiences. I love when Ashton Warner says, "if you don't like noise, don't be a teacher" (p. 147). I sometimes suspect that today's professionals are allergic to the voices of children, because classrooms are too often solemnly silent. When I visit some schools, I am reminded of tombs or prisons where students are confined with reams of worksheets to complete as punishment. Classrooms should be alive with conversation as children try out new ways of thinking and behaving. Rather than responding to teachers' questions for recall of information, they should be revising questions for one another based on the experiences the teacher provides for them. Ashton Warner says togetherness breeds learning, or, as she elegantly put it, "what an unsung creative medium is relationship!" (p. 147).

· 11 ·

Cynthia Ballenger

BECAUSE YOU LIKE US:
THE LANGUAGE OF CONTROL*

ALEXANDRA: Cynthia Ballenger, author of Teaching Other People's
Children: Learning and Literacy in a Bilingual Classroom (1999), *is a
prominent teacher researcher, one of my favorite writers on classroom life. Because her point of departure is often a puzzling moment, an odd remark by a
student, or the nagging sensation that she just doesn't understand what is happening, she shares her vulnerability and uncertainty in a way that is unusually
refreshing. Classroom researchers often feel compelled to tell the story of "best
practice," but Ballenger is more often than not making visible her own shortcomings and hard-learned lessons in the service of those who may share similar
predicaments.*

*In this article, she sheds light on a fascinating dimension of classic classroom
management dilemmas: misbehaving children who, as she says, "followed their
own inclinations rather than my directions in almost everything" (p. 153).
Through careful observation and dialogue with others, Ballenger skillfully analyzes cultural differences between the Haitian children in her charge, other
Haitian teachers, and her own North American upbringing and ways of asking children to comply with her requests. This reflection over time and careful
analysis of ways of speaking to small children who do not share her cultural
background lead to experimentation, and ultimately, improved teaching.*

*In teacher education today there is a great deal of concern that teachers need
more exposure to culturally responsive pedagogy and must cultivate a height-
ened cultural awareness. Ballenger's cultural experimentation, what she refers
to as "trying on this Haitian way," may be an important first step for teachers,
and parents, and in fact, all of us, who should, as she suggests, first learn about*

From the *Harvard Educational Review* 62, no. 2 (1992): 199–208.

the unfamiliar cultural norms we encounter in our interactions with children and their families, and then examine our own enculturation as we come to realize there are multiple ways to solve the puzzles of teaching.

This article is the result of a year spent in conversations about teaching—difficult conversations in which I, a seasoned teacher and fledgling sociolinguist, was only rarely the informed party.* Mike Rose, in *Lives on the Boundary* (1989), uses the metaphor of "entering the conversation" to describe the process of learning to participate in academic discourse. In my case, there was a multitude of different conversations I was trying to enter, and in each I had a different role to play.

During that same time I was teaching preschool, as I have done for most of the past fifteen years. The school was in the Haitian community in Dorchester, Massachusetts, and primarily served the children of Haitian immigrants. I went there because in my previous work as an early childhood special education teacher I had noticed that more and more Haitian children were being referred to my class. These children were arriving attended by all kinds of concerns from the educational professionals: they were "wild," they had "no language," their mothers were "depressed." There were certainly some children I saw who had genuine problems, and yet time and time again I found that, after a period of adjustment, they were responsive, intelligent children; their mothers were perhaps homesick and unhappy in a strange, cold country, but generally not clinically depressed. During that period, however, we did make many mistakes, and I became interested in learning the Haitian culture and language in order to see the children more clearly. After a period at graduate school studying sociolinguistics, I took a position as a preschool teacher in a bilingual school where both Haitian Creole and English were spoken and where, as I came to understand, Haitian culture was quite central. I was the only teacher at this school who was not Haitian and, although by this time I spoke Creole, I was still getting to know the culture.

*Earlier versions of this work have been presented at the Penn Ethnography in Educational Research Forum in February 1991 and the Brookline Teacher-Researcher Seminar in June 1990. My research was carried out as a member of that seminar with teachers and children at my school. In this article, all teachers' and children's names have been changed.

During that time I was one of two instructors of a course in child development that a local college offered for Haitian people who wished to work in day-care centers. My Haitian co-instructor and I designed this course based on the model of a conversation about child rearing—a dialogue between Haitians and North Americans about their attitudes on the subject. I was also a new member of the Brookline Teacher-Researcher Seminar (BTRS), a group of public school teachers and academic researchers who are attempting to develop a common language and a shared set of values with which to approach classroom issues (Michaels & O'Connor, 1990; Phillips, 1991). As a graduate student in sociolinguistics, I had done research; as a teacher, I had thought about teaching; I was now involved in trying to approach issues in ways that incorporated both of these perspectives. The work that I will report on here was part of these conversations. I will try to let the reader hear some of the different voices that I heard.

In this article, I will discuss the process I went through in learning to control a class of four-year-old Haitian children. Researchers who regard language as the principal vehicle by which children are socialized into their particular family and culture have consistently regarded control and discipline as central events—events where language patterns and cultural values intersect in visible ways (Boggs, 1985; Cook-Gumperz, 1973; Watson-Gegeo & Gegeo, 1990). When, as in my case, the adult does not share the same cultural background and the same experience of socialization as the children, one becomes very aware of learning how to enter and manage the relevant conversation. Although it can be argued that my participation in the events I relate here was in some ways informed by sociolinguistic theory, I present this more as a story than as a research report. This is my attempt to discuss this experience in a way that will not deny access to the conversation to those who helped form my understanding of it. I must stress, however, that all of these conversations would not have been possible if there hadn't been room in the preschool day for talk—the school was run jointly by the teachers and we spent considerable time each day together—and if there had not been some financial support for the Brookline Teacher-Researcher Seminar (Phillips, 1991). This support, in the form of small stipends, xeroxing, money for an occasional day off to reflect, and a sense of being valued, combined with the nature of the school where I was teaching, made my situation luxurious compared with that of many teachers faced with problems similar to mine.

THE PROBLEM

Having had many years of experience teaching in early childhood programs, I did not expect to have problems when I came to this Haitian preschool three years ago. However, I did. The children ran me ragged. In the friendliest, most cheerful, and affectionate manner imaginable, my class of four-year-olds followed their own inclinations rather than my directions in almost everything. Though I claim to be a person who does not need to have a great deal of control, in this case I had very little—and I did not like it.

My frustration increased when I looked at the other classrooms at my school. I had to notice that the other teachers, all Haitian women, had orderly classrooms of children who, in an equally affectionate and cheerful manner, *did* follow directions and kept the confusion to a level that I could have tolerated. The problem, evidently, did not reside in the children, since the Haitian teachers managed them well enough. Where then did it reside? What was it that the Haitian teachers did that I did not do?

The group of Haitian preschool teachers whom I was teaching in the child-development course recognized the problem in their own terms. As part of the course, they were all interning in various day-care centers, some with me at the Haitian school, the majority in other centers. Many of the teachers in the other centers were extremely concerned about behavior problems. What they told me and each other was that many of the children in their centers were behaving very poorly; many felt that this was particularly true of the Haitian children. They felt that the way in which they were being instructed as teachers to deal with the children's behavior was not effective. One woman explained to me that when she was hit by a four-year-old, she was instructed to acknowledge the anger he must be feeling, then to explain to him that he could not hit her. She told me that, from her point of view, this was the same as suggesting politely, "Why don't you hit me again?"

When I talked with Haitian parents at my school, I again heard similar complaints. From the point of view of many of the people I talked with, the behavior tolerated in their neighborhood schools was disrespectful; the children were allowed to misbehave. A common refrain in these conversations was, "We're losing a generation of children"; that is, the young children here now, who were not brought up first in Haiti, were not being brought up with the same values. However, when I asked for specific advice about things I might do to manage the children better, the teachers and I could never identify any behaviors of mine that I could try to change.

I took my problem to the Brookline Teacher-Researcher Seminar. The members of BTRS have come to share a focus on language—the language of instruction; children's language in a wide variety of situations; the language of science talk, of book talk, of conflict; and so on. Thus, in our conversations, the BTRS group encouraged me to approach my problem by discovering what it was that the Haitian teachers *said* to the children in situations where directions were being given. The Seminar members have also come to believe that an important part of a research project is examining where a particular research question comes from in one's own life—why it seems important, what its value is to the teacher-researcher. In many cases, this is a matter of investigating one's own socialization, a kind of self-reflection that became an important part of my investigation.

SITUATIONS AS TEXTS

I began to write down what the Haitian teachers said to the children in situations where the children's behavior was at issue. I then carried these texts to the various conversations of which I was a part: the Haitian teachers in the child development course, the North American teachers in the Brookline Seminar, and the parents and teachers at the school where I was teaching. I will present here some texts that I consider typical in their form and content, and then share some of the responses and the thinking engendered by these texts among the people with whom I had been conversing.

I present first Clothilde's account of an event at her day-care center. Clothilde is a middle-aged Haitian woman and a student in the child-development course. She has a great deal of experience with children—both from raising her own and from caring for other people's—and many of her classmates turn to her for advice. The text below is from a conversation in which she had been complaining to me about the behavior of the Haitian children in the day-care center where she was student teaching. She felt that the North American teachers were not controlling the children adequately.

One day, as Clothilde arrived at her school, she watched a teacher telling a little Haitian child that the child needed to go into her classroom, that she could not stay alone in the hall. The child refused and eventually kicked the teacher. Clothilde had had enough. She asked the director to bring her all the Haitian kids right away. The director and Clothilde gathered the children into the large common room. The following is the text of what she told me she said to the children:

> *Clothilde:* Does your mother let you bite?
> *Children:* No.
> *Clothilde:* Does your father let you punch kids?
> *Children:* No.
> *Clothilde:* Do you kick at home?
> *Children:* No.
> *Clothilde:* You don't respect anyone, not the teachers who play with you or the adults who work upstairs. You need to respect adults—even people you see on the streets. You are taking good ways you learn at home and not bringing them to school. You're taking the bad things you learn at school and taking them home. You're not going to do this anymore. Do you want your parents to be ashamed of you?

According to Clothilde, the Haitian children have been well-behaved ever since. Other Haitian teachers with whom I have shared this text have confirmed that that was what the children needed to hear. However, they also said that Clothilde will have to repeat her speech because the children won't remain well-behaved indefinitely without a reminder.

The next text involves an incident at my school. Josiane, who has taught for many years both here and in Haiti, was reprimanding a group of children who had been making a lot of noise while their teacher was trying to give them directions:

> *Josiane:* When your mother talks to you, don't you listen?
> *Children:* Yes.
> *Josiane:* When your mother says, go get something, don't you go get it?
> *Children:* Yes.
> *Josiane:* When your mother says, go to the bathroom, don't you go?
> *Children:* Yes.
> *Josiane:* You know why I'm telling you this. Because I want you to be good children. When an adult talks to you, you're supposed to listen so you will become a good person. The adults here like you, they want you to become good children.

Finally, we have Jérémie's father speaking to him. Jérémie is a very active four-year-old, and the staff had asked his father for help in controlling his behavior:

> *Father:* Are you going to be good? (Jérémie nods at each pause.)
> Are you going to listen to Miss Cindy?
> Are you going to listen to Miss Josiane?
> Because they like you.
> They love you.
> Do it for me.
> Do it for God.
> Do you like God?
> God loves you.

REFLECTING

The content and the form of these texts are different from what I, and many other North American teachers, would probably have said in the same circumstances. I shared these and other texts and observations with many parents and teachers, both Haitian and North American. I asked them to reflect with me on how these conversations were different and what underlay them. What follows is a blend of many people's observations and self-reflections, including my own. Here I want to note that I am assuming that the North American teachers, including myself, shared similar training and enculturation. Although we differed in many ways, I would characterize our culture—as Heath does in *Ways with Words* (1983)—as "mainstream culture." The Haitian teachers also shared some, although not all, values and assumptions. Although I am trying to distill these conversations in order to identify "typical" practices of Haitian or North American teachers, I do not mean to imply that all North American or all Haitian teachers are the same.

The Haitian preschool teachers had clear insights into behavior characteristic of North American teachers. Clothilde commented that the North American teachers she knows frequently refer to the children's internal states and interpret their feelings for them; for example, "you must be angry," "it's hard for you when your friend does that," and so on. Clothilde pointed out to me that in her speech she makes no reference to the children's emotions; other Haitian teachers I have observed also do not do this as a rule.

Rose, another Haitian teacher, also commented that North American teachers often make reference to particular factors in the child's situation that, in the teacher's opinion, may have influenced his or her behavior. For example, Michael, whose mother had left him, was often told that the teachers understood that he missed his mother, but that he nevertheless needed to share his toys. When a child pushes or pinches another child sitting next to him or her, many North American teachers will suggest that, if the child does not like people to sit so close, he or she should say so rather than pinch. Rose felt, and from my observation I concurred, that Haitian teachers rarely do this. Josiane suggested further that if she were concerned about an individual child and his or her particular problems, instead of articulating them for him or her, her goal would be "to make him or her feel comfortable with the group." If the child were misbehaving, she felt she would say, "You know I'm your friend," and then remind him or her that "we don't do that." In fact, I have seen her do exactly that many times, with excellent results.

These examples suggest to me a difference in focus between the North American and Haitian teachers. It seems that North American teachers characteristically are concerned with making a connection with the individual child, with articulating his or her feelings and problems. On the other hand, Clothilde, Josiane, and the many other Haitian people I spoke with and observed, emphasize the group in their control talk, articulating the values and responsibilities of group membership. For example, we have seen that both North American and Haitian teachers make reference to the family, but in different ways. North American teachers are likely to mention particular characteristics of a child's family, characteristics that are specific to that family and are seen as perhaps responsible for the child's individual actions. The Haitian teachers emphasize instead what the families have in common. The families do not differ in their desire that the children respect adults, that the children behave properly, and that their behavior not shame them. The children's answers, when they are given in unison as in Josiane's text above, present a vivid enactment of the sort of unity the Haitian teachers' approach may engender.

Another difference the Haitian teachers noted is the use of consequences. North American teachers typically present the particular consequences of an act of misbehavior. For example, I often say something like, "He's crying because you hit him," or, "If you don't listen to me, you won't know what to do." Haitian teachers are less likely to differentiate among particular kinds of misbehavior; they condemn them all, less in terms of their results than as examples of "bad" behavior. Clothilde is typical of the Haitian teachers in that the immediate consequences are not made explicit; she does not explain why she is against biting or punching. She instead refers to such behavior as "bad," and then explains to the children the consequences of bad behavior in general, such as shame for the family. Jérémie's father simply tells Jérémie to be good, to be good for those who love him. Josiane, too, tells the children to be good because the people who like them want them to be good. I have heard other Haitian teachers refer to the impression that bad behavior would create in a passer-by, or to the necessity of modeling good behavior for younger children. But Haitian teachers rarely mention the specific consequences of particular acts, a clear difference from North American teachers.

In the Haitian texts, one has the impression that the children share the adult's understanding of what bad behavior is. Clothilde's series of rhetorical questions, like "Do your parents let you kick?," is an example of the form that many Haitian teachers adopt when addressing children about their behavior. The children understand their role without difficulty; they repeat the expected answers in choral unison. The choice of this form—that is, questions to which the answer is assumed—emphasizes the fact that the children already know that their behavior is wrong.

In the North American control situation, on the other hand, the child often appears to be receiving new information. If there is a consensus about behavior—certain behavior is bad, certain other behavior is good—we don't present it this way. North Americans frequently explain the consequences of particular actions as if they were trying to convince the child that there was a problem with his or her behavior. As presented in school, misbehavior is considered wrong not because of anything inherent in it, but because of its particular consequences, or perhaps because the behavior stems from feelings that the child has failed to identify and control.

These differences, as I came to recognize them, seemed significant enough to account for some of the difficulties I had been experiencing in my classroom. But what to do about them?

PRACTICE

With the overwhelming evidence that these children were used to a kind of control talk other than what I had been providing, I have since begun to adopt some of the style of the Haitian teachers. I assume that I am not very good at it, that I have no idea of the nuances, and I continue to include many of the ways I have typically managed behavior in my teaching. Nevertheless, I have developed a more or less stable melange of styles, and my control in the classroom has improved significantly. In addition, I find that I love trying out this Haitian way. I was struck by an experience I had the other day, when I was reprimanding one boy for pinching another. I was focusing, in the Haitian manner, on his prior, indisputable knowledge that pinching was simply no good. I also used my best approximation of the facial expression and tone of voice that I see the Haitian teachers use in these encounters. I can tell when I have it more or less right, because of the way that the children pay attention. As I finished this particular time, the other children, who had been rapt, all solemnly thanked me. They were perhaps feeling in danger of being pinched and felt that I had at last been effective. This solemn sort of response, which has occurred a few other times, gives me the sense that these situations are very important to them.

The following anecdote may suggest more about the way in which these interactions are important to the children. Recently I was angrily reprimanding the children about their failure to wait for me while crossing the parking lot:

> *Cindy:* Did I tell you to go?
> *Children:* No.
> *Cindy:* Can you cross this parking lot by yourselves?
> *Children:* No.
> *Cindy:* That's right. There are cars here. They're dangerous. I don't want you to go alone. Why do I want you to wait for me, do you know?
> "Yes," says Claudette, "because you like us."

Although I was following the usual Haitian form—rhetorical questions with "no" answers—I had been expecting a final response based on the North American system of cause and effect, something like, "Because the cars are dangerous." Claudette, however, although she understands perfectly well the dangers of cars to small children, does not expect to use that information in this kind of an interaction. What, then, *is* she telling me? One thing that she is saying, which is perhaps what the solemn children also meant, is that, from her point of view, there is intimacy in this kind of talk. This is certainly the feeling I get from these experiences. I feel especially connected to the children in those instances in which I seem to have gotten it right.

THE LARGER CONTEXT

North American teachers generally think of reprimands—particularly of young children who are just learning to control their behavior—as put-downs, and are reluctant to give them. North American preschool teachers, in particular, will take great pains to avoid saying "no" or "don't." In contrast, I have learned from working with Haitian children and teachers that there are situations in which reprimands can be confirming, can strengthen relationships, and can, in a sense, define relationships for the child, as seems to have been the case for Claudette in the example given above.

Such an opportunity may be lost when we go to great lengths to avoid actually telling a child that he is wrong, that we disagree or disapprove. When we look at the difference between the ways in which things are done at home and at school, and the negative consequences that may result from these mismatches for children coming from minority cultural backgrounds, the area of misbehavior and the way it is responded to seem particularly important because it affects so directly the nature of the relationship between child and teacher.

I was not unaware when I began that this subject was a hotbed of disagreement: North Americans perceive Haitians as too severe, both verbally and in their use of physical punishment, while Haitians often perceive North American children as being extraordinarily fresh and out of control.* Haitian immigrant parents here are at once ashamed and defiantly supportive of their community's disciplinary standards and methods. In order to represent the views of Haitians I spoke with independent of my process of understanding, I asked them to reflect again on our two cultures after they had heard my interpretations.

People, of course, offered many varied points of view, yet everybody emphasized a sense of having grown up very "protected" in Haiti, of having been safe there both from getting into serious trouble and from harm. This sense of being protected was largely based on their under-

---

*It must be stated that the consequences of this disagreement are, of course, vastly more painful for the powerless. Contact with schools, with social service institutions, with the police, is in many cases highly problematic for Haitian families. The Haitian family, in these situations, is frequently met with a lack of understanding that leads easily to a lack of respect. Mainstream assumptions about "proper" ways of talking and dealing with children's behavior often stand in the way of distinguishing a functioning family, for example, from a dysfunctional one, in distinguishing a child whose parents are strict in order to help him or her succeed from one whose family simply does not want to deal with the child's problems. Such assumptions often stand in the path of appropriate help as well. The school where I taught was often called upon to discuss cultural differences with social service groups, hospitals, and other schools. Occasionally, we were asked to provide some assistance for particular cases. But, of course, there were countless instances in which Haitian families were involved with these various powerful institutions and the families were without such aid.

standing that their entire extended family, as well as many people in the community, were involved in their upbringing. Haitian families in the United States, some pointed out, are smaller and less extended. The community here, while tight in many ways, is more loosely connected than in Haiti. This change in social structure was bemoaned by the people I spoke with, especially with reference to bringing up children. They attributed to this change their sense that this generation of children, particularly those born here, is increasingly at risk. They are at risk not only of falling away from their parents' culture, but also, and consequently, of falling prey to the drugs, crime, and other problems of urban life that they see around them.

And yet everyone I spoke with also recalled some pain in their growing up, pain they relate to the respect and obedience they were required to exhibit to all adults, which at times conflicted with their own developing desire to state their opinions or make their own choices. This pain was nevertheless not to be discarded lightly. For many of the Haitian people with whom I spoke, religious values underlie these twin issues of respect and obedience; respect for parents and other adults is an analogue for respect and obedience to God and God's law.

Many people seemed to agree with the ambivalence expressed by one Haitian lawyer and mother who told me that, while she had suffered as a child because of the uncompromising obedience and respect demanded of her in her family, she continued to see respect as a value she needed to impart to her children. She said to me, "There must be many other ways to teach respect." She was one of many Haitians who told me of instances where a child from a poor family, a child with neither the clothes nor the supplies for school, had succeeded eventually in becoming a doctor or a lawyer. In these accounts, as in her own case, it is in large measure the strictness of the family that is regarded as the source of the child's accomplishment, rather than the talent or the power of the individual.

Presumably, there is some tension in all societies between individual and community. In these accounts is some suggestion of the form this tension sometimes takes within Haitian culture. For my part, I am struck and troubled by the powerful individualism underlying the approach I characterize as typical of me and many North American teachers. It appears that North Americans do speak as if something like the child's "enlightened self-interest" were the ultimate moral guidepost. In comparison to the language used by the Haitian teachers, North American teachers' language seems to place very little emphasis on shared values, on a moral community.

The process of gaining multicultural understanding in education must, in my opinion, be a dual one. On the one hand, cultural behavior that at first seems strange and inexplicable should become familiar; on the other hand, one's own familiar values and practices should become at least temporarily strange, subject to examination. In addition to the information I have gained that helps me to manage and form relationships with Haitian children in my classroom, I also value greatly the extent to which these conversations, by forcing me to attempt to empathize with and understand a view of the world that is in many ways very different from my customary one, have put me in a position to reexamine values and principles that had become inaccessible under layers of assumptions.

I am not teaching Haitian children this year, although I continue to visit them. Next year I expect to have a classroom with children from a wide range of backgrounds. It is difficult to say how my last experience will illuminate the next—or, analogously, how my experience can be of use to teachers in different kinds of classrooms. I do believe that teachers need to try to open up and to understand both our own assumptions and the cultural meaning that children from all backgrounds bring to school. It seems to me that accommodation must be made on all sides so that no group has to abandon the ways in which it is accustomed to passing on its values. I have been fortunate that the knowledge and collaboration of so many people, Haitian and North American, were available to help me begin to understand my own experience. All of these conversations have been their own rewards—I have made new friends and, I believe, become a better teacher.

REFERENCES

Boggs, S. (1985). *Speaking, talking and relating: A study of Hawaiian children at home and at school*. Norwood, NJ: Ablex.

Cook-Gumperz, J. (1973). *Social control and socialization.* London: Routledge & Kegan Paul.

Heath, S. B. (1983). *Ways with words.* Cambridge, Eng.: Cambridge University Press.

Michaels, S., & O'Connor, M. C. (1990). *Literacy as reasoning within multiple discourses: Implications for policy and educational reform.* Newton, MA: Education Development Center.

Phillips, A. (February, 1991). *Hearing children's stories: A report on the Brookline Teacher-Researcher Seminar.* Paper presented at the Penn Ethnography in Educational Research Forum, Philadelphia, PA.

Rose, M. (1989). *Lives on the boundary.* New York: Penguin.

Watson-Gegeo, K., & Gegeo, D. (1990). *Disentangling: The discourse of conflict and therapy in the Pacific Islands.* Norwood, NJ: Ablex.

MAUREEN: Cynthia Ballenger's article is an excellent example of teacher research. She experienced a problem in her own classroom, actually in her teaching, and set out to discover the source and solution to it. We are all then able to profit from what she has learned about identity, culture, language, and the tensions that exist between the pull to conformity within a community and the needs and rights of the individual.

I do, however, have some disagreement with the duality she offers pertaining to the connections we as teachers make to an individual child as opposed to the emphasis we place on the importance of the group. Teachers and parents need to understand that both are important and one may take precedence over the other in particular situations. We need to maintain an alternating balance between the two. Teachers need to be able to swing from an emphasis on the individual to the greater needs of the group as a whole in the classroom, while parents have to juggle individual children's needs and those of the family, while teaching children how to function in groups. This facility of recognizing when and how to move back and forth between the individual and the group is essential to healthy communal living in a democracy.

I also have some questions about the centrality of control and discipline in this piece. Such a narrow focus does not fully take into account the incredible complexity of teaching and learning. New teachers are overly concerned about classroom management techniques and ask for tips on how to control a class and what discipline models are most effective. I believe that these issues occur when children are not sufficiently challenged by an imaginative and rewarding curriculum. In a classroom where children are involved in solving problems, whether they are seeking new ways to tessellate a geometric figure, working out a new human rights doctrine for their school, or arguing over the ultimate outcome of an exciting novel, one hears a muted buzz in the room signifying involvement, enthusiasm, and effort. The children are engaged with powerful ideas and are disciplining themselves.

While Ballenger's focus in this piece is on discipline, ultimately her work can help us to think about differences in students' cultural backgrounds and how that can affect classroom climate and the culture created by the members of a classroom as they develop shared understandings.

SUGGESTED RESOURCES AND FURTHER READING

To learn more about moon observations, space science, and astronomy, see http://www.nasa.gov.

For more information on the National Writing Project, see http://www.writingproject.org.

For an exciting online collection of classroom videos collected by the Carnegie Foundation for the Advancement of Teaching, see http://gallery.carnegiefoundation.org.

Brookline Teacher Research Seminar (2003). *Regarding children's words: Teacher research on language and literacy*. New York: Teachers College Press.

■ PART IV ■

ON EQUITY AND ISSUES OF SOCIAL JUSTICE

Persistent and unjust inequalities in our schools measured by funding and resources, achievement gaps based on race and class, and teacher quality, are issues of grave concern in education. The need for action has never been more urgent. Some have taken the struggle for justice to the courts, others to the streets. The issues raised in the following essays are explosively provocative, and if we ignore them or choose to do nothing about them, we risk a future of ever-widening gaps between the wealthy and the poor, unsolvable social ills, and a society so segregated that hatred and misunderstanding become a fixed feature of our collective cultural identity as Americans. Parents and teachers can play an active role in addressing issues of equity and social justice and in searching for solutions in our schools and communities.

12

Peggy McIntosh

WHITE PRIVILEGE:
UNPACKING THE INVISIBLE KNAPSACK*

ALEXANDRA: I first read this well-known piece by Peggy McIntosh, Associate Director of the Wellesley College Center for Research on Women and the founder and co-director of the national Seeking Educational Equity and Diversity (S.E.E.D.) Project on Inclusive Curriculum, in a University of Washington course on multicultural education taught by Professor James Banks, a renowned scholar in the field. It had a profound effect on me. Like McIntosh, I had a long-standing interest in issues of gender equity, going back to my high school days, and saw racism as something that didn't matter so much to me as long as I did my best to not be racist. Reading McIntosh's list of the effects of white privilege forced me to consider, one by one, what those assertions meant for a person of color. I was put in another's shoes, forced to look at myself and see what I could not previously see.

Once McIntosh shed light on the "matrix of white privilege," I started to pay attention. I noticed racial stereotyping in television and print advertising, I picked up on the suspicious glances of white shop clerks as they watched people of color browse in stores, and I saw how real estate markets worked to perpetuate racially segregated neighborhoods and schools. I return to McIntosh's list often, trying to heed her advice to make others aware of the unfair and unseen advantages white people enjoy and to debunk the "myth of meritocracy." I use #15 on the list ("I am never asked to speak for all the people of my racial group") in my courses on the first day of class, when we collaboratively create a list of ground rules for how we want our class to be. Most students suggest

*From Independent School 49, no. 2 (1990): 31–36. [Essay excerpted from 1988 White Privilege and Male Privilege: A Personal Account of Coming to See Correspondences Through Work in Women's Studies, Working Paper 189 (Wellesley, MA: Wellesley College Center for Research on Women, 1988).

things like "listen respectfully," and I always explain that while someone might volunteer information based on their experiences as members of a particular social group, no one should be expected to speak for that group, and we add that to the list.

I believe McIntosh's piece on white privilege has endured as a classic text because she successfully translates a personal viewpoint born of experience into a universal truth. While each reader may find some points that seem either outdated or not personally relevant, her list expands your thinking about where white privilege can be found. As she elucidates "interlocking oppressions" you begin to recognize the cumulative forces keeping poor people of color from realizing their dreams. I believe we all have an obligation to talk openly about these issues with children, to make the unseen visible, so that future generations can work actively to reconstruct the balance of power and privilege.

I was taught to see racism only in individual
acts of meanness, not in invisible systems
conferring dominance on my group.

Through work to bring materials from women's studies into the rest of the curriculum, I have often noticed men's unwillingness to grant that they are overprivileged, even though they may grant that women are disadvantaged. They may say they will work to improve women's status, in the society, the university, or the curriculum, but they can't or won't support the idea of lessening men's. Denials that amount to taboos surround the subject of advantages that men gain from women's disadvantages. These denials protect male privilege from being fully acknowledged, lessened, or ended.

Thinking through unacknowledged male privilege as a phenomenon, I realized that, since hierarchies in our society are interlocking, there was most likely a phenomenon of white privilege that was similarly denied and protected. As a white person, I realized I had been taught about racism as something that puts others at a disadvantage, but had been taught not to see one of its corollary aspects, white privilege, which puts me at an advantage.

I think whites are carefully taught not to recognize white privilege, as males are taught not to recognize male privilege. So I have begun in an untutored way to ask what it is like to have white privilege. I have come to see white privilege as an invisible package of unearned assets that I can count on cashing in each day, but about which I was "meant" to remain oblivious. White privilege is like an invisible weightless knapsack of special provisions, maps, passports, codebooks, visas, clothes, tools, and blank checks.

Describing white privilege makes one newly accountable. As we in women's studies work to reveal male privilege and ask men to give up some of their power, so one who writes about having white privilege must ask, "Having described it, what will I do to lessen or end it?"

After I realized the extent to which men work from a base of unacknowledged privilege, I understood that much of their oppressiveness was unconscious. Then I remembered the frequent charges from women of color that white women whom they encounter are oppressive. I began to understand why we are justly seen as oppressive, even when we don't see ourselves that way. I began to count the ways in which I enjoy unearned skin privilege and have been conditioned into oblivion about its existence.

My schooling gave me no training in seeing myself as an oppressor, as an unfairly advantaged person, or as a participant in a damaged culture. I was taught to see myself as an individual whose moral state depended on her individual moral will. My schooling followed the pattern my colleague Elizabeth Minnich has pointed out: whites are taught to think of their lives as morally neutral, normative, and average, and also ideal, so that when we work to benefit others, this is seen as work that will allow "them" to be more like "us."

DAILY EFFECTS OF WHITE PRIVILEGE

I decided to try to work on myself at least by identifying some of the daily effects of white privilege in my life. I have chosen those conditions that I think in my case attach somewhat more to skin-color privilege than to class, religion, ethnic status, or geographic location, though of course all these other factors are intricately intertwined. As far as I can tell, my African American coworkers, friends, and acquaintances with whom I come into daily or frequent contact in this particular time, place, and line of work cannot count on most of these conditions.

1. I can, if I wish, arrange to be in the company of people of my race most of the time.

2. If I should need to move, I can be pretty sure of renting or purchasing housing in an area that I can afford and in which I would want to live.

3. I can be pretty sure that my neighbors in such a location will be neutral or pleasant to me.

4. I can go shopping alone most of the time, pretty well assured that I will not be followed or harassed.

5. I can turn on the television or open to the front page of the paper and see people of my race widely represented.

6. When I am told about our national heritage or about "civilization," I am shown that people of my color made it what it is.

7. I can be sure that my children will be given curricular materials that testify to the existence of their race.

8. If I want to, I can be pretty sure of finding a publisher for this piece on white privilege.

9. I can go into a music shop and count on finding the music of my race represented, into a supermarket and find the staple foods that fit with my cultural traditions, into a hairdresser's shop and find someone who can deal with my hair.

10. Whether I use checks, credit cards, or cash, I can count on my skin color not to work against the appearance of financial reliability.

11. I can arrange to protect my children most of the time from people who might not like them.

12. I can swear, or dress in second-hand clothes, or not answer letters without having people attribute these choices to the bad morals, the poverty, or the illiteracy of my race.

13. I can speak in public to a powerful male group without putting my race on trial.

14. I can do well in a challenging situation without being called a credit to my race.

15. I am never asked to speak for all the people of my racial group.

16. I can remain oblivious of the language and customs of persons of color, who constitute the world's majority, without feeling in my culture any penalty for such oblivion.

17. I can criticize our government and talk about how much I fear its policies and behavior without being seen as a cultural outsider.

18. I can be pretty sure that if I ask to talk to "the person in charge" I will be facing a person of my race.

19. If a traffic cop pulls me over, or if the IRS audits my tax return, I can be sure I haven't been singled out because of my race.

20. I can easily buy posters, postcards, picture books, greeting cards, dolls, toys, and children's magazines featuring people of my race.

21. I can go home from most meetings of organizations I belong to feeling somewhat tied in rather than isolated, out of place, outnumbered, unheard, held at a distance, or feared.

22. I can take a job with an affirmative action employer without having coworkers on the job suspect that I got it because of race.

23. I can choose public accommodation without fearing that people of my race cannot get in or will be mistreated in the places I have chosen.

24. I can be sure that if I need legal or medical help my race will not work against me.

25. If my day, week, or year is going badly, I need not ask of each negative episode or situation whether it has racial overtones.

26. I can choose blemish cover or bandages in "flesh" color that more or less match my skin.

ELUSIVE AND FUGITIVE

I repeatedly forgot each of the realizations on this list until I wrote it down. For me white privilege has turned out to be an elusive and fugitive subject. The pressure to avoid it is great, for in facing it I must give up the myth of meritocracy. If these things are true, this is not such a free country; one's life is not what one makes it; many doors open for certain people through no virtues of their own.

In unpacking this invisible knapsack of white privilege, I have listed conditions of daily experience that I once took for granted. Nor did I think of any of these perquisites as bad for the holder. I now think that we need a more finely differentiated taxonomy of privilege, for some of these varieties are only what one would want for everyone in a just society, and others give license to be ignorant, oblivious, arrogant, and destructive.

I see a pattern running through the matrix of white privilege, a pattern of assumptions that were passed on to me as a white person. There was one main piece of cultural turf; it was my own turf, and I was among those who could control the turf. My skin color was an asset for any more I was educated to want to make. I could think of myself as belonging in major ways and of making social systems work for me. I could freely disparage, fear, neglect, or be oblivious to anything outside of the dominant cultural forms. Being of the main culture, I could also criticize it fairly freely.

In proportion as my racial group was being made confident, comfortable, and oblivious, other groups were likely being made unconfident, uncomfortable, and alienated. Whiteness protected me from many kinds of hostility, distress, and violence, which I was being subtly trained to visit, in turn, upon people of color.

For this reason, the word "privilege" now seems to me misleading. We usually think of privilege as being a favored state, whether earned or conferred by birth or luck. Yet some of the conditions I have described here work systematically to overempower certain groups. Such privilege simply confers dominance because of one's race or sex.

EARNED STRENGTH, UNEARNED POWER

I want, then, to distinguish between earned strength and unearned power conferred systemically. Power from unearned privilege can look like strength when it is in fact permission to escape or to dominate. But not all of the privileges on my list are inevitably damaging. Some, like the expectation that neighbors will be decent to you, or that your race will not count against you in court, should be the norm in a just society; others, like the privilege to ignore less powerful people, distort the humanity of the holders as well as the ignored groups.

We might at least start by distinguishing between positive advantages, which we can work to spread, and negative types of advantage, which unless rejected will always reinforce our present hierarchies. For example, the feeling that one belongs within the human circle, as Native Americans say, should not be seen as privilege for a few. Ideally it is an unearned entitlement. At present, since only a few have it, it is an unearned advantage for them. This paper results from a process of coming to see that some of the power that I originally saw as attendant on being a human being in the United States consisted in unearned advantage and conferred dominance.

I have met very few men who are truly distressed about systemic, unearned male advantage and conferred dominance. And so one question for me and others like me is whether we will be like them, or whether we will get truly distressed, even outraged, about unearned race advantage and conferred dominance, and, if so, what we will do to lessen them. In any case, we need to do more work in identifying how they actually affect our daily lives. Many, perhaps most, of our white students in the United States think that racism doesn't affect them because they are not people of color; they do not see "whiteness" as a racial identity. In addition, since race and sex are not the only advantaging systems at work, we need similarly to examine the daily experience of having age advantage, or ethnic advantage, or physical ability, or advantage related to nationality, religion, or sexual orientation.

Difficulties and dangers surrounding the task of finding parallels are many. Since racism, sexism, and heterosexism are not the same, the advantages associated with them should not be seen as the same. In addition, it is hard to disentangle aspects of unearned advantage that rest more on social class, economic class, race, religion, sex, and ethnic identity than on other factors. Still, all of the oppressions are interlocking, as the members of the Combahee River Collective pointed out in their "Black Feminist Statement" of 1977.

One factor seems clear about all of the interlocking oppressions. They take both active forms, which we can see, and embedded forms, which as a member of the dominant group one is taught not to see. In my class and place, I did not see myself as a racist because I was taught to recognize racism only in individual acts of meanness by members of my group, never in invisible systems conferring unsought racial dominance on my group from birth.

Disapproving of the systems won't be enough to change them. I was taught to think that racism could end if white individuals changed their attitudes. But a "white" skin in the United States opens many doors for whites whether or not we approve of the way dominance has been conferred on us. Individual acts can palliate, but cannot end, these problems.

To redesign social systems we need first to acknowledge their colossal unseen dimensions. The silences and denials surrounding privilege are the key political tool here. They keep the thinking about equality or equity incomplete, protecting unearned advantage and conferred dominance by making these subjects taboo. Most talk by whites about equal opportunity seems to me now to be about equal opportunity to try to get into a position of dominance while denying that systems of dominance exist.

It seems to me that obliviousness about white advantage, like obliviousness about male advantage, is kept strongly inculturated in the United States so as to maintain the myth of meritocracy, the myth that democratic choice is equally available to all. Keeping most people unaware that freedom of confident action is there for just a small number of people props up those in power and serves to keep power in the hands of the same groups that have most of it already.

Although systemic change takes many decades, there are pressing questions for me and, I imagine, for some others like me if we raise our daily consciousness on the perquisites of being light-skinned. What will we do with such knowledge? As we know from watching men, it is an open question whether we will choose to use unearned advantage to weaken hidden systems of advantage, and whether we will use any of our arbitrarily awarded power to try to reconstruct power systems on a broader base.

———————

MAUREEN: I remember vividly the night one of my graduate students described her fear of driving through an all-white, affluent neighborhood adjacent to our campus. I was stunned and angered. It was a revelation that she was so afraid of being stopped by an officer that she locked all her doors and drove carefully at just under the speed limit. My anger was directed not only at that community but also at my own ignorance. Why had I never realized that women of color might be uneasy driving at night in an all-white community?

Since then, I have given Peggy McIntosh's paper to all my classes, and we explore together the white privilege that still exists in our country fifty years after Brown v. Board of Education of Topeka. *It is the catalyst for many more open discussions of ethnicity, gender, and exceptionality that can and should be a required part of the curriculum.*

At first some students react negatively to the idea that they are privileged, but as the discussion warms, new perspectives emerge and the journals that all my students keep begin to reflect new attitudes and new identifications. Especially in times of unrest when bias spreads because of ignorance and fear, we need to spend time with young children building on their natural warmth and affinity to peoples from other countries. The eradication of prejudice can and should be a major concern of educators in every part of the world.

13

Diana Hess

MOVING BEYOND CELEBRATION: CHALLENGING CURRICULAR ORTHODOXY IN THE TEACHING OF *BROWN* AND ITS LEGACIES*

ALEXANDRA: Diana Hess is Associate Professor in Curriculum and In-struction at the School of Education, University of Wisconsin-Madison. Her scholarly interests include social studies, democracy education, and teaching le-gal and constitutional cases and issues in schools. In this important article, pub-lished a year after the fiftieth anniversary of the landmark Brown v. Board of Education of Topeka *United States Supreme Court case, Hess explores the incongruity between the academic world, where impassioned debate about the case and its importance in history persisted especially during the anniversary year, and the world of K–12 schooling, where* Brown *continues to be given iconic status devoid of controversy. After exploring five perspectives on the meaning and legacy of* Brown *within scholarly and civil rights literature, ranging from "simple icon" to "irrelevant," Hess shows how secondary history texts and social studies teachers treat* Brown *as iconic, and why such treatment persists despite current controversial debates about segregation and inequitable schooling in America.*

Reading Hess reminds us how easy it is in K–12 schooling to succumb to the all too familiar "redemptive narratives" of civil rights history—Brown, Rosa Parks, Martin Luther King Jr.—and consequently to treat certain social prob-lems as if they were resolved long ago (p. 200). Arguing that by doing so we risk inauthentic teaching with respect to the social-political context of education, sending harmful messages about issues of race by ignoring them, Hess makes a persuasive case for confronting controversy and including studies of controver-sial issues in secondary social studies teaching.

Even young children can have a strong sense of fairness and justice, and are able to explore difficult issues. For example, in my sixth-grade class, as part of

*From *Teachers College Record* 107, no. 9 (2005): 2046–2067.

*a unit on Freedom Summer, we learned about the Little Rock Nine and corre-
sponded through e-mails to Melba Pattillo Beals, who promptly replied to our
burning questions thanks to an interactive Web site published by Scholastic. We
read Christopher Paul Curtis's novel* The Watsons Go to Birmingham—
1963, *and then we watched and were deeply moved by Spike Lee's documentary*
4 Little Girls *about the Birmingham bombing. Students were inspired by
novels such as* Just Like Martin *by Ossie Davis, in which characters their age
were engaging in civil rights demonstrations, and they asked to look again and
again at documentary footage from the excellent PBS series* Eyes on the
Prize. *They learned to sing protest songs of the times. They interviewed parents and relatives who were teenagers during the 1950s and 1960s to better
understand how issues of race unfolded in the not-so-distant past and published
an anthology of their findings. Without proper educational experiences in deliberating public issues of historical and contemporary relevance, as Hess notes, the
future of democracy is at risk of increasing fragility.*

On May 15, 2004, the National Museum of American History unveiled
its exhibit celebrating the 50th anniversary of the landmark United
States Supreme Court case, *Brown v. Board of Education of Topeka* (1954).[1]
The exhibit powerfully illuminates life under de jure segregation—
sometimes labeled "Apartheid America"—while vividly illustrating the
challenges faced in crafting a political and legal movement to dismantle
that system of separate and unequal. After documenting some of the
complications involved in enforcing the Supreme Court's decision, the
exhibit closes with these stirring words:

> When the U.S. Supreme Court struck down school segregation, it ad-
> vanced the cause of human rights in America and set an example for all the
> peoples of the world. The American dream of ethnic diversity and racial
> equality under the law is a dream of liberty and justice for all.

As these words imply, the Smithsonian exhibit primarily celebrates the
Court's decision in the case. As such, it is remarkably devoid of the controversies surrounding the legacies of the *Brown* ruling, which have
been so prominently and passionately articulated in the popular media,

in recently published scholarly analyses, and at the myriad conferences organized to mark the 50th anniversary of this landmark case. In these venues, by contrast, attention has focused not only on celebrating the importance of the case, but also on explicating the contemporary realities of persistent racial inequality, especially with respect to education.

While many people considered the *Brown* ruling to be essential and laudable, particularly in the context of 1954, some are also greatly dismayed by the minimal impact it wielded in solving the problem of race-based inequality of educational opportunity. As civil rights attorney Bert Neuborne recently put it, "*Brown* unlocked the law and stopped it from standing in the way of justice. But it is a failure until we find a way to adequately educate poor kids."[2] Forty years after the decision, Thurgood Marshall's cocounsel, Judge Robert Carter, wrote, "For most black children, *Brown*'s Constitutional guarantee of equal education opportunity has been an arid abstraction, having no effect whatever on the educational offerings black children are given or the deteriorating schools they attend" (Patterson, 2001, p. 210).

By the 50th anniversary of the *Brown* decision, the former United States secretary of education, Rod Paige, said that there is "an emerging de facto apartheid in our schools, a contemporary crisis that is similar, perhaps identical, to the situation in the 1950s South" (Ware, 2004, p. 43).

While rightfully extolling the hard-won victory of *Brown* in the context of the 1950s, the Smithsonian exhibit ignores the persistence of racial inequality in the United States evidenced by the achievement gap, the income gap, the access to health care gap, and so on. In addition, the exhibit glosses over the fact that the vast majority of schools are still segregated. In the exhibit, there is no simmering crisis with respect to race and schooling, no ongoing lack of educational opportunity, no divisiveness over educational outcomes and their national origins. An instantiation of "official knowledge," the museum instead presents *Brown* as an icon of American democracy, a case to be remembered with reverence and extolled as achievement.[3] It is impossible to overlook the incongruity between the Smithsonian's presentation of *Brown*'s legacy to the public as a grand democratic achievement and academics' versions of *Brown*'s legacy as a matter of debate.

The same disjuncture exists, perhaps not surprisingly, with respect to the way in which *Brown* is often presented to high school students.

Like the Smithsonian museum, schools function to solidify public memories, to persuade the masses of "future citizens" to accept and embrace particular national narratives. Thus, in schools, *Brown* and its legacies tend to be presented as iconic—stripped of the controversies that have animated deliberations in the world outside of school. An object of uncritical devotion, *Brown* is often taught not simply as a correctly decided court case, but as an all-important symbol that continues to shape contemporary ideas about justice, equality, and the power of the Supreme Court. As one high school teacher explained, "*Brown* is not just a decision of our high court, but is also an integral part of our social consciousness. It represents the power of our legal system to spur social changes of great magnitude and the strength of the rule of law in the face of popular opposition" (Brandsberg-Engelmann, 2002, p. 66). Another high school teacher, Erik Shager (2002), put the matter more succinctly: For many teachers, the case is the "slam dunk of all Supreme Court decisions" (p. 71).

In this article, I explore why the legacy of *Brown* is both so controversial in the academy and civil rights community and so settled in the school curriculum. To do so, I begin by categorizing and illustrating five perspectives on *Brown*'s meanings and legacies, drawn from scholarly literature about the decision. Next, I illustrate how high school social studies textbooks and teachers often present *Brown* without attention to the full range of these differing perspectives, and I advance some explanations for why these differing perspectives are not commonly presented to secondary school students. After evaluating the opportunities and costs afforded by teaching *Brown* and its legacy as iconic, I present alternative possibilities to engage young people in deliberating which perspectives deserve support and why. These alternatives, I will argue, are more consistent with the kind of democratic education that contemporary U.S. society demands and deserves.

IN THE ACADEMY: PERSPECTIVES ON *BROWN*

In academic circles and in the civil rights community, the meaning of the *Brown* decision, especially its effects on promoting racial justice in the United States, is contested terrain. Typifying U.S. society more generally, the range of opinion spans the political spectrum, including perspectives from the simplistic to the nuanced. In this section, I discuss five perspectives distilled from this literature. These modes of thought are hardly mutually exclusive, and although they are separable, they blur at their margins. It is possible, probable in fact, for some to subscribe to more than one perspective simultaneously, and this is important. Also, these perspectives, although helpful in furthering the claims of this article, are not ends in themselves. They simply illustrate the diverse streams of thought that exist around *Brown* and its legacies. Located along a continuum according to the perceived consequences of the Supreme Court decision, these perspectives include *Brown* as simple icon, *Brown* as liberation referent, *Brown* as unfulfilled promise, *Brown* as well-intentioned error, and *Brown* as irrelevant. Below, I discuss each perspective's central features, elaborating thereafter their significance for schools.

Brown as an Icon

First, it may be worth reiterating that celebrating *Brown* is not unwarranted. As Michael Klarman (1994) pointed out, "Constitutional lawyers and historians generally deem *Brown v. Board of Education* to be the most important U.S. Supreme Court decision of the twentieth century, and possibly of all time" (p. 81). Roger Wilkins (1996) went further, writing that *Brown* "may have been the seminal civil rights event of the twentieth century" (p. 14).

Although many will agree about the import of the decision, those within this first analytic category or perspective tend to think of *Brown* in somewhat less complicated terms. Those who construct *Brown* as an icon tend to believe that the Supreme Court did the right thing, at the right time, and for the right reasons. More significantly, though, they see the consequences of *Brown* as manifestly positive. In a clear and forceful manner, the decision proclaimed that what James Patterson (2001) called "the very heart of constitutionally sanctioned Jim Crow" (p. 204) was legally and morally wrong, thereby sending a powerful democratic message that American apartheid had to end. Those who subscribe to this view of *Brown* consider the decision to have effected change, almost single-handedly positioning racism and discrimination as things of the past.

Given this understanding (or misunderstanding), those who subscribe to this view of the *Brown* decision argue that it deserves its status as an icon; in short, it deserves an uncomplicatedly laudatory label.[4] As Jack Balkin noted, "With the decision in *Brown*, the symbolic weight of federal law and the federal Constitution was now placed on the side of African Americans and the civil rights movement and against their opponents" (Balkin & Ackerman, 2001, p. 24). Within this view, the weight of the *Brown* decision tipped the balance against an unjust system, using schools to fell the pillars of an unjust society.

Brown as Liberation Referent

The first perspective is similar to the second one, as proponents of both consider *Brown* to have been positively decided and generally positive in outcome—perhaps viewing American history itself to be teleologically driven toward positive outcomes. However, the central thrust of this view is that *Brown* did not effect change in isolation, but instead functioned as a catalyst does in a complex reaction. At the core of this view is the fact that the *Brown* decision became a symbol for other "rights" movements—a sort of liberation referent. The legacy of the decision, then, exceeded its history as the story of integrating Black and White Americans. It deserves not only to be a simple icon of societal shift, but to also be appreciated as a lever within and across multiple movements. As Ellen Condliffe Lagemann (1996) pointed out, *Brown* "set the stage for the civil rights movement, Martin Luther King, the women's movement, the Lau decision, and Hispanics, Asian groups, the American Association of Retired Persons, and other groups concerned about equality in this country" (p. 11). Similarly, the Supreme Court's 2003 decision in *Lawrence v. Texas*, which struck down state laws banning homosexual sodomy, has been hailed by some as the *Brown v. Board of Education* for gay Americans (Graff, 2003). Piggybacking on perceptions of its success, *Brown* as liberation referent followed "naturally" from its status as an icon.

Brown as Unfulfilled Promise

Unlike the first two perspectives, in this one, the problematic legacies of *Brown* per se diminish its status as an icon or liberation referent. Instead, this view stresses most heavily that *Brown* represents an unfulfilled promise. If the goal of *Brown* was to create equal educational opportunities for students of color through desegregation, then even a cursory analysis of the current educational landscape in the United States provides evidence that that goal remains unmet. Gloria Ladson-Billings and William Tate noted in 1995 that students of color were more segregated than ever, and the same holds true nearly 10 years later, particularly in light of court orders and policies dismantling desegregation plans and even despite decreases in residential segregation (Ladson-Billings, 2004; Lee, 2004; Orfield & Lee, 2005). Moreover, as Ladson-Billings and Tate argued, often when school desegregation has occurred, its benefits have not gone to children of color, but to Whites. Similarly, Raskin (2003) argued that the refusal of the Burger and Rehnquist courts to stay the course initiated by *Brown* has resulted in the ironic and pernicious reality that "in many parts of America, there are 100-percent white suburban schools and 100-percent black or minority schools, and they are all perfectly lawful because the segregation is not commanded by the state" (p. 159). In 1980, 63% of African American students attended predominantly minority schools. By 1998, the figure was 70% (Orfield & Yun, 1999). Between 1991 and 2003, in fact, the level of segregation increased in all regions of the country; by 2003, 78% of African American students in the Northeast were attending majority-minority schools (a 3% rise over the period), while in the Border and Southern regions, 71% and 74% attended such schools, respectively (a 10% rise in both regions; see Lee, 2004). As Raskin aptly elaborated, whether the government has segregated by law or allowed it to happen in practice is a distinction that "surely escapes most elementary children" (p. 159). Recall that *Brown* was based on the idea that the very experience of segregation was harmful to African American children and, as Chief Justice Warren wrote in the opinion, it "may affect their hearts and minds in a way unlikely ever to be undone" (*Brown v. Board of Education*, 1954, p. 483).

In sum, in this view, *Brown* was decided correctly, but rather than catalyzing positive social change, it failed as a historical experiment. In a sense, the next perspective is akin to this one, but rather than finding fault in the failed legacies of *Brown* or arguing that the decision was the right one that an unready society derailed, its proponents locate the failure of *Brown* in the decision itself.

Brown as Well-Intentioned Error

Frustration with the difference between the progress that many civil rights advocates hoped *Brown* would spark and the persistence of race-based unequal educational opportunities and outcomes have caused some to question the fundamental premises of the *Brown* decision. For example, Derrick Bell (2001) argued that instead of ordering the desegregation of schools, a better path for improving the educational opportunities for African American students would have been to equalize the resources allotted to segregated schools. Instead of the more ambiguous order (in *Brown II*) to desegregate "with all deliberate speed," Bell advocates the following in response to the question, "What should *Brown* have said?":

> Effective immediately on receipt of this Court's mandate, school officials of the respondent school districts must: 1) ascertain through standardized tests and other appropriate measures the academic standing of each school district as compared to nationwide norms for school systems of comparable size and financial resources. This data will be published and made available to all patrons of the district. 2) All schools within the district must be equalized in physical facilities, teacher training, experience, and salary with the goal of each district, as a whole, measuring up to national norms within three years. (p. 197)

Implicit in Bell's alternative is the view that improving educational opportunities did not have to be achieved via desegregation. Instead, improving the quality of education offered to African American students could occur through an outpouring of resources. It is interesting to note that this solution might have prevented what is widely considered a particularly harmful consequence of the *Brown* decision: the loss of teaching and school administrative positions for some 20,000 African American educators. Likewise, this solution might have contributed less to the logic of inferiority underlying the *Brown* decision, including the idea that all-Black classrooms were harmful to Black students who only stood to benefit from contact with White pupils.

Others who characterize the decisions in *Brown* zero in on the ponderous phrasing of *Brown II*—"with all deliberate speed"—viewed by many at the time as an open invitation to resistance, which, of course, is what occurred in much of the nation. By not setting a firm deadline in the *Brown II* decision, the Court compromised the overall impact of *Brown*. Civil rights lawyer Oliver Hill (2000) argued that "there's no question about" whether "all deliberate speed" (p. 623) was a mistake; Chief Justice Earl Warren admitted as much to him on two separate occasions. Although Bell is arguing that desegregation per se was the wrong strategy, Hill finds fault not with ordering the integration of the schools, but with the slow pace implicit in the Court's language. What both share, however, is the view that the Court's decision itself was fundamentally flawed.

Brown as Irrelevant

Unlike the claims I have described above, some legal scholars believe that *Brown* simply did not matter very much. That is, rather than creating change single-handedly or serving as a catalyst for change over time, rather than acting in isolation or helping launch multiple social movements, rather than being decided rightly or wrongly, rather than being derailed in implementation by an unwilling society or the language of the decision, *Brown* itself was basically irrelevant. Gerald Rosenberg (1999) advanced this position by arguing that the changes in the social fabric of desegregation were prompted by the Civil Rights Act of 1965 rather than the *Brown* decision. Thus, vis-à-vis school desegregation and *Brown*, Rosenberg questioned whether litigation was the right mechanism for furthering civil rights goals at all. In doing so, he explicitly challenged conventional wisdom about the power of courts in the United States, especially of the Supreme Court.

For Rosenberg (1999), it is misguided to expect the courts to act as the great engine of societal reform and naïve to claim that *Brown* is an example of the judiciary at its majestic best. In his words, such notions support the "romantic belief in the triumph of rights over politics" (p. 221).

Although this review of the different perspectives on *Brown* and its legacy is comprehensive rather than exhaustive, the foregoing differences of opinion on central and important questions support my premise. In the world outside of school—perhaps especially in the academy, but not only in that site—there exists no monolithic agreement about *Brown*, its legacies, and the extent to which it has shaped contemporary society. While within the academy, then, competing visions of *Brown* flourish; within schools, the story is seemingly very different.

IN THE WORLD OF SCHOOLING: *BROWN* IN THE CURRICULUM

Over the years, I have asked many legal and educational experts a basic curriculum question: Which Supreme Court cases should students learn and why? Law professors, high school teachers, judges, and two Supreme Court justices (Sandra Day O'Connor and Ruth Bader Ginsberg) have all, and without exception, included *Brown* on their lists. This seemingly universal view—that *Brown* is a case of such import that all students need to learn it in schools—is reflected in many states' official educational policies. *Brown* is mentioned in state social studies standards more frequently than any other case; it receives prominent attention in virtually all government, law, and history textbooks; it shows up on many state tests; and it is included in Web-based circular resources about the Supreme Court (Hess & Marri, 2002).[5] Agreement has thus crystalized around *Brown*'s import for schools, and yet the kind of attention *Brown* has garnered in the academy has yet to significantly infiltrate classrooms.

In this section, I will discuss the descriptions of *Brown* in textbooks and describe some teachers' reactions to the very notion that *Brown*'s dimensions can be controversial, both toward the aim of explaining the treatment of *Brown* in the curriculum, and more specifically, why its controversies are not taught in schools. What I will argue below is suggestive only; to date, no systematic surveys or large-scale studies have investigated teachers' conceptions of Supreme Court cases and their resultant treatments in the classroom. Moreover, despite data suggesting that the majority of social studies teachers do rely heavily on textbooks, textbooks cannot serve as an index of what occurs in classrooms. (It is also the case, I should note, that studies of school texts have not generally focused on *Brown*'s coverage, though one study by the American Bar Association [in press] found that *Brown* was the "most frequently mentioned" Supreme Court case in 21 leading high school texts.) Thus, the evidence I will array stands as indicators rather than quantifiable measures per se. That said, the content analysis of state standards and textbooks and the informal surveys of teachers' views that I provide below are instructive. Although more research is warranted, the analysis proffered below points in useful directions for those future studies.

Brown in Textbooks: A Simple Icon

I reviewed the treatment of *Brown* and its legacy in 16 history and government textbooks used in U.S. secondary schools (see Appendix). Eight of the 12 history books that I reviewed are among the most widely adopted in the nation (American Textbook Council, 2005). Not surprisingly in light of the consensus around its importance, *Brown* is included in every one of these government, civics, and United States history textbooks. More surprisingly, the case is included in all the world history books as well. One world history text, *World History: The Human Odyssey* (Spielvogel, 1998), goes so far as to give the impression that there was no civil rights movement before *Brown*, explaining, "The civil rights movement had its beginnings in 1954, when the United States Supreme Court took the dramatic step of striking down the practice of racially segregated public schools" (p. 960). Another textbook, *World History: People and Nations* (Miller, Eckel, Haynes, & Parker, 2000), assigns somewhat less credit to *Brown* as a catalyst but does call the decision a "turning point" that "encouraged the growing civil rights movement of the 1950s and 1960s" (p. 768). That *Brown* receives attention in world history textbooks implies that it is conceived of as not just an important event for the United States, but also as important within the context of world history writ large.

Yet, whether world history or U.S. history texts, virtually all the textbooks emphasized the changes supposedly sparked by *Brown*. Far less attention is given to the persistence of racial inequality as a long-term outcome despite or because of *Brown*. Consistent with the American Bar Association's (in press) finding that "history textbooks typically treat *Brown* as a story in itself and part of a larger one—a landmark of the civil rights movement and a seminal event in our nation's history," I likewise found laudatory labels such as *landmark, historic*, and *important* used to describe the case in most of the textbooks. For example, the section on *Brown* in *Magruder's American Government* text (McClenagahn, 2003) begins its treatment of the case by stating, "Finally, in an historic decision in 1954, the Court reversed *Plessy v. Ferguson*" (p. 603).

Here, *Brown* marked the end of the long struggle, the apex of democratic achievement. Textbooks produced by these major publishers emphasize the ways in which civil rights legislation and post-*Brown* Supreme Court decisions fostered desegregation. Absent from these texts are the critiques of *Brown*'s legacy that have recently gained such prominence in academic and civil rights circles. In such portrayals, *Brown* is simply an icon.

Only one textbook I reviewed, *Civics for Democracy: A Journey for Teachers and Students* (Isaac, 1992), dealt forthrightly with the Supreme Court decisions after *Brown* that slowed down desegregation, or in some cases, caused school resegregation. In a section titled "The Movement Loses Ground," this text states,

> Yet, in 1974, the Court weakened its commitment to school integration by ruling in *Milliken v. Bradley* that desegregation plans did not have to include the suburbs. By 1980, the Court had completely rejected busing as a method for improving black schooling but offered no alternative. The number of single-race schools increased rapidly. (p. 48)

Not surprisingly, this unusual textbook comes from an unusual source. It was written as a product for Ralph Nader's Center for Study of Responsive Law and Essential Information. Likely the least widely adopted text of all those I studied, its exceptionalism was not only the probable cause of its marginalization but a product of its marginality.

Millions of students in the United States learn about most subjects, including history, from a single source: their classroom textbook (see Apple & Christian-Smith, 1991); Goodlad, 1984). That the major textbooks do not consider *Brown* to be anything but a simple icon not only inhibits students' understanding of this history, but also curtails their understanding of their present-day circumstances. Although textbooks alone cannot fully illuminate the knowledge taught in classrooms, they certainly reveal the challenges that teachers may face; in order to teach about *Brown* as a controversy, teachers would need to do independent research, a task that the next section suggests would be an anathema to many.

Teachers' Views of *Brown*: A Simple Icon

In order to find out how teachers consider *Brown* and its legacy, the implication being that their perceptions affect their teaching of *Brown* in their classrooms, I asked 60 teachers from across the country who attended the Supreme Court Summer Institutes in 2002 how they taught *Brown* and its legacy. Did they present multiple and competing perspectives about the case and its effects, or did they teach it as a historical conflict that was correctly decided?

Many of the teachers seemed flabbergasted by the question, as if the very suggestion that anything about *Brown* and its legacy could be viewed as controversial was unthinkable. One teacher responded, "Treating *Brown* as a controversy would be like letting a Holocaust denier into my classroom." Another remarked that to do so would violate her dedication to serving as an "antiracist role model" for her students. A third teacher remarked she would likely be thought of as racist if she presented *Brown* or its legacy as controversial. A fourth teacher was the first to inject into the discussion the possibility of *Brown*'s moral and practical complexities; she explained, "It's not that I teach *Brown* as a mistake, but we do talk about whether integration was the right approach to improving educational opportunity. We analyze how much progress has really been made." Considering the discussions that I had with teachers, I noticed how few expressed sentiments similar to those conveyed by the last teacher.

In light of the aforementioned textbook narratives and seemingly common teacher perceptions, it's worth considering the general forces that prevent teachers from engaging controversy in the world of school before discussing the particularities of treating *Brown* as one.

In the Classroom: Controversy Avoidance

The argument that classrooms are typically places where controversy is avoided is hardly new. James Banks (1996) has noted this as one of the defining differences between "school" and "academic" knowledge. School knowledge is often presented as "static" and "settled," while academic knowledge is, almost by definition, a cauldron of competing perspectives and ideologies. Likewise, scholars who have investigated the content of history textbooks agree that textbooks present history as questions for which there are clear answers, instead of as controversies for which there could be multiple and competing answers (Loewen, 1995; Zimmerman, 2002). As James Loewen explained, "The stories that history textbooks tell are predictable; every problem has already been solved or is about to be solved. Textbooks exclude conflict or real suspense" (p. 13).

While there are multiple reasons that textbooks present history as a series of answered questions, one is the fear that adding controversy to the curriculum generates controversy, as opposed to simply reflecting it. And there is little support in the public at large, and even within schools, for the idea that controversy, even when dealt with well, is inherently educational. As one of Jonathan Zimmerman's (2002) students remarked, "You'll never see a parents' group called 'Americans in Favor of Debating the Other Side' in our schools" (p. 197).

This is not to suggest that controversy is always avoided. Catherine Cornbleth's (2002) year-long study of history classes provides evidence that some teachers present students with multiple perspectives and divergent views. But Cornbleth did not find many instances in which students were engaged in deliberations about controversial issues. Similarly, Simon's (2001) study of moral and existential issues in high school classes showed clearly that although authentic issues do arise, discussions of them are "alarmingly truncated." The teachers she studied "seemed reluctant to organize their courses or class time in ways that would invite students to delve into these issues on a regular basis or in a sustained way" (p. 220).

Recent survey research provides further empirical support for the claim that social studies courses typically shun controversy (Levine & Lopez, 2004). A random sample of 10–25-year-olds in the United States was asked to pick the one theme that had been most emphasized in their social studies or American history classes. Their top choice was "the Constitution or the U.S. system of government and how it works." The second most common choice was "great American heroes and the virtues of the American system of government." Only 11% selected "problems facing the country today," and only 9% chose "racism and other forms of injustice in the American system."

These findings led the researchers to conclude that conservative critics of social studies education who charge that the curriculum is infused with left-wing perspectives on important contemporary issues are simply wrong. By contrast, in most social studies courses, students are encountering an extremely traditional view of history that emphasizes a narrative of progress and heroes, while shunning analysis of contemporary problems facing the nation. It is then, of course, no surprise that the representation of *Brown* in textbooks would tend to fit this pattern, treating the case as a simple icon. After all, treating it in accordance with most of the other academic models would force discussion of more contentious contemporary issues.

Controversy Avoidance Factors Specific to *Brown*

Alongside the general resistance to controversial issues in schools, there are factors specific to teaching *Brown* that may account for why so few teachers engage their students in the controversies or differing viewpoints noted above. One factor may be that some teachers lack awareness of just how controversial *Brown* and its legacy have become in the world outside of high school history textbooks. The controversies are clearly not aired in most textbooks, are rarely exposed at professional development activities, and are most prominent in legal and social science journals that teachers do not commonly read. Moreover, because most teachers in the United States are White, they are less apt to know that within the African American community, *Brown* and its legacy have been controversial for quite some time.[6]

What critical race theorists have identified as "interest convergence" may help to explain why *Brown* is likely to be presented as a simple icon. Derrick Bell (1995) explained interest convergence as it relates to *Brown v. Board of Education* as follows:

> The interests of blacks in achieving racial equality will be accommodated only when it converges with the interests of whites. However, the Fourteenth Amendment, standing alone, will not authorize a judicial remedy providing effective racial equality for blacks where the remedy sought threatens the superior societal status of middle- and upper-class whites. (p. 22)

Bell is arguing that the *Brown* decision had particular economic and political advantages that Whites in policy-making positions recognized. These include the widely held view that the abolition of de jure school segregation would enhance America's reputation in the world, that African Americans would be unwilling to serve in the military unless the formal segregationist policies were eradicated, and that economic growth in the South was being held back by racist policies. Thus, *Brown* is an example of what happens when the interests of Whites and African Americans converge. Most White teachers may not be familiar with "interest convergence" alone, much less how it applies to *Brown*.

And yet, as the concept of interest convergence implies, it is important to ask why *Brown* isn't commonly taught as a controversy, or put differently, whose interests are served by teaching *Brown* as though it were a simple icon.

Merely celebrating *Brown* serves the interests of those who want to believe that racial discrimination was largely a problem of the past. This claim both overstates the efficacy of *Brown* and deemphasizes contem-

porary racial inequalities. For some, in fact, the idolization of *Brown* as
a grand achievement because it outlawed segregation has even impeded
their recognition that they themselves teach in, or have children attending, segregated schools.

I first learned about this perspective from a high school history
teacher who told me that his students could barely believe that there was
a time in the United States when the law was used to segregate schools.
As a consequence, this teacher said that for his students, there was nothing controversial about *Brown* or its legacies. I then asked him to describe the student population in his school, which he explained was
virtually all White. Knowing that he lived near a racially diverse city, I
asked where the students of color went to school. He told me that there
was another high school—less than 5 miles away—that enrolled almost
all the African American students. How, I asked the teacher, can your
students believe that segregation was a thing of the past when they attend a segregated school themselves?

The teacher elucidated the ways in which interest convergence functioned to support *Brown* as a simple icon. He responded that the students made a distinction between de jure and de facto segregation,
though they might not use those labels. His students could simultaneously believe that *Brown* was a grand achievement because it called for
the end of state-sanctioned segregation while they attended a virtually
all-White school. They saw their segregated school as fulfilling the
mandates of *Brown* because it was not segregated *by law*. To these students, the idea that *Brown* forced the desegregation of schools was such
a powerful idea that it shrouded the reality of segregation, arguably perpetuating the same inequalities, but now without legal recourse. Thus,
the interests of these White students were catered to by not problema-
tizing *Brown* and its legacy. They did not have to confront the continuing or worsening racial inequalities in educational opportunities. The
teacher felt that it would be extremely challenging to interest his students in an analysis of the complexities of *Brown* and its legacy because
to do so would directly confront their privilege relative to other students in less resourced schools. Consequently, this teacher spent little
time on *Brown*, leaving the students' prior beliefs about the decision un-
challenged and intact.

Up to this point, I have concentrated on reasons for teaching *Brown* as an icon that are largely negative, such as the paucity of controversy in the curriculum generally, the tendency of textbooks to treat historical issues as closed questions, and ways in which celebrating *Brown* shifts emphasis from dealing with contemporary problems related to equality in the United States. Other, more positive, reasons also help explain why *Brown* is more likely to be celebrated than problematized in schools.

Brown as a Moral Example

For instance, teachers may focus on the majesty of *Brown* as a moral exemplar that they hope will shape their students' views. One high school social studies teacher recently remarked to me, "I teach *Brown* because it is such a clear example of how a democracy, when it works the way it is supposed to, can make progress. It is obvious to my students that segregation was wrong and that the Court was right—few things in our history are just so manifestly good." In this regard, one is compelled to consider how an iconic perspective on *Brown*, even if oversimplified, may serve to promote antiracist convictions within racially privileged students. Although I contend that regarding *Brown* as an icon is more likely to undermine the development of critical dispositions in students, it is also important to acknowledge that an iconic approach does not necessarily run counter to the pursuit of democratic educational ends.

As historian McNeill (see Zimmerman, 2002) wrote, sometimes what is needed is "an appropriately idealized version of the past that may allow a group of human beings to come close to living up to its noblest ideas" (p. 222).

Brown can deliver a number of moral messages, but the most essential, in my view, pertains to the seemingly elusive goal of equality in the United States: what it is, why it is so important, and why individuals should be committed to advancing it. However, many teachers may see the differing viewpoints about *Brown* in the world outside of schools and textbooks as quibbles in the academy that, if given airtime, may serve to undermine the very moral commitments they are trying to build in students. According to this line of thinking, *Brown* is a part of United States history that young people can easily feel proud of because it serves as such a powerful example that wrongs can be righted. Thus, presenting

Brown as an icon is a perfect example of a redemptive narrative. The story of *Brown*, with its powerful heroes, its injustices overcome, and its unanimous decision, is employed to do much more than simply teach young people about a court case. Instead, its primacy rests with its utility as a moral example, one that may challenge students to consider issues of racial inequality as much as it may reinforce notions that "we" as a nation have already overcome racism.

These complexities raise a number of questions. What accounts for why *Brown* and its legacy are commonly considered great achievements? In other words, although there are, of course, forces that work to keep controversy out of the curriculum generally, are there forces specific to *Brown* that account for teachers' general impression of it as a simple icon? Moreover, should more teachers engage secondary school students in analyzing *Brown* and its legacies from different academic perspectives? That is, should the iconic status of *Brown* and its effects become matters that students deliberate? Or are there sound educational reasons for transmitting *Brown* to students in a celebratory and triumphant fashion? On the question of deliberating *Brown* and its effects, I would like to present some arguments in support of such an approach.

THE CASE FOR CONTROVERSY

Notwithstanding the possibility that taking a noncontroversial approach to *Brown* and its legacy could help students build moral understandings and commitments that are valuable, I believe that the arguments against teaching *Brown* as a triumphalist tale are more compelling. Although I am sympathetic to how challenging it is for teachers to help students understand different perspectives, debate opposing views, challenge the status quo, and make decisions about real issues, I believe that it is a democratic imperative. In my view, traditional social studies curriculum and teaching offer an inadequate approach to democratic education because they fail to provide students with experience in deliberating public issues—something that engaged citizens should "know" how to do. Still, the question is whether multiple and competing perspectives about *Brown* and its legacy are the kind of problems that young people should deliberate.

Although much of the debate about *Brown* and its legacy originates in the academy, the differing perspectives are not simply academic concerns. In fact, they inform policies that ultimately influence students' lives. Consider that civil rights organizations, such as the National Association for the Advancement of Colored People (NAACP), have held conferences about whether school desegregation is a failed policy, and that a wide range of institutions, from lawmaking bodies to the media, continue to participate in the debate around affirmative action. All of this is evidence that the meaning of *Brown* and its legacy are continually being debated and contested. For teachers or textbooks to present *Brown* and its legacy as noncontroversial is inauthentic to the broader social and political context of schools.

In addition, and more problematic, presenting *Brown* and its legacy as noncontroversial downplays the importance of race in our society. Ladson-Billings (1996) wrote, "Issues of race are avoided in U.S. classrooms for the same reasons that they are avoided in everyday life. We have not found ways to talk about them without feelings of rancor and guilt" (p. 101).

Ignoring issues of race does not solve them, and moreover, it signals to students of color that issues of particular concern to them are not important enough for the curriculum (Epstein, 1997). It also signals to White students, I would add, that these issues do not concern them, as if race is "someone else's problem" rather than something structured by unequal *relations* between groups. Given the prominence of *Brown* in the curriculum, ignoring its controversies affirms the belief that racial inequalities are a past problem now solved, a problem not part and parcel of the contemporary world in which we live. In actuality, issues related to race may be more productively discussed in schools than in other venues. As Gutmann (1999) wrote, "Schools have a much greater capacity than most parents and voluntary associations for teaching children to reason out loud about disagreements that arise in democratic politics" (p. 58). Public schools' greater capacity lies in the fact that they contain more ideological diversity than one would expect to find in many families or associations. This diversity of views (and, by extension, diversity about which issues matter the most) provides a way to promote "rational deliberations of competing conceptions of the good life and the good society" (p. 44).

Another issue that should be considered in teaching *Brown* centers on how the case, when taught as iconic, may promote a view of the Supreme Court that is itself a matter of controversy: namely, the view that the Court functions only to mitigate against injustice. Because of the way *Brown* is taught in the curriculum, it is likely that young people form ideas about the Court from this particular case that then become part of their conceptual framework for thinking about the judicial branch of government more generally. One such generalization is that the Supreme Court's primary and more frequently enacted function in United States democracy is to liberate people who are suffering under the heavy hand of a discriminatory majority. Klarman (1994) traced this perspective to *Brown* when he wrote, "The conventional assessment of the Court's countermajoritarian capacity has been distorted, I believe, by a single decision—*Brown*. Because that ruling rescued us from our racist past, the conventional story line runs, the Court plainly can and does play the role of heroic defender of minority rights from majoritarian oppression" (p. 82). Thus, the conventional presentation of *Brown* may only serve to reinforce a view of the Supreme Court as an agent of social justice—a position that is itself a matter of controversy.

How *Brown* Could Be Taught

I have argued that the way *Brown* is typically presented in the school curriculum deserves re-visioning. A brief summary of three alternatives may clarify the distinction that I am drawing between celebrating *Brown* and its legacy and educating about it.

The first approach is to directly infuse the controversies about *Brown* that exist in the academy into the school curriculum—that is, to teach students the different ways in which *Brown* and its legacy are viewed and have them deliberate core questions about these perspectives. For example, what accounts for the differing interpretations of *Brown*? Whose interests are advanced by each interpretation? Which interpretations do students think have the most merit? And are there other interpretations that they can create? My main point here is to engage students directly in learning the different perspectives about the meaning of *Brown* and its legacies rather than to suggest that there is one right answer that students should build and believe.

A second approach that could complement the first is to use *Brown* as a launching pad for investigating contemporary issues related to race and class in the United States. For example, students could examine what accounts for the resegregation that Gary Orfield, John Yun, and Chungmei Lee have so thoroughly documented (Lee, 2004; Orfield & Lee, 2005; Orfield & Yun, 1999). Students could then deliberate an array of policy options to address the persistent educational inequalities in the United States.

A third approach to treating *Brown* and its legacy as controversies would be to have students focus on what happened in their own schools and communities as a consequence of *Brown* and what contemporary issues that history has created. As an example, a group of students in an experimental civics course at Northwestern High School in Maryland spent the spring of 2003 creating an oral history project on school integration and resegregation in their county from 1955 to 2000. The class, composed entirely of students of color, learned the techniques of oral history and then interviewed people who had insider knowledge about what transpired during this time. The students interviewed an African American who had been the first to desegregate a White school in 1956, a civil rights lawyer who had sued the county to institute busing, and teachers.

The students heard a wide range of sharply competing opinions about how *Brown* and its legacy played out in their county. One of the course teachers, Peter Levine, explained that "a major goal [of the project] is to help our students see history not only as the record of state actions, powerful people, and downtrodden victims, but also as a story of communities making difficult decisions."

Students discussed possible answers to the question, "What should have been done to address school segregation in 1955?" They generated a long list ranging from "leave it alone," to "integrating the teaching staff first," to "busing to achieve equal racial distribution in all schools."[7]

This project captured the differing perspectives about *Brown* and its legacy—the nuances of its successes and limitations. As an exemplar of democratic education, it went far beyond merely celebrating the landmark court case and its aftermath. Instead, the project illustrates well the point Parker (2003) stressed when he argued that "problems and differences are the essential assets for cultivating democrats" (p. 78).

By contrast, teaching *Brown* and its legacies as altogether positive fails to take advantage of the real debate that exists about how to tackle the continuing problems of inequality that vex the United States. Moreover, when teachers teach controversial questions as if there is one best answer, they deprive their students of the opportunity to do the necessary work of democracy, making them dangerously susceptible to the blind acceptance of the political conclusions of others. Even if the decision to deny a controversy is made with the best of intentions—and I believe that is often the case when *Brown* is celebrated in the curriculum—I fear the result. Orthodoxy is, by definition, the enemy of inquiry. Redemptive narratives, such as presenting *Brown* and its effects as unequivocally positive, while alluring, do not promote a more egalitarian United States. I end this article with a charge to high school social studies teachers across the country: Teach *Brown* not as an icon that deserves mere celebration, but as an ongoing controversy from decision through legacy, in the hope that such teaching will help young people deal with the important and thorny issues that are part and parcel of the world in which we live.

APPENDIX: TEXTBOOKS REVIEWED FOR COVERAGE OF *BROWN*

American History

Joyce Appleby, Alan Brinkley, and James M. McPherson, *The American Journey: Building a Nation* (Glencoe, 2003), and Joyce Appleby, Alan Brinkley, Albert S. Broussard, James M. McPherson, and Donald A. Ritchie, *The American Republic Since 1877* (Glencoe/McGraw-Hill, 2003). (This pair of books was treated as a single entry.)*

Paul Boyer and Sterling Stuckey, *The American Nation in the Modern Era* (Holt, Rinehart & Winston, 2003).

Henry W. Bragdon, Samuel P. McCutcheon, and Donald A. Ritchie, *History of a Free Nation* (Glencoe, 1998).*

Andrew Cayton, Elizabeth Israels Perry, Linda Reed, and Alan W. Winkler, *America: Pathways to the Present* (Prentice Hall, 2003).*

Gerald A. Danzer, J. Jorge Klor de Alva, Larry S. Krieger, Louis E. Wilson, and
  Nancy Woloch, *The Americans* (McDougal Littell, 2003).*

Gary B. Nash, *American Odyssey: The United States in the Twentieth Century* (Glencoe/
  McGraw-Hill, 2002).*

World History

Roger B. Beck, Linda Black, Larry S. Krieger, Phillip C. Naylor, and Dahia Ibo
  Shabaka, *Modern World History: Patterns of Interaction* (McDougal Littell, 2003).

Elisabeth Gaynor Ellis and Anthony Esler, *World History: Connections to Today* (Prentice Hall, 2003).*

Mounir A. Farah and Andrea Berens Karls, *World History: The Human Experience*
  (Glencoe/McGraw-Hill, 2001).*

William Travis Hanes III, ed., *World History: Continuity and Change* (Holt, Rinehart
  & Winston, 1999).*

Sue Miller, ed., *World History: People & Nations* (Holt, Rinehart & Winston, 2000).

Jackson S. Spielvogel, *World History: The Human Odyssey* (National Textbook Company, 1999; Glencoe, 2003).

American Government

Katherine Isaac, *Civics for Democracy: A Journey for Teachers and Students* (Essential
  Books, 1992).

Steven Kelman, *American Government* (Holt, Rinehart, & Winston, 2003).

William A. McClenaghan, ed., *Magruder's American Government* (Prentice Hall, 2003).

Richard C. Remy, *United States Government: Democracy in Action* (Glencoe/McGraw-
  Hill, 2000).

*The author thanks Amy Stuart Wells, the two anonymous TCR reviewers,
Simone Schweber, Kristen Buras, Gloria Ladson-Billings, Eric Freedman,
Jonathan Ivry, Keith Barton, Paulette Dillworth, Hilary Conklin, and Michael
Olneck for their helpful feedback on prior drafts of this manuscript.*

NOTES

1. Information about the exhibit, Separate Is Not Equal: *Brown v. Board of Education*, can be accessed at http://americanhistory.si.edu/Brown/index.html.

---

*According to the research of the American Textbook Council (2005), these history textbooks have been widely
adopted.

2. Bert Neuborne made this comment on May 18, 2004, while serving as a panelist in a session entitled, "Social Forces/Social Actors on *Brown*," at *Brown* Plus Fifty: A Renewed Agenda for Social Justice, National Commemorative Conference, New York University.

3. With this reading of the Smithsonian exhibit, I do not wish to suggest that celebrating *Brown* is unwarranted; my point is simply that celebration alone necessarily "occludes" *Brown*'s complicated past and present.

4. In a compelling book on a seemingly unrelated topic, Simone Schweber (2004) has explained how consensus crystalizes around curricular subjects, typically prompting overly simplistic treatments in the classroom. Although Schweber's book analyzes the representations of the Holocaust in public high school classrooms rather than a Supreme Court case, her underlying notion that the Holocaust became iconic in public discourse and that schools subsequently treated it as morally simple rather than intellectually complex is similar to my argument here.

5. There are other reasons that *Brown* is an integral part of the historical canon of cases taught in the secondary school curriculum. According to an analysis of the cases that appear in state standards documents, the cases deemed most important for young people to learn were those that generate little contemporary social controversy, those that the Supreme Court "got right" (Hess & Marri, 2002). As an illustration, *Roe v. Wade* (1973) is clearly one of the most important Supreme Court decisions of the 20th century, yet it is only listed in four states' social studies standards. Likewise, the famous affirmative action case, *Bakke v. California* (1976), appears only in three states' standards. Because both of these cases continue to generate tremendous social debate, they tend not to appear in state social studies standards.

6. I wish to thank Paulette Dilworth at Indiana University and Mary Curd Larkin of Street Law, Inc., for helping me understand the nature and history of the controversies related to *Brown* and its legacy to the African American community.

7. I learned about this project from Peter Levine. For an explanation of the activities that the students engaged in and the content of their discussions, go to http://www.peterlevine.ws/hsclassthread.htm. The students created an online historical exhibit—including the oral histories, a slide show, and a deliberative poll—that can be found at http://www.princegeorges.org/Northwestern_history/animatedintro.htm.

REFERENCES

American Bar Association. (In press). *A review of the treatment of law-related content in secondary U.S. history, civics, and government textbooks*. Chicago: American Bar Association Division for Public Education.

American Textbook Council. (2005). *Widely adopted history textbooks*. Retrieved June 27, 2005, from www.historytextbooks.org/adoptions.htm.

Apple, M. W., & Christian-Smith, L. K. (Eds.). (1991). *The politics of the textbook*. New York: Routledge.

Balkin, J. M., & Ackerman, B. A. (2001). *What* Brown v. Board of Education *should have said: The nation's top legal experts rewrite America's landmark civil rights decision*. New York: New York University Press.

Banks, J. A. (1996). *Multicultural education, transformative knowledge, and action: Historical and contemporary perspectives*. New York: Teachers College Press.

Bell, D. A. (1995). *Brown v. Board of Education* and the Interest Convergence Dilemma. In K. Crenshaw (Ed.), *Critical race theory: The key writings that formed the movement* (pp. 20–29). New York: New Press.

Bell, D. A. (2001). Revised decisions: Dissenting. In J. M. Balkin & B. A. Ackerman (Eds.), *What* Brown v. Board of Education *should have said: The nation's top legal experts rewrite America's landmark civil rights decision* (pp. 185–200). New York: Nee York University Press.

Brandsberg-Engelmann, J. (2002). Teaching *Brown v. Board of Education*. *Social Education, 66*, 66–67.

Brown v. Board of Education of Topeka, 347 U.S. 484 (1954).

Cornbleth, C. (2002). Images of America: What youth do know about the United States. *American Educational Research Journal, 39*, 519–552.

Epstein, T. (1997). Sociocultural approaches to young people's historical understanding. *Social Education, 61*, 28–32.

Goodlad, J. I. (1984). *A place called school*. New York: McGraw-Hill.

Graff, E. J. (2003). *The High Court finally gets it right*. Retrieved June 29, 2003, from http://www.sodomylaws.org/lawrence/lweditorials020.htm.

Gutmann, A. (1999). *Democratic education* (rev. ed.). Princeton, NJ: Princeton University Press.

Hess, D., & Marri, A. (2002). Which cases should we teach? *Social Education, 66*, 53–59.

Hill, O. (2000). Transcript of a symposium on *Brown v. Board of Education*: An exercise in advocacy. *Mercer Law Review, 52*, 581–630.

Isaac, K. (1992). *Civics for democracy: A journey for teachers and students*. Washington, DC: Essential Books.

Klarman, M. J. (1994). How *Brown* changed race relations: The backlash thesis. *Journal of American History, 81*, 81–118.

Ladson-Billings, G. (1996). Multicultural issues in the classroom: Race, class, and gender. In R. W. Evans & D. W. Saxe (Eds.), *Handbook on teaching social issues* (pp. 100–110). Washington, DC: National Council for the Social Studies.

Ladson-Billings, G. (2004). Landing on the wrong note: The price we paid for *Brown*. *Educational Researcher, 33*(7), 3–13.

Ladson-Billings, G., & Tate, W. F. (1995). Toward a critical race theory of education. *Teachers College Record, 97*, 47–68.

Lagemann, E. C. (1996). An American dilemma still. In E. C. Lagemann & E. C. Miller (Eds.), Brown v. Board of Education: *The challenge for today's schools* (pp. 1–8). New York: Teachers College Press.

Lee, C. (2004). Is resegregation real? Cambridge, MA: Civil Rights Project, Harvard University.

Levine, P., & Lopez, M. H. (2004). *Themes emphasized in social studies and civics classes: New evidence* [CIRCLE Fact Sheet]. College Park: The Center for Information & Research on Civic Learning & Engagement, University of Maryland.

Loewen, J. W. (1995). *Lies my teacher told me: Everything your American history textbook got wrong*. New York: New Press.

McClenagahn, W. A. (Ed.). (2003). *Magruder's American Government*. Needham, MA: Prentice Hall.

Miller, S., Eckel, J., Haynes, R., & Parker, C. J. (Eds.). (2000). *World History: People and nations*. Austin, TX: Holt, Rinehart and Winston.

Orfield, G., & Lee, C. (2005). *Why segregation matters: Poverty and educational inequality*. Cambridge, MA: Civil Rights Project, Harvard University.

Orfield, G., & Yun, J. T. (1999). *Resegregation in American schools*. Cambridge, MA: Civil Rights Project, Harvard University.

Parker, W. (2003). *Teaching democracy: Unity and diversity in public life*. New York: Teachers College Press.

Patterson, J. T. (2001). Brown v. Board of Education: *A civil rights milestone and its troubled legacy*. Oxford: Oxford University Press.

Raskin, J. B. (2003). *Overruling democracy: The Supreme Court vs. the American People*. New York: Routledge.

Rosenberg, G. N. (1999). African-American rights after *Brown*. *Journal of Supreme Court History, 24*, 201–225.

Schweber, S. A. (2004). *Making sense of the Holocaust: Lessons from classroom practice.* New York: Teachers College Press.

Shager, E. (2002). Review of J. T. Patterson, Brown v. Board of Education: *A civil rights milestone and its troubled legacy. Social Education, 66,* 70–71.

Simon, K. G. (2001). *Moral questions in the classroom: How to get kids to think deeply about real life and their schoolwork.* New Haven, CT: Yale University Press.

Spielvogel, J. J. (Ed.). (1998). *World history: The human odyssey* (2nd ed.). Belmont, CA: West/Wadsworth.

Ware, L. (2004, May/June). The unfulfilled promise. *The Crisis Magazine, 111,* 43.

Wilkins, R. (1996). Dream deferred but not defeated. In E. C. Lagemann & L. P. Miller (Eds.), Brown v. Board of Education: *The challenge for today's schools* (pp. 14–18). New York: Teachers College Press.

Zimmerman, J. (2002). *Whose America? Culture wars in the public schools.* Cambridge, MA: Harvard University Press.

––––––––––––

MAUREEN: This article by Diana Hess is academic in tone but makes an important point for all parents and teachers. We often deprive our children of a healthy exchange of ideas, of the awareness of differing points of view. Sometimes it's because we want to protect them; sometimes it's because we want them to follow our advice or our point of view. But if we want them to grow in understanding and sensitivity, we need to keep reminding them that not everyone agrees about most socio-political issues. Understanding the nature of this diversity of opinion leads to intellectual enlightenment.

Using the Supreme Court decision in Brown v. *Board of Education of* Topeka *in 1954, Hess examined most of the social studies textbooks used in secondary schools and found that the case is treated as an icon, the catalyst that started the civil rights movement in America. In academic circles, however, she found a wide spectrum of opinions of its role and its importance. She asks us to examine this variety of viewpoints and the controversies surrounding the decision so that we may make an informed decision about its place in history.* Brown *is just one example of the taken-for-granted approach of many texts in American history that need to be opened to exploration and enlightenment rather than used as propaganda in the effort to create a dedicated, unquestioning citizenry.*

In teaching literature, for example, we search for multiple explanations of content so as to magnify the complexity of the writing. Hess points out that even educators often see issues from a narrow point of view. As parents and as teachers, we must search for multiple meanings to enlarge our vision and to open windows on possibility. We must have conversations about alternative viewpoints so as to recognize students' varied knowledge and experience, and must always try to generate new questions, new explorations.

14

Gloria Ladson-Billings

CULTURALLY RELEVANT TEACHING*

ALEXANDRA: Gloria Ladson-Billings, an internationally acclaimed author and scholar, is Professor of Education at the University of Wisconsin-Madison and former President of the American Educational Research Association. In this excerpt from one of her best-loved books, she weaves together stories of classroom life, teachers' biographies, her own personal history, and theory about culturally relevant teaching in prose that is remarkably accessible and compelling. She explains that in her search for exemplary teachers the practices she observed in these classrooms made sense to her because of her own experiences as an African American student.

The portraits of teachers and students that follow are affirming and hopeful, and we come to understand that the teachers' belief in the students' potential for academic excellence is key to developing relationships based on trust and motivating students to achieve the high expectations these teachers have for them. One teacher, Ann Lewis, describes a particularly memorable metaphor of a troubled student who has been perceived as being "in the kitchen junk drawer," but she sees him as a "piece of crystal . . . up there in the china cabinet" (p. 216). Ladson-Billings argues that teachers must be attentive to students' individual cultural backgrounds as well as to the collective culture growing in the classroom community. She illustrates the necessary pedagogical competency with vivid examples of literacy and mathematical learning.

What is also noteworthy is that two of the teachers profiled, Ann Lewis and Julia Devereaux, take quite different approaches to teaching literacy, which represent current political differences between whole-language, holistic methods and direct reading and phonics instruction. Where some authors would use

---

*From *The Dreamkeepers: Successful Teachers of African American Children* (San Francisco: Jossey-Bass, 1994).

these differences to further polarize the political debates about so-called best practice, Ladson-Billings's analysis shows that the underlying ideologies and beliefs in students' capabilities are the same for both teachers. Furthermore, she provides six important tenets that both teachers' literacy programs employ. These are so clearly spelled out that when she comes to the portrait of the fourth teacher, a novice student of hers at the University of Wisconsin, we can feel why he is unable to connect with a group of four students he is seeking to teach how to convert improper fractions into a mixed number. So universally important are these six tenets for practice, and the five that follow the four teacher portraits, that it hardly matters whether they are derived from instruction in literacy, mathematics, or any other subject matter. Furthermore, Ladson-Billings suggests that the teachers' choice of methods and their own cultural background matter less than their uncompromising commitment to helping all students realize their potential.

———————

Hold fast to dreams
For if dreams die
Life is a broken winged butterfly. . . .
—Langston Hughes

In this chapter I offer a more contextualized examination of the activities of four classrooms, three in which culturally relevant teaching was practiced and one in which it was not. The context for two of the classes is a reading lesson and for the other classes it is a math lesson.

THE FOCUS ON LITERACY

One of the critical national indicators of educational progress (and national development) is the literacy rate. Arnove and Graff assert that national literacy campaigns are not unique to the twentieth century; many charismatic leaders have used literacy campaigns for "salvation, redemption, and re-creation." They suggest that in the twentieth century, especially since 1960, "literacy has been seen as a process of consciousness-raising aimed at human liberation."[1] National literacy campaigns have been a part of the social and political fabric of such countries as Brazil, Cuba, and Guineau Bissau. However, the aim of literacy campaigns in the United States has been individual and personal advancement. Nightly public service messages on television exhort citizens to sign up at local libraries and schools for reading instruction. An explanation of this trend is presented by Ferdman: "In a society tending toward homogeneity, it is easy to think of literacy simply in terms of specific skills and activities. Given broad cultural consensus on the definition of literacy, alternative constructions are either remote or invisible, and so literacy becomes a seemingly self-evident personal attribute that is either present or absent."[2] But Ferdman further contends that in a multiethnic society the "cultural framework" for literacy must be considered. Thus in citing deCastell and Luke,[3] Ferdman points out that "being literate has always referred to having mastery over the processes by means of which culturally significant information is coded."

The following passage is central to Ferdman's argument: "In a culturally heterogeneous society, literacy ceases to be a characteristic inherent solely in the individual. It becomes an interactive process that is constantly redefined and renegotiated, as the individual transacts with the socioculturally fluid surroundings."

In the context of this study of culturally relevant teaching, the construction of literacy among African Americans is especially important. Gadsden contends: "For African American learners, in particular, literacy has been an especially tenuous struggle, from outright denial during slavery, to limited access in the early 1900s, to segregated schools with often outdated textbooks well into the 1960s, to—many might argue—marginal acceptance of their culture and capacity as learners even into the 1990s."[4]

My father completed only about four years of formal schooling. His school was a one-room classroom that he, his four brothers, and his two sisters attended. By the time my father was in what was considered to be fourth grade, he had learned as much as his older siblings who had stopped attending school to help with farming chores at home. In an attempt to escape the harsh discipline of his stepmother when he was about 12 years old, he and an older brother ran

*away from home to live with an adult sister in Philadelphia. By the time he ar-
rived, school was but a distant memory. He kept up his reading with the newspaper every day and the Bible every night.*

*When I reached junior high school, my father would thumb through my
textbooks and read them as if he actually found them interesting.*

The next section of this chapter describes culturally relevant literacy
instruction in Ann Lewis's and Julia Devereaux's classrooms. They make
literacy a communal activity and demonstrate ways to make learning to
read and write a more meaningful and successful enterprise for African
American learners.

Ann Lewis: A Literacy Revival

Lewis is an Italian American woman in her midforties. Active in school
and community politics, she has lived most of her life in the largely
African American community where she teaches. Some of the older
teachers and administrators in the district were her teachers. Lewis re-
members herself as less than an ideal student:

> I grew up in the community and my greatest desire was to teach here, basi-
> cally because I spent so much time with quality teachers and those teachers
> encouraged me to teach. As strict as those teachers were with me, they
> pushed me to do what was right. I was a difficult child in class and that's why
> I started teaching—to give other so-called difficult children a real chance.

Lewis did not take a traditional route to teaching. Having married
soon after high school, she began her adult life as a homemaker, mother,
and wife. But the breakup of her marriage meant that she needed to
work to support herself and her children. She secured a job as a teacher's
aide in a local elementary school. Her decision to work in the schools
came in the early 1970s, at a time when schools and school districts described as economically disadvantaged received additional state and federal
funds to hire community people, particularly parents, as paraprofession-
als. Familiarity with both the school and the home culture made the

teachers' aides a special resource. Students and parents who were intimidated by the formality and cultural barriers between themselves and the school's more formal staff often sought out the teachers' aides for assistance and support.

Aware that teachers' aides were an important resource and that turnover among the teaching staff was on the increase, the school district proposed and implemented a program to encourage the aides to attend the local community college, transfer to the state university, and then enroll in the university's fifth year teacher accreditation program. With a critical mass of teachers' aides enrolling in the program, the district, in conjunction with the community college, could offer courses in the school district so that the aides were able to keep their jobs. Lewis was among the first group of aides to take advantage of the program.

Although many aides enthusiastically began the district-sponsored program, time and circumstances kept most from completing it. Lewis was one of the few who endured and completed it. She began as a certified teacher in the district in 1977.

By 1983 Lewis had built a reputation in the school district for her assertive, even aggressive, advocacy of teachers' rights. She had been elected president of the teachers' association and was a self-appointed watchdog for the school board, attending every meeting and taking public issue with positions she felt were not in the best interests of the teachers. Not known for her diplomacy or tact, she often locked horns with board members and school administrators about what she perceived as violations of the teachers' contract. This kind of behavior is risky in a small district such as Pinewood, where board members and district administrators can have an inordinate amount of influence on the day-to-day running of the school. Lewis felt that, perhaps because they shared the feelings of board members and district administrators, or because they saw it as a way to ingratiate themselves with their superiors, her principals attempted to apply subtle forms of harassment. She received many of the students that no other teacher wanted. I suggested to Lewis that maybe these students were assigned to her because of a principal's confidence in her ability to work with them, whereas her colleagues could not. Lewis gave me a look indicating that I might be out of touch with the reality of urban schools.

In the spring of 1983 Lewis seriously rethought her decision to teach. She knew she still loved being in the classroom. Further, because of her reputation as an excellent teacher, many parents requested (and even demanded) that their children be placed in her class. Thus administrative attempts to stack her class with "troublemakers" were thwarted by these concerned parents who saw that Lewis offered a special intellectual opportunity for their children. But she was weary of her battles with the district and school board. She felt as if she were working two jobs; and her "night job" was affecting her performance on her "day job."

One piece of good fortune for Lewis was a friendship with a colleague who had gone on to become an administrator in the district. Now a principal, her friend told Lewis about the Bay Area Writing Project and suggested that Lewis and another teacher take advantage of the seven-week program, which was offered at the University of California at Berkeley. Because none of her other colleagues were interested in giving up seven weeks of their summer, Lewis faced no competition for the scholarship offered.

Today Lewis credits this experience with renewing her enthusiasm for teaching:

> I can't tell you how that experience changed me. It's not so much that the philosophy was radical or revolutionary. In fact, it was kind of like a recognition that the way I thought about teaching was all right. It was the intellectual activity, you know, the thinking. Because I wasn't bombarding my kids with worksheets, I think some of the other teachers thought I wasn't working hard. But I was trying to get at their thinking, to remind them that they *could* think, that thinking was allowed in school. I came back here in the fall and totally restructured my class around writing (and later literature) and I had the research to back it up.

When my study began, Lewis was in the seventh year of her revised curriculum. Each year and each class of fifth or sixth graders brought new permutations to her ideas and her thinking about the kind of education the community required.

During the first year of my observations, I visited Lewis's sixth-grade class regularly but randomly, that is, I went there every week but at varied times. I felt that appearing at different times helped me to see the different moods of the classroom.

Fall 1990 marked the second year of Lewis's participation in the study. In this second year I began to appear at a set time each week. Although Lewis's teaching was not circumscribed by a predictable schedule (of reading, math, science, and so on) literacy teaching was more likely in the mornings. My field notes describe my first visit that year:

I arrived at the school at 8:45 on Thursday morning. The school grounds were quiet. I noticed that the lawn was freshly cut, a sure sign of the beginning of the school year. I stopped at the main office to sign in and speak to the principal. The secretary informed me that the principal was covering a class because they had been unable to get a substitute. As I walked through the inner courtyard I noticed the vice principal talking with two black girls who looked to be about twelve years old. He seemed to be reprimanding—or perhaps counseling—them. The noise level of the class next to Ann Lewis's was high. Students were talking, the teacher was shouting. I noticed the contrast when I walked into Ann's class, which was unusually quiet. The students were listening as one of them read aloud.

The class was studying *Charlie Pippin* by Candi Dawson Boyd. [The novel] is about an eleven-year-old African American girl who attempts to win the approval of her father, a decorated Vietnam War veteran who has buried all his feelings about the war within him. The girl feels alienated from her father and wants to find a way to reach him. Ann and her students were about twenty pages into the book.

There were twenty-nine students in the class (twenty African Americans). When the student who was reading finished, an African American boy, Jerry, asked, "Is she [the story's protagonist] going to stay eleven years old in this book?"

Lewis responded with a question, "What about in *Driving Miss Daisy*? Did the main character stay the same age?"

Students (in unison): "No."

Ann: "How do you know?"

Jerry: "Because she was using one of those walkin' things when she got old."

Ann: "A walker?"

Jerry: "Yeah, and then she was in the old folks home."

Ann: "Can you *see* without a video?"

Calvin (another African American boy): "Yes, you can see when you're reading. So we'll see how old Charlie is in the book!"

Ann reminded the students about a previous discussion about "connotation" and "denotation" and said, "Remember we said 'hungry' makes you think one way but 'famished' makes you think another way?"

Calvin asked if the discussion could go back to talking about the book and Ann encouraged him. "She got feelings her dad doesn't understand and he got feelings she don't understand."

Ann: "Do you know anybody who ever feels like this?"

Calvin: "*Me*!"

Ann drew a Venn diagram to represent similarities and differences between Calvin and the character in the story. "You have your own video of your entire life in your head. Every time you read, you can get an image of how the story connects with your life. Do you want to get back to the story?"

"Yeah!," the class says in unison.

A third boy began to read. When he finished, Lewis said, "Close your eyes. Let's put on your video." She then re-read a section of the book describing the mother in the story. "How can you relate this to your life?" One of the African American girls commented "That's just like when I kiss my mom."

Students took turns reading passages from the book. For some, this was the first "chapter" book they'd read in school. Some of these slower readers had trouble with some of the words. Lewis encouraged them and urged other class members to help. "Remember, we're all a team here. We've got to help each other." When Charlene (an African American girl) asked a question about a dispute the main character had with her father, Lewis suggested the students role-play to understand better. Two students struggled a bit with the role-play. Two others gave it a try and got a round of applause from the rest of the class.

After the role-play Ann asked, "What do we know about Charlie's dad?" The class erupted with excitement—many wanted to contribute. Lewis began to develop a "character-attribute web" on the board. As the students became more excited, she encouraged them to settle down by explaining which part of the brain they were using. "We're not in the limbic [she pointed to a bulletin-board diagram of the brain], we're in the cerebellum. Let's not deteriorate into reptilian. Okay, you now have two minutes to talk with someone about other attributes of Charlie's dad."

When the two minutes were up, many students contributed to the attribute web. Ann filled the board with the student responses and shouted, "That was perfect! You're a *perfect* class. If you're perfect raise your hand!" Twenty-nine hands were in the air.

Over the course of the next several months, *Charlie Pippin* became the centerpiece for a wide range of activities. One group of students began a Vietnam War research group. One group member who assumed a leadership position was a very quiet Vietnamese girl whose relatives had fought in the war. She brought in pictures, maps, letters, even a family member to talk to the class about Vietnam. In the book, the main character—Charlie—had made origami to sell to her classmates. Lewis taught her students how to make origami. She introduced them to Eleanor Coerr's *Sadako and the Thousand Paper Cranes*. A second group of students researched nuclear proliferation. They asked Lewis to rent the video "Amazing Grace," which is about a young boy's and a professional athlete's stand against nuclear weapons. The entire study took place against the backdrop of an impending war between the United States and its allies and Iraq.

Several of the students decided that, like Sadako, they could make paper cranes to symbolize their opposition to war. In a way, the students believed that their efforts might even prevent the war. Although Lewis gave them no extra time to make their cranes, they found many opportunities to do so. By January 15, the date that then-President George Bush had set to move into Kuwait, Lewis's class had folded and hung up in their classroom window 1,039 paper cranes—tiny paper birds that stood as a symbol of their commitment to peace.

It is interesting to note that Lewis's reference to the parts of the brain, and later class discussions about learning taxonomies, grew out of her own experiences at that time: She was taking a graduate course and shared much of her learning and experiences with the students. She brought readings and the language from her graduate studies into her sixth-grade classroom. The students seemed eager to hear about what she was learning and to enjoy the vision of her as a student and of themselves as "graduate students."

Thus during this year I witnessed a class of students engaged in reading, writing, and speaking activities with increasing levels of competence and confidence. One of the hallmarks of Lewis's class was the intellectual leadership demonstrated by the African American boys. Although most of them had had previous problems, including poor academic performance, truancy, suspensions, recommendation for special-education placement, and at least one threatened expulsion, Lewis's class represented an opportunity for a new academic beginning.

One of Lewis's star students, a boy named Larry, had had a particularly troubling history. Although he was short and slightly built, he was the oldest child in the class. He had been left back several times and was thirteen in a class made up of eleven-year-olds. He had been traumatized by the drive-by shooting of a favorite aunt. Other teachers in the school referred to him as "an accident just waiting to happen." None wanted him in their classrooms. Lewis referred to Larry as "a piece of crystal."

> He's strong and beautiful but fragile. I have to build a safe and secure place for him and let him know that we—the class and I—will be here for him. The school has been placing him in the kitchen junk drawer. I want him to be up there in the china cabinet where everyone can see him.

By the end of the school year, Larry had been elected president of the school's sixth grade. He was involved in peer-conflict mediation and was earning A's and B's in every subject. He was among the academic leaders of Lewis's class.

While Larry represented a special example of accomplishment, the classroom was a special place for all the children, including the nine non-African Americans. (They were Latino, Pacific Islander, and Vietnamese.) The work was challenging and exciting. The students were presumed to have some level of literacy, which formed the foundation for increased competency. Reading, writing, and speaking were community activities that Lewis believed all students could participate in—and they did.

Julia Devereaux: "Gimme that old-time [religion] teaching."

If one were to design a "controlled study" Devereaux and Lewis would be closely matched on more variables than any other two teachers in my study. The two women are the same age and both have lived in the school community most of their lives. They attended the same state university (at different times) and were elementary, junior high, and senior high school classmates. In 1988 Devereaux succeeded Lewis as president of the teachers' association. Although weary of both the internal and external politics of the association, Lewis agreed to assist Devereaux in her first term as president.

The two obvious differences between the two that are important in this study are that Devereaux is African American whereas Lewis is white and that Devereaux believes in direct reading instruction, particularly using a basal text, whereas Lewis is committed to a whole-language approach to literacy.

Devereaux teaches at a school in the district that has made a commitment to training the teachers in a method espoused by a well-known African American educator in Chicago who established her own school for inner-city students. It is a no-frills, no-nonsense approach to teaching and learning. This basic-skills approach emphasizes phonics as the appropriate way to teach reading. "Classic" books in the European and African American tradition are a part of the curriculum. Devereaux transferred voluntarily to this school because of its philosophy; she was one of eight teachers the school sent to Chicago to receive training in this pedagogical approach.

Devereaux's family has always been a mainstay of the community. Her parents worked hard to raise a family there. Her father brought the family to California from Louisiana in the 1950s. He began work as a night custodian as a retail store and later became a bail bondsman. Her mother began as a window dresser at another retail store and went on to become assistant manager. Eventually her father opened a grocery store where both parents worked. Later, he studied for and earned his real-estate license and today is a well-respected realtor in the community.

Devereaux's family is active in the local Catholic church. Devereaux herself leads a Girl Scout troop. But her family is also known for a series of tragedies it has suffered. Both Devereaux and her sister were victims of violent crimes. Both have worked hard to put the trauma of the assaults behind them.

During the three years of my study, Devereaux taught fourth grade; however, she has taught every grade from second to eighth. Her classroom is a beehive. Students always seem to be all over the place, except when it is "reading time." Devereaux convenes the class for reading at 9:00 A.M. During the first twenty to thirty minutes of the day, the students may be involved in a variety of activities, including games, journal writing, handwriting, and spelling assignments, while Devereaux ties up loose ends, collecting monies for various projects or field trips, ordering books and materials, checking papers, or visiting with students. But, at 9 o'clock all this activity comes to a halt.

Each of the twenty-five students in Devereaux's class this semester pulls out a basal reader and places it on top of the desk. Twenty-one of the twenty-five are African American, four are Latino. There are fifteen girls and ten boys.

Devereaux's reading lessons seem almost scripted. She begins with a phonics drill. A student goes to the front of the room, takes the pointer, and begins the drill by pointing to the chart above the chalkboard. The student points to the letter *b*: "Beating drum, beating drum, ba, ba, ba," she says. The class repeats in unison. She continues, "B sounds, 'bound.' What does 'bound' mean?" One student raises his hand and says, "Bound means to leap." The drill leader continues the drill through the consonants. Although this is a fourth-grade class, the words and terms they are asked to define seem sophisticated; they include "justice," "kinsman," "fatigue," "depositor," "lay waste," "preserve," "reunion," and "veranda." There is a high degree of participation in the drill. The drill leader calls on many different students.

At the conclusion of the drill, Devereaux thanks her and moves to the front of the room. She asks students to recap the last story they read.

Depending on which skills were emphasized in the lesson and whether the students mastered those skills, she reviews some skills at the end of the story review.

One morning, Devereaux introduces the lesson by saying, "Today we're going to be reading about the first woman jockey." She directs the students' attention to a word list on the board. The following words are there: "influence," "atmosphere," "outlet," "developing," "demonstrate," "concentrate," and "equestrian." The students first attempt to define the words in words of their own and then use their glossaries. As they pronounce the words, Devereaux reminds them to sound them out phonetically.

She then begins calling on the students in round-robin fashion to read the story aloud. They seem eager to get a turn. She tries to divide the reading selection up so that everyone gets a turn. "Who haven't I heard from today?" she asks. Two hands go up. She calls on these students next. The entire class reads the last two paragraphs aloud in unison. Throughout the reading she asks a variety of recall questions. The entire experience seems rather ordinary, even boring.

I am anxious to talk to her about what she's doing.

I know it seems old-fashioned but I believe the students benefit from the structure. It's as if it were important for them to know what comes next. I have children in here who other teachers told me could not read. Heck, *they* told me they couldn't read. But I look them squarely in the eye in the beginning of the school year and tell them, you *will* read, and you will read *soon*. I tell my entire class we all have to know how to read and it's everybody's responsibility to make sure that everyone learns to read well. I pair up the better readers with the poorer ones and tell them that *the pair* gets a reading grade. They are allowed to do any number of things to help each other read. Although the school doesn't want us to do it I let them take their readers home. I also use some of those old, out-of-date basals as at-home readers for them. All students have a reading log in which they list what they read aloud to their parents the night before. The parents sign the logs. I award prizes for completing the reading logs. You may have noticed how quiet things got when the reading lesson began. I'm pretty easygoing about a lot of things, but I keep my reading time sacred.

Devereaux does a number of things to encourage reading. She has her own Book of the Month Club. Each month, Devereaux announces a book to read. Up to ten students may sign up to read it. She often purchases the books with her own money. The book club meets to talk about the book on their own time—at lunch with the teacher, in early-morning hours before school, or after school. No grades are given for participation in the club. Its reward is intrinsic.

The proof of Devereaux's pudding is indeed in the tasting. She suggested that I select her most difficult student, Michael, look at his cumulative file, and then listen to him read. Michael's file was two inches thick. He had been in a series of foster homes. His natural mother was a drug addict and had neglected him. Every teacher from first grade on had recommended that he be placed in a special day class. Everyone agreed he could not learn to read; he lacked the requisite skills and needed remedial attention that no one had the time to give him.

I asked Michael if he was willing to read something to me. His face lit up. He selected a book entitled *The Trouble with Tuck* from the shelf. It was a story about a girl and her dog. Although his reading was halting, Michael employed phonics skills and decoded the words that were not familiar. I asked him how long he had been such a good reader. "Only since I been in Miss Devereaux's class."

"Why is that?" I asked.

"I don't know, she just told me that I could read if I wanted to and she was going to help me want to. She said you can't stay in her class if you don't read. I want to stay."

Michael's reading partner was Jabari. Devereaux selected him because she knew that Jabari was very competitive and would personally take on the challenge of helping Michael to read. She supplied the pair with a variety of high-interest books about sports and athletes, rap stars, Hollywood actors. Devereaux often found reading tasks for Michael, such as reading the daily bulletin, food labels, baseball cards, cookbook directions, the telephone directory, maps; she tried to help him see the purpose of literacy. Michael also learned to take advantage of Devereaux's passion for reading. He was quick to ask her if he could read instead of doing some other task and she usually permitted him to do so. After all, here was a kid that everyone said would never read.

In third grade I was selected to go to the Reading Teacher. As I described earlier, the Reading Teacher was the person who worked with the accelerated group. As members of the special reading group we became a part of a special reading incentive program. We were rewarded for the number of books we read. To prove that we had actually read the books we said we had, we had to sign up for a "book talk" with a teacher who had read the book. We scheduled these book talks during early mornings before school, at recess or lunchtime, or after school. It was exciting to sit down with an adult and talk about what we had read. We received certificates for reading twenty-five, fifty, or seventy-five books. If we read a hundred books we received a certificate and a pin. I did not rest until I got my certificate and pin. I reached that lofty plateau by the middle of fourth grade.

Lewis Versus Devereaux

On the surface Ann Lewis and Julia Devereaux employ very different strategies to teach reading. In some ways their differences represent the larger debate about literacy teaching, that of whole-language versus basal-text techniques. However, beneath the surface, at the personal ideological level, the differences between these instructional strategies lose meaning. Both teachers want their students to become literate. Both believe that their students are capable of high levels of literacy.

More specifically, several overarching tenets may be called from both teachers' literacy programs. In sum, these tenets include the following:[5]

1. **Students whose educational, economic, social, political, and cultural futures are most tenuous are helped to become intellectual leaders in the classroom.** Both teachers direct a lot of their pedagogy toward African American boys. In Lewis's and Devereaux's classrooms it is "cool" or "def" to choose academic excellence. The teachers make the students' culture a point of affirmation and celebration. This means that they have to work actively against the constant and repeated denigration of Africa, Africans, and African Americans. By disrupting the notion of African American males as social outcasts, the teachers pro-

vide academic support for these boys and at the same time give the other students a new view of their fellow students.

2. **Students are apprenticed in a learning community rather than taught in an isolated and unrelated way.** The mention of this tenet here is a restatment of the idea. Both teachers treat their students as if they already know something. Rather than teach skills in an isolated, disconnected way, the two embed reading instruction within larger contexts. Even in Devereaux's more structured approach, the teaching of skills is contextualized.

3. **Students' real-life experiences are legitimized as they become part of the "official" curriculum.** Even though both of these teachers select literature for their students they depend heavily on the experiences of their students to make the literature come alive. They are not writing on blank slates; instead, they are challenging conventional scripts by importing the culture and everyday experiences of the students into the literacy learning.

4. **Teachers and students participate in a broad conception of literacy that incorporates both literature and oratory.** What counts as literarily worthy is broadly defined in both classrooms. The students are allowed to ask their own questions and search for their own answers. By building on the students' knowledge, Lewis and Devereaux are able to teach complex ideas and skills without worrying that they are teaching above the students' reading level. Using multiple teaching strategies ensures that every child develops his or her reading ability without being ridiculed or embarrassed.

5. **Teachers and students engage in a collective struggle against the status quo.** Both teachers help their students understand that societal expectations for them are generally low. However, they support them by demonstrating that their own expectations are exceptionally high. Thus they indicate that to prove the prevailing beliefs wrong, teacher and students must join together.

6. **Teachers are cognizant of themselves as political beings.** In the case of both Lewis and Devereaux, the political nature of their work is manifested in their teacher association activities. Both have developed a sociopolitical and cultural vision that they know they need to move away from cultural-deficit explanations for African American students'

low achievement levels and toward models of cultural excellence. They talk often with their students about the political nature of their work. The students are reminded that their progress toward cultural excellence is the mightiest weapon they possess to fight against a mediocre status quo.

MATH IN A CULTURALLY RELEVANT CLASSROOM

Margaret Rossi is an Italian American woman in her midforties. She began her teaching career in the late 1960s, when she was a Dominican nun. She has taught in both private and public schools and in both wealthy white communities and low-income communities of color. When this study was being done, she was teaching sixth grade. She was identified by a group of African American parents as a very effective teacher. In an ethnographic interview Rossi revealed that she knew that her students characterized her as "strict," but that she believed they respected her for being a demanding yet caring teacher.[6]

One morning, before an observation session, I met Rossi in the courtyard outside of her classroom. Although we exchanged pleasantries it was apparent that her mind was on the lesson she intended to teach. Earlier, she had talked to her students about the African origins of algebra; they had learned that the first definitive evidence of the use of algebra had appeared in the writings of Ahmes, an Egyptian mathematician who lived around 1700 B.C. or earlier. They learned that, much later, the Greeks had contributed to the early development of algebra. Rossi felt that the "setting of the context" was important for motivating her students to learn algebra. She attempted to make them see that it had clear relations to their own heritage. There was no reason for them to think of it as "foreign." As she said to me, tongue-in-cheek, "It's not Greek to them!"

Rossi gave her room key to one of her students and asked her to go in and take care of some housekeeping chores. When the bell rang the students filed noisily in. They settled down after they entered the room and took their seats. At 8:35 Rossi greeted them with a cheery "good morning" and the students responded in kind. What followed the good morning greeting was a whirlwind of activity, perhaps too complex to explain fully here. However, I will attempt to summarize what transpired.

The entire time I observed her class that morning, Rossi and her students studied mathematics. Although they were engaged in problem solving through algebraic functions, no worksheets were handed out, no problem sets were assigned. The students, and Rossi, posed the problems.

Observing from a pedagogical standpoint, I saw Rossi make a point of getting every student involved in the lesson. She continually assured them that they were capable of mastering the problems. They cheered each other on and celebrated when they were able to explain how they arrived at their solutions. Rossi's time and energy were completely devoted to mathematics. Taking attendance, collecting lunch money, and all other tasks were handled by students in an unobtrusive, almost matter-of-fact manner that did not interfere with the mathematics discussion.

Rossi moved around the classroom as students posed questions and suggested solutions. She often asked, "How do you know?" to push the students' thinking. When students asked questions, Margaret was quick to say, "Who knows? Who can help him out here?" By recycling the questions (and consequently, the knowledge) Margaret helped her students understand that they were knowledgeable and capable of answering their own questions and those of others. However, Rossi did not shrink from her own responsibility as teacher. From time to time she worked individually with students who seemed puzzled or confused. By asking a series of probing questions, she was able to help students organize their thinking about a problem and develop their own problem-solving strategies. The busy hum of activity in her classroom was directed toward mathematics. Every so often, she would suggest a problem and the students would work frantically to solve it. Each time she did this, a new set of questions and possible solutions came up. I was amazed at how comfortable the students seemed as the discussion proceeded. No one student or group of students dominated the session. Responses and questions came from all over the classroom.

As I sat taking notes, I heard a student exclaim, "This is easy!" Others nodded their heads in agreement. Never missing an opportunity to make mathematics accessible to her students, Rossi used such expressions to make a comment that reminded them how intelligent and capable they were.

At one point that morning, Rossi directed the students' attention to a page in the pre-algebra textbook she had scrounged up for the class. Rather than assign pages in the text, she showed the students how the textbook representation of what they had been doing appeared different. "Don't let it scare you," she urged. "You know how to solve problems like these." Rossi was thus assuring them that the good work they were doing in her class would carry through to district and state assessments; she knew that her students would be required to perform on standardized tests and that their performance might prove to be a significant factor in their mathematics placement the following year when they went on to middle school.

On another level Rossi may also have been reassuring her students that what they were doing was "legitimate." Because so much of this work was not out of a textbook, students (and perhaps their parents) may have wondered if they were doing "real" algebra.

By 9:59 it was time to prepare for recess. For almost an hour and a half Rossi and her students had been occupied with mathematical problem solving. She never once needed to stop to discipline or reprimand a student. The few instances in which students seemed to be off-task were quickly remedied when Rossi or another student posed a problem that brought their attention back to the discussion. Rossi told the students how proud she was of the way they had worked. She also told them that they were doing work that some eighth graders couldn't. At 10 A.M., twenty-six happy sixth graders marched out to recess. Rossi smiled but she had a look of sadness in her eyes. She turned to me after the last student had left the room:

> They're so smart but so few teachers recognize it. I'm so afraid they will meet the same fate as last year's class. We work so hard to get them into algebra and then they go to the middle school where they're treated like they don't know anything. Last year's students were so bored with the math they had—it was actually arithmetic—that they started cutting math class to come back over here for me to teach them. When I explained that I couldn't teach them they just stopped going to math class altogether and failed for nonattendance.

TELLING ISN'T TEACHING

I have described the classrooms of Ann Lewis, Julia Devereaux, and Margaret Rossi as examples of best practices. In this section, I describe a lesson carried out by Alex Walsh, one of my own student teachers.

Walsh was a twenty-two-year-old white student enrolled in a prestigious teacher preparation program. His student teaching assignment was in an upper-middle-class, predominately white community known for its excellent public school system. Alex was looking forward to the experience. He had been assigned to a sixth-grade class. His cooperating teacher was active on many district committees and had requested a student teacher who was comfortable taking the initiative and working independently. The class would probably have been characterized as an open classroom. Students worked at their own pace and in cooperative groups. One student who had cerebral palsy was mainstreamed into the class; a full-time teacher's aide worked with her. There were no African American students in the class but it was a culturally diverse class. The students represented several language groups—Spanish, Japanese, Chinese, Arabic—but all were fluent in English. Many of the students came from professional homes—the homes of doctors, attorneys, accountants, college professors.

It was my unofficial policy not to visit my student teachers on the same day that I visited the teachers participating in my study. It would be too easy to make unfair comparisons between the experts and the novices. However, on one particular day visiting both could not be avoided. After observing Margaret Rossi, I headed across the freeway to visit Alex Walsh.

Although the physical distance between the two schools was less than five miles, in resources—personnel, material, and students—they were worlds apart. Walsh's school was in a district that performed at the ninety-fifth percentile on standardized tests while the teachers in my study were working in a district that performed below the tenth percentile.

When I arrived in Walsh's classroom, the students were working on mathematics. The cooperating teacher was working with a group of twelve or thirteen students. Six or seven other students were working independently at their desks, and Walsh was working at a table in the back of the room with four boys—two white, two Latino. As I settled into a chair near Walsh's group I could hear him trying to explain how to change an improper fraction into a mixed number.

None of the students seemed to be paying attention to him. Two of the boys were poking each other with pencils; another was listening to his Walkman (although he denied it when questioned about why he had his hat pulled down over his ears). The fourth boy was staring out the window. After Walsh finished his explanation, he called on one of the pencil-pokers to solve a problem. The boy seemed to have no idea what to do. When asked if anyone could help, none of the others responded. Walsh gave his explanation another try.

This time he stopped many times to reprimand the boys for playing, giggling, and not paying attention. At the end of his explanation, he gave the boys three problems to solve. None of them was able to solve the problems. "This stuff is stupid!" remarked one boy. "I'm not doin' this," said another as he pushed his paper and pencil toward the center of the table. The other boys laughed. Walsh said "Okay, let's try doing the first one together." He began explaining the steps needed to change the improper fraction. The boys were not following. Walsh's patience wore thin. "Look!" he shouted. "I'm trying to teach you guys how to do this and you're not even paying attention."

Unsuccessfully, the boys tried to stifle a giggle. That was the last straw. Walsh sternly ordered them back to their seats and assigned them a page from their texts. The boys grumbled that they did not know how to do the problems, but Walsh ignored their complaints and told them he expected to see the problems before the math session was over. He glanced up at me. His face was red, perhaps from anger, perhaps from embarrassment—or both.

During our postobservation conference, I began by asking, "Tell me what you taught today." Walsh started telling me what he had intended and referred me to his lesson plan. "Yes," I commented, "You seem to have had a plan that fit your intent, but what did you teach?" Once again, he began to explain his intentions. He told me about how he had thought out the plan and how the boys had subverted it. "I could see that, Alex," I remarked. "But what did you *teach*?" He looked at me dejectedly and sighed. "I guess I didn't teach anything," he said. I nodded in agreement. "Right, now we can talk about what went wrong."

Clearly, it is not fair to compare Alex Walsh's abilities with Margaret Rossi's. Rossi's seventeen years of experience *should* make her more skilled at teaching than Walsh. She has had the opportunity to make mistakes and grow as a teacher. And I am sure she has also had times when she "didn't teach anything." However, juxtaposing the two sessions illustrates just how different experts are from novices. If Walsh could have observed any of the teachers in my study, perhaps he might have learned some of the following:[7]

1. **When students are treated as competent they are likely to demonstrate competence.** Culturally relevant teaching methods do not suggest to students that they are incapable of learning. These teachers provide intellectual challenges by teaching to the highest standards and not to the lowest common denominator.

   In Lewis's class, the students were expected to do more than read for literal meaning. Their responses to what they read were even more important than parroting back what the author had written. As they read books, Lewis asked what they thought the text meant and what connections they could make between the text and their own lives. Although Devereaux's reading class was more structured, the intellectual challenge was still there. Devereaux expected all students to become literate and she provided a variety of vehicles through which the students could develop their literacy. Rossi's decision to use challenging mathematics to motivate and teach her students proved to be an excellent way to improve both their mathematical skills and their conceptual skills. Doing algebra allowed them to build upon their competence and develop the confidence to meet even higher intellectual challenges.

2. **When teachers provide instructional "scaffolding," students can move from what they know to what they need to know.** In the classes of all three teachers, students are allowed (and encouraged) to build upon their own experiences, knowledge, and skills to move into more difficult knowledge and skills. Rather than chastise them for what they do not know, these teachers find ways to use the knowledge and skills the students bring to the classroom as a foundation for learning.

3. **The focus of the classroom must be instructional.** Although a classroom is a complex and dynamic place, the primary enterprise must be to teach. In culturally relevant classrooms, instruction is foremost. Even when Lewis was reprimanding the students, she was instructing (explaining different parts of the brain). Devereaux's insistence on a sacrosanct reading period is her way of letting the students know that the time cannot be violated, not even by her personal relationship with them. Rossi's fast-paced, challenging mathematics leaves no room for off-task, noninstructional behavior. The message that the classroom is a place where teachers and students engage in serious work is communicated clearly to everyone.

   Walsh's students did not take him seriously. Perhaps his inability to be effective with them came in part from his status as a student teacher; however, I have seen student teachers who are capable of managing a class. Walsh's group of students set their sights on disrupting his lesson; they were learning not to learn. Walsh's decisions to send them back to their seats with assignments they could not do (such as changing improper fractions to mixed numbers) taught them that instruction was not that important *and* that it could be used as a form of punishment.

4. **Real education is about extending students' thinking and abilities.** At no point in my student teacher's lesson did he assess what his students already knew. By building on some success—starting with something they had already mastered—he may have been more successful in engaging the students in the skills he intended to teach. As it was, his students decided that what he was talking about had nothing to do with them and he was unable to make the necessary connections. In contrast, Lewis, Devereaux, and Rossi move their students to newer learning after establishing what they know and are able to do. Rather than a "drill-and-kill" approach to knowledge acquisition, their approach makes student learning a more contextualized, meaningful experience.

5. **Effective teaching involves in-depth knowledge of both the students and the subject matter.** The limited nature of the student teaching experience made Walsh's ability to build the necessary relationships between himself and his students difficult. If they knew more about one another, the children would have developed a greater commitment to learning because of their commitment to their teacher.

Lewis, Devereaux, and Rossi know their students well. They know which ones respond to subtle prodding and which ones need a more forceful approach. For them, good teaching starts with building good relationships. Rossi knew that one of her students was considered a candidate for special education. However, she believed that it was important to include him as a part of the class and hold him responsible for meeting high standards. To ensure that these expectations did not frustrate him, she spent more time with him, guaranteeing incremental success. Devereaux knew that Michael had a troubled home life. She knew that his poor reading ability was tied to the problems he confronted at home. So she worked to fill his school day with literacy experiences. By calling on him to read—directions, daily messages, and recreational materials—she cemented her relationship with him while he built his knowledge base and skills.

This chapter provided three examples of culturally relevant teaching in the basic skill areas of reading and math. Although each teacher has her own distinctive style, all share some essential qualities that were absent from the student teacher's practices. Despite his seemingly more desirable school environment, which resembled his own background, his effectiveness was compromised by the combination of his inexperience and his more assimilationist teaching orientation. Like many novices, the student teacher struggled with organizing students for instruction, but he also struggled with what he considered teaching to be. In his mind, teaching was the same as telling, and he did not question the hierarchical relationship he was attempting to establish between himself and the students. He assumed that the relationship between the students and himself was a one-way relationship: He would instruct; they would learn. He failed to treat them as if they knew anything and showed little enthusiasm for the material. He could not situate the lesson in the students' experience. For all of his efforts, his attempts to teach the students were futile. He gave up in frustration, believing the students had relinquished their privilege of being taught.

NOTES

1. Arnove, R., and Graff, H. "National Literacy Campaigns: Historical and Comparative Lessons." *Phi Delta Kappan*, 1987, 69(3), 202–206.

2. Ferdman, B. "Literacy and Cultural Identity." *Harvard Educational Review*, 1990, 60(2), 181–204.

3. deCastell, S., and Luke, A. "Defining Literacy in North American Schools: Social and Historical Conditions and Consequences." *Journal of Curriculum Studies*, 1983, 15, 373–389.

4. Gadsden, V. (ed.). "Literacy and the African American Learner." *Theory into Practice*, 1991, 31(4), 275.

5. For further elaboration of these tenets, see Ladson-Billings, G. "Liberatory Consequences of Literacy," *The Journal of Negro Education*, 1992, 61, 378–391.

6. Spradley, J. *The Ethnographic Interview*. Troy, Mo.: Holt, Rinehart & Winston, 1979.

7. The summary statements on pp. 186–190 are taken from Ladson-Billings, G. "Making Math Meaningful in Cultural Contexts." In W. Secada, E. Fenemma, and L. Byrd (eds.), *New Dimensions in Equity*. New York: Cambridge University Press, 1994.

———————

MAUREEN: After reading this chapter by Gloria Ladson-Billings from her acclaimed book The Dreamkeepers, *I am more than ever convinced that there is no one formula for successful classroom teaching. It seems that publishers offer new foolproof systems for the teaching of reading or math almost every year, which often means teachers are constantly forced to adopt and to learn new curriculum programs. I always think they should be called "teacher-proof," for that is how they are designed. The teachers follow the guide, use the book and provided activities, and are promised success in their endeavors. Teachers are not robots, however. It is difficult to program them and seldom are any two alike. That's no surprise. Neither are children.*

Ladson-Billings beautifully demonstrates this in her descriptions of the two teachers who differ markedly in their philosophies and methodologies. It is not the materials, but teachers' relationships with their students that count. Both had high expectations, celebrated their cultures, and created caring communities for their classes. "Real education is about extending students' thinking and abilities," she says (p. 229). It is not about drilling information to achieve a high test score. The teachers Ladson-Billings observed knew their students, subject matter, and effective pedagogy. This knowledge included what we describe as pedagogical content knowledge and culturally relevant teaching. Both are essential for excellence in education. She reminds us that successful teachers do not punish their students for what they cannot or do not know. They investigate new ways to approach subject matter based on the knowledge and background of each of their students and awaken in them an appetite for learning.

This is an important point for us all. Children have an innate desire to learn. Both parents and teachers, and ultimately all adults, have the responsibility for providing safe, stimulating environments and caring, supportive systems to enable the world's children to grow and to achieve success.

· 15 ·

Sonia Nieto

PROFOUNDLY MULTICULTURAL QUESTIONS*

ALEXANDRA: Sonia Nieto's book on multicultural education, The Light in Their Eyes *(1999), is always inspirational to my graduate students. When Nieto was a keynote speaker at a conference at the City College of New York in the fall of 2006, her moving oratory in defense of urban teachers earned a well-deserved standing ovation. A professor emerita of Language, Literacy, and Culture at the University of Massachusetts, Amherst, she is the author of* Affirming Diversity: The Sociopolitical Context of Multicultural Education *(1992) and more recently* What Keeps Teachers Going? *(2003) and* Why We Teach *(2005). In this brief article she raises difficult questions with no easy answers, asking us to critically examine the political nature of education, while making the argument that American schools are more segregated and inequitably funded than ever.*

I cannot help but wonder what would happen if those who read Nieto's alarming statistics and troubling evidence of widespread inequity were to pose these questions at PTA and school board meetings. Imagine impassioned communities of parents and educators coming together to talk frankly about issues including tracking, resources, segregation, teacher quality, or school financing. Imagine parents and educators finding answers for what can be done to bring about change for the betterment of all students. Without such grassroots efforts, it's likely that most people will continue to believe that some multicultural curriculum or professional development experience in culturally relevant pedagogy will suffice for now. Nieto's powerful questions should haunt us and move us to action.

*From *Educational Leadership* 60, no. 4 (2003): 6–10.

I still recall the question that my friend Maddie, also an educator, asked me a number of years ago when I was describing an initiative to bring a multicultural program to a particular urban school district. A supporter of multicultural education, she was nonetheless becoming frustrated by the ways in which many districts were implementing it. She was especially concerned that many students from that particular district were doing poorly in school, and she asked impatiently, "But can they do math?"

Her question stayed with me for a long time—and prompted me to think about what it means to provide an education that is both multicultural and equitable. (Nieto, 1999). Sadly, issues of equity and access are not always linked with multicultural education. Sometimes, multicultural education is seen as little more than a way to promote self-esteem, or simply as a curriculum that substitutes one set of heroes for another. When that happens, we may end up with young people who feel good about themselves and their heritage but who have few skills that prepare them for life; or alternatively, who know how to do math and science and read, but who know little about their cultural backgrounds and are even ashamed and embarrassed by them.

Let me make clear that I strongly believe in multicultural education. That first exhilarating course that I took on the subject nearly 30 years ago put into words many of the ideas I had wanted to express since becoming a teacher. More recently, the term *culturally responsive pedagogy* has come into use and been advocated persuasively (Gay 2000; Ladson-Billings, 1994). An outgrowth of multicultural education, culturally responsive pedagogy is founded on the notion that—rather than deficits—students' backgrounds are assets that students can and should use in the service of their learning and that teachers of all backgrounds should develop the skills to teach diverse students effectively.

Despite my great support for these philosophies, however, I am also concerned that they can be used in simplistic ways that fail to address the tremendous inequities that exist in our schools. For example, to adopt a multicultural basal reader is far easier than to guarantee that all children will learn to read; to plan an assembly program of ethnic music is easier than to provide music instruction for all students; and to train teachers in a few behaviors in cultural awareness or curriculum inclusion is easier than to address widespread student disengagement in learning. Although these may be valuable activities, they fail to confront directly the deep-seated inequalities that exist in schools. Because they are sometimes taken out of context—isolated as prepackaged programs or "best practices"—multicultural education and culturally responsive pedagogy can become Band-Aid approaches to serious problems that require nothing short of major surgery.

I define multicultural education as an anti-racist education that is firmly related to student learning and permeates all areas of schooling (Nieto, 1994). It is a hopeful way to confront the widespread and entrenched inequality in U.S. schools because its premise is that students of all backgrounds and circumstances can learn and achieve to high levels, and—even more essential—that they deserve to do so. Multicultural education needs to be accompanied by a deep commitment to social justice and equal access to resources. Multicultural education needs, in short, to be about much more than ethnic tidbits and cultural sensitivity.

For instance, although educators may call attention to the fact that the curriculum in U.S. schools is becoming more multicultural (an overblown claim in any event), they may neglect to note that the achievement gap between white students and students of color is growing. Although the gap was reduced by about half between 1970 and 1988, it has been widening since then. The reversal is evident in grades, test scores, dropout rates, and other indicators, and it has taken place in every type of school district and in all socioeconomic groups (D'Amico, 2001). Just one example: The average 12th grade low-income student of color reads at the same level as the average 8th grade middle-class white student (Kahlenberg, 2000). In terms of high school completion, 88 percent of white students have graduated from high school, but the rate for Hispanics is just 56 percent (U.S. Census Bureau, 2000a). Given these alarming statistics, the claim that education is equally available to all is more of a fiction than ever. Multicultural education and culturally responsive pedagogy by themselves cannot solve these problems.

It makes sense, then, to look carefully at two factors besides cultural differences that influence student learning: the sociopolitical context of education, and school policies and practices. The former includes societal ideologies, governmental policies and mandates, and school financing. School policies and practices—specifically, curriculum, pedagogy, tracking, testing, discipline, and hiring—can also either promote or hinder learning among students of different backgrounds.

Besides focusing on matters of culture and identity, educators also need to ask profoundly multicultural questions—that is, troubling questions that often go unanswered or even unasked. The answers tell us a great deal about what we value because the questions are about equity, access, and social justice in education. Here are a few of the questions that we must address if we are serious about giving all students of all backgrounds an equal chance to learn.

WHO'S TAKING CALCULUS?

I use "calculus" as a place marker for any number of other high-status and academically challenging courses that may open doors for students to attend college and receive advanced training. For instance, we find that although slightly more than 12 percent of white students are enrolled in calculus, only 6.6 percent of African Americans and 6.2 percent of Latinos and Native Americans are enrolled. In the case of physics, the numbers are 30.7 percent for whites, 21.4 percent for African Americans, 18.9 percent for Hispanics, and 16.2 percent for Native Americans (National Center for Education Statistics [NCES], 2002). This situation has serious implications for reforming such policies as rigid tracking, scheduling, and counseling services. Access to high-level and demanding academic courses has a long-term and dramatic effect in terms of college attendance and subsequent quality of life. For instance, the 2000 U.S. Census reported that annual average earnings for those with a bachelor's degree were nearly double the amount for those with just a high school diploma: $45,678 compared with $24,572 (U.S. Census Bureau, 2000b).

WHICH CLASSES MEET IN THE BASEMENT?

Language-minority students and students with special needs are too often hidden away in the basement—or in the hall closet, or the room with the leaky ceiling on the fourth floor, or the modular unit separated from the rest of the school. Administrators offer seemingly logical reasons for placing these students in these areas: There's no other available space in the building; these students were the last to arrive and therefore need to be placed where there's room; now they're closer to the English as a Second Language teacher. But placing programs for marginalized students in less desirable places is a powerful metaphor for the low status and little attention that they receive. It also serves in many cases to segregate these students from the so-called "regular" (English-speaking) or so-called "normal" (non-special needs) students, in this way creating an even greater gulf between them and the rest of the school.

The continuing segregation of students on the basis of race and ethnicity is a trend that has been escalating for the past 20 years. According to Gary Orfield (2001), most of the progress made toward desegregating schools in the two decades prior to 1988 has been lost in the past 15 years. For African Americans, the 1990s witnessed the largest backward movement toward segregation since the *Brown v. Board of Education* decision. Latinos are now the most segregated of all ethnic groups—not just in race and ethnicity, but also poverty. U.S. schools are becoming more separate and unequal than ever.

WHO'S TEACHING THE CHILDREN?

The question of who is teaching the children is inextricably linked to matters of social justice in education. Teachers working in poor urban schools tend to have less experience and less preparation than do those in schools that serve primarily white and middle-class students (Editorial Projects in Education, 1998). In addition, poor urban districts are more likely to hire teachers out of field than are suburban and middle-class school districts (David & Shields, 2001). These situations would be deemed unacceptable in more affluent districts.

Related to teachers' experience and training is the issue of teachers' race and ethnicity. Although all educators—teachers, administrators, curriculum coordinators, and others—need to develop the attitudes and skills to be effective with our increasingly diverse student population, we need a concerted effort to recruit a more diverse faculty. At present, the number of students of color in U.S. classrooms is growing dramatically at the same time that the number of teachers of color is declining. In 1972, just 22 percent of students in public schools were considered "minority"; by 1998, it was 37 percent (NCES, 2000a). The teaching force, on the other hand, is about 87 percent white. These trends show little sign of changing (U.S. Census Bureau, 2001).

The growing gap is problematic because mounting evidence indicates that a higher number of teachers of color in a school—particularly African American and Hispanic—can promote the achievement of African American and Hispanic students (Clewell, Puma, & McKay, 2001; Dee, 2000). In fact, one study found that a higher number of teachers of color can have an even greater impact on the achievement of white students (Meier, Wrinkle, & Polinard, 1999). Another study found that having same race and gender role models was "significantly and consistently predictive of a greater investment in achievement concerns" on the part of young people (Zirkel, 2002, p. 371).

Associated with teacher quality is the question of teachers' influence on their students. The proof is growing that all teachers—regardless of race, ethnicity, or gender—who care about, mentor, and guide their students can have a dramatic impact on their futures, even when these students face tremendous barriers related to poverty, racism, and other social ills (Flores-González, 2002; Noddings, 1992; Valenzuela, 1999). Stanton-Salazar, for instance, suggests that mentoring and support from teachers can provide students with the social capital they need to succeed, thus creating networks that "function as pathways of privilege and power"—pathways not generally available to poor students of color (1997, p. 4).

HOW MUCH ARE CHILDREN WORTH?

What do we pay for education, and how does the answer differ according to students' race, ethnicity, social class, and above all, home address? The well-known facts are that school financing is vastly unequal and that students with wealthier parents are fortunate to live in towns that spend more on their education, whereas young people who live in financially strapped urban or rural areas are much less fortunate (Kozol, 1991). Regrettably, the children who need the most get the fewest funds and resources (NCES, 2000b).

We also need to ask what our most vulnerable students are worth in terms of attention and care. A recent court case is a good example of the low value placed on students who attend poor urban schools. In June 2002, an appeals court in New York State ruled that youngsters who drop out of the New York City schools by 8th grade nevertheless receive "a sound basic education" (cited in Gonzalez, 2002). The result of this astonishing ruling was to overturn a 2001 landmark decision that had found the state's formula for funding public schools unfair because it favored schools in suburban areas. The majority opinion in the appeals ruling, written by Judge Alfred Lerner, said in part,

> the skills required to enable a person to obtain employment, vote, and serve on a jury are imparted between grades 8 and 9. (cited in González, 2002)

Although Judge Lerner conceded that such a meager education might qualify young people for only the lowest-paying jobs, he added, "Society needs workers at all levels of jobs, the majority of which may very well be low-level" (cited in González, 2002). I am left wondering whether Judge Lerner would want this level of education for his own children or would think it fair and equitable.

These, then, are some of the profoundly multicultural questions that I suggest we ask ourselves. Certainly they are not the only questions that we can ask, but they give us an inkling of the vast inequities that continue to exist in U.S. public schools. My questions are not meant to diminish the noble efforts of educators who struggle daily to reach students through culturally responsive education or through an accurate representation in the curriculum of students' histories and cultures. But as we focus on these approaches—approaches that I wholeheartedly support—we also need to ask troubling questions about equity, access, and fair play. Until we do something about these broader issues, we will be only partially successful in educating all our young people for the challenges of the future.

REFERENCES

Clewell, B. C., Puma, M., & McKay, S. A. (2001). *Does it matter if my teacher looks like me? The impact of teacher race and ethnicity on student academic achievement*. New York: Ford Foundation.

D'Amico, J. J. (2001). A closer look at the minority achievement gap. *ERS Spectrum, 19*(2), 4–10.

David, J. L., & Shields, P. M. (2001). *When theory hits reality: Standards-based reform in urban districts, final narrative report*. Menlo Park, CA: SRI International.

Dee, T. S. (2000). *Teachers, race, and student achievement in a randomized experiment*. Cambridge, MA: National Bureau of Economic Research.

Editorial Projects in Education. (1998). *Education Week: Quality counts 1998*. Bethesda, MD: Author.

Flores-González, N. (2002). *School kids, street kids: Identity and high school completion among Latinos*. New York: Teachers College Press.

Gay, G. (2000). *Culturally responsive teaching: Theory, research, and practice*. New York: Teachers College Press.

González, J. (2002, June 27). Schools ruling defies logic. *New York Daily News*, p. 24.

Kahlenberg, R. D. (2000). *Economic school integration* (Idea Brief no. 2). Washington, DC: The Century Foundation.

Kozol, J. (1991). *Savage inequalities: Children in America's schools*. New York: Crown.

Ladson-Billings, G. (1994). *The dreamkeepers: Successful teachers of African American children*. San Francisco: Jossey-Bass.

Meier, K. J., Wrinkle, R. D., & Polinard, J. L. (1999). Representative bureaucracy and distributional equity: Addressing the hard question. *Journal of Politics, 61*, 1025–1039.

National Center for Education Statistics. (2000a). *Editorial projects in education, 1998*. Washington, DC: U.S. Department of Education, Office of Educational Research and Improvement.

National Center for Education Statistics. (2000b). *Trends in disparities in school district level expenditures per pupil*. Washington, DC: U.S. Department of Education, Office of Educational Research and Improvement.

National Center for Education Statistics. (2002). *Digest of education statistics, 2001*. Washington, DC: U.S. Department of Education, Office of Educational Research and Improvement.

Nieto, S. (1994). Affirmation, solidarity, and critique: Moving beyond tolerance in multicultural education. *Multicultural Education, 1*(4), 9–12, 35–38.

Nieto, S. (1999). *The light in their eyes: Creating multicultural learning communities.* New York: Teachers College Press.

Noddings, N. (1992). *The challenge to care in schools: An alternative approach to education.* New York: Teachers College Press.

Orfield, G. (2001). *Schools more separate: Consequences of a decade of resegregation.* Cambridge, MA: The Civil Rights Project, Harvard University.

Stanton-Salazar, R. D. (1997). A social capital framework for understanding the socialization of racial minority children and youth. *Harvard Educational Review,* 67(1), 1–40.

U.S. Census Bureau. (2000a). *Educational attainment in the United States: March 1999* (P20-528). Washington, DC: U.S. Department of Commerce.

U.S. Census Bureau. (2000b). *Educational attainment in the United States (Update): March 2000.* Washington, DC: U.S. Department of Commerce.

U.S. Census Bureau. (2001). *Statistical abstract of the United States: Education* [Online]. Available: www.censusgov/prod/2001pubs/statab/sec04.pdf.

Valenzuela, A. (1999). *Subtractive schooling: U.S.–Mexican youth and the politics of caring.* Albany, NY: SUNY Press.

Zirkel, S. (2002). "Is there a place for me?": Role models and academic identity among white students and students of color. *Teachers College Record, 104*(2), 357–376.

MAUREEN: The questions Sonia Nieto asks about multicultural education are pertinent and perplexing. Even though educators have made an effort to introduce multicultural education and what is now called culturally responsive pedagogy into our schools, Nieto reminds us that the way they are implemented is often simply as Band-Aids, temporary tourniquets applied to hemorrhaging problems of inequity. She cites amazing statistics to show the widening gap between students of color and white students because of the sociopolitical climate and attitudes that influence practices and policies in American education. She echoes the concerns of many of her scholarly colleagues when she states, "U.S. schools are becoming more separate and unequal than ever" (p. 237).

As the achievement gap widens and the population becomes ever more diverse, we must ensure that every child receives the attention needed to succeed. One thing I have noticed in working with student teachers is that they are of-

ten asked to work with students who present the most puzzling learning difficulties or are struggling with language, even though novices are less equipped to solve complex learning problems. These children require the most highly skilled and trained professionals to diagnose their needs. Nieto points out that similar shortcomings of teacher expertise are found in urban schools. Yet good teachers who care about their students can help even the most needy students overcome hurdles and difficulties. The future of the democratic ideal rests in the promise of equal access to the riches of the curriculum.

John Dewey has written that what every parent wishes for his or her own child should be wished for all children, because "education is the fundamental method of social progress and reform" (Dewey, 1897, p. 80). Parents must look beyond advocacy solely for their own children and begin to think in broader terms about all the children in our nation's schools.

Lisa Delpit

EBONICS AND CULTURALLY
RESPONSIVE INSTRUCTION*

MAUREEN: Lisa Delpit's fascinating look at the significance of dialects and the controversies surrounding their use in classrooms has application to even wider problems we as Americans face in an emerging global approach to schooling. Most urban schools report increasing numbers of languages among the student body. There are over one hundred in New York City, but increasingly large numbers are found in suburban districts as well.

Delpit wisely points out that children's literature provides an opportunity to explore the tales and folklore of diverse cultures as well as the opportunity for children to experience the dialect of many languages. Certainly this is an entry point for children to become acquainted with cultures other than their own and, perhaps, to introduce the broader issue of racism.

One cannot read the daily paper or listen to the nightly news without worrying about the growth of intolerance in the world. The focus on unanimity in all things moral and sacred flies in the face of the democratic principles that helped make America strong and invincible. One cannot but wonder what hatred lies beneath the recent growth in bigotry and violence heaped especially upon recent immigrants in not only this country but also the rest of the world.

What can we as teachers and parents do?

We need to learn as much as we can about other cultures as they touch our lives and the lives of our children. We need to know what value systems are operating, what rules govern behavior, what degrees of acceptance of differing lifestyles are in operation. After I was married, I lived in Iran for ten months. My husband, an Italian engineer who learned languages easily and rapidly,

*From *Rethinking School Reform: Views from the Classroom*, ed. L. Christensen and S. Karp (Milwaukee, WI: Rethinking Schools, 2003), 79–88.

had worked there for five years prior to our marriage. Because he read, wrote, and spoke fluent Farsi, his knowledge of the country and its peoples was remarkable. I learned a great deal from him about the value of studying a country's history and customs.

Now, in the community where I live, there are many immigrants from Iran who have made their home here. Often, there is a good deal of negative discussion about their habit of "bargaining" while shopping in all commercial establishments in the community. My explanation that these recent immigrants are only practicing what is commonplace in their old communities is met first with astonishment and then with understanding of the custom. Most Americans do not know that it is not only acceptable but also imperative to bargain in Iran.

The exploration and discovery of the world's diversity ought to be a priority in our curricula; we must teach children that it is this diversity that has always enhanced and enriched our country and our culture.

The "Ebonics Debate" has created much more heat than light for most of the country. For teachers trying to determine what implications there might be for classroom practice, enlightenment has been a completely nonexistent commodity.

I have been asked often enough, "What do you think about Ebonics? Are you for it or against it?" My answer must be neither. I can be neither for Ebonics nor against Ebonics any more than I can be for or against air. It exists. It is the language spoken by many of our African-American children. It is the language they heard as their mothers nursed them and changed their diapers and played peek-a-boo with them. It is the language through which they first encountered love, nurturance and joy.

On the other hand, most teachers of those African-American children who have been least well-served by educational systems believe that their students' life chances will be further hampered if they do not learn Standard English. In the stratified society in which we live, they are absolutely correct. While having access to the politically mandated language form will not, by any means, guarantee economic success (witness the growing number of unemployed African Americans holding doctorates), not having access will almost certainly guarantee failure.

So what must teachers do? Should they spend their time relentlessly "correcting" their Ebonics-speaking children's language so that it might conform to what we have learned to refer to as Standard English? Despite good intentions, constant correction seldom has the desired effect. Such correction increases cognitive monitoring of speech, thereby making talking difficult.

To illustrate, I have frequently taught a relatively simple new "dialect" to classes of preservice teachers. In this dialect, the phonetic element "iz" is added after the first consonant or consonant cluster in each syllable of a word. (Maybe becomes *miz-ay-biz-ee* and apple, *iz-ap-piz-le*.) After a bit of drill and practice, the students are asked to tell a partner in "iz" language why they decided to become teachers. Most only haltingly attempt a few words before lapsing into either silence or into Standard English. During a follow-up discussion, all students invariably speak of the impossibility of attempting to apply rules while trying to formulate and express a thought. Forcing speakers to monitor their language typically produces silence.

Correction may also affect students' attitudes toward their teachers. In a recent research project, middle-school, inner-city students were interviewed about their attitudes toward their teachers and school. One young woman complained bitterly: "Mrs. ____ always be interrupting to make you 'talk correct' and stuff. She be butting into your conversations when you not even talking to her! She need to mind her own business." Clearly this student will be unlikely to follow the teacher's directives or to want to imitate her speech style.

GROUP IDENTITY

Issues of group identity may also affect students' oral production of a different dialect. Researcher Sharon Nelson-Barber, in a study of phonologic aspects of Pima Indian language, found that in her first through third grades, the children's English most approximated the standard dialect of their teachers. But surprisingly, by fourth grade, when one might assume growing competence in standard forms, their language moved significantly toward the local dialect. These fourth graders had the *competence* to express themselves in a more standard form, but chose, consciously or unconsciously, to use the language of those in their local environments.

Nelson-Barer believes that by age eight or nine, these children became aware of their group membership and its importance to their well-being, and this realization was reflected in their language.[1] They may also have become increasingly aware of the schools' negative attitude toward their community and found it necessary—through choice of linguistic form—to decide with which camp to identify.

What should teachers do about helping students acquire an additional oral form? First, they should recognize that the linguistic form a student brings to school is intimately connected with loved ones, community, and personal identity. To suggest that this form is "wrong," or even worse, ignorant, is to suggest that something is wrong with the student and his or her family. To denigrate your language is, then, in African-American terms, to "talk about your mama." Anyone who knows anything about African-American culture knows the consequences of that speech act!

On the other hand, it is equally important to understand that students who do not have access to the politically popular dialect form in this country are less likely to succeed economically than their peers who do. How can both realities be embraced in classroom instruction?

It is possible and desirable to make the actual study of language diversity a part of the curriculum for all students. For younger children, discussions about the differences in the ways television characters from different cultural groups speak can provide a starting point. A collection of the many children's books written in the dialects of various cultural groups also can provide a wonderful basis for learning about linguistic diversity,[2] as can audiotaped stories narrated by individuals from different cultures, including taping books read by members of the children's home communities. Mrs. Pat, a teacher chronicled by Stanford University researcher Shirley Brice Heath, had her students become language "detectives," interviewing a variety of individuals and listening to the radio and television to discover the differences and similarities in the ways people talked.[3] Children can learn that there are many ways of saying the same thing, and that certain contexts suggest particular kinds of linguistic performances.

Some teachers have groups of students create bilingual dictionaries of their own language form and Standard English. Both the students and the teacher become engaged in identifying terms and deciding upon the best translations. These can be done as generational dictionaries too, given the proliferation of "youth culture" terms growing out of the Ebonics-influenced tendency for the continual regeneration of vocabulary. Contrastive grammatical structures can be studied similarly, but, of course, as Oakland, California's policy suggests, teachers must be aware of the grammatical structure of Ebonics before they can launch into this complex study.

Other teachers have had students become involved with standard forms through various kinds of role-play. For example, memorizing parts for drama productions will allow students to practice and "get the feel" of speaking Standard English while not under the threat of correction. A master teacher of African-American children in Oakland, Carrie Secret, has used this technique and extended it so that students videotaped their practice performances and self-critiqued them as to the appropriate use of Standard English. (But I must add that Carrie's use of drama and oration goes much beyond acquiring Standard English. She inspires pride and community connections which are truly wondrous to behold.) The use of self-critique of recorded forms may prove even more useful than I initially realized. California State University–Hayward professor Etta Hollins has reported that just by leaving a tape recorder on during an informal class period and playing it back with no comment, students began to code-switch—moving between Standard English and Ebonics—more effectively. It appears that they may have not realized which language form they were using until they heard themselves speak on tape.

Young students can create puppet shows or role-play cartoon characters—many "superheroes" speak almost hypercorrect Standard English! Playing a role eliminates the possibility of implying that the *child's* language is inadequate and suggests, instead, that different language forms are appropriate in different contexts. Some teachers in New York City have had their students produce a news show every day for the rest of the school. The students take on the personae of famous newscasters, keeping in character as they develop and read their news reports. Discussions ensue about whether Tom Brokaw would have said it that way, again taking the focus off the child's speech.

DISCOURSE STYLE AND LANGUAGE USE

Although most educators think of Black Language as primarily differing in grammar and syntax, there are other differences in oral language of which teachers should be aware in a multicultural context, particularly in discourse style and language use. Harvard University researcher Sarah Michaels and other researchers identified differences in children's narratives at "sharing time."[4] They found that there was a tendency among young white children to tell "topic-centered" narratives—stories focused on one event—and a tendency among black youngsters, especially girls, to tell "episodic" narratives—stories that include shifting scenes and are typically longer.

While these differences are interesting in themselves, what is of greater significance is adults' responses to the differences. C. B. Cazden reported on a subsequent project in which a white adult was taped reading the oral narratives of both black and white first graders, with all syntax dialectal markers removed.[5] Adults were asked to listen to the stories and comment about the children's likelihood of success in school.

The researchers were surprised by the differential responses given by black and white adults. In responding to the retelling of a black child's story, the white adults were uniformly negative, making such comments as "terrible story, incoherent" and "[n]ot a story at all in the sense of describing something that happened." Asked to judge this child's academic competence, all of the white adults rated her below the children who told "topic-centered" stories. Most of these adults also predicted difficulties for this child's future school career, such as "This child might have trouble reading," that she exhibited "language problems that affect school achievement," and they theorized that "family problems" or "emotional problems" might hamper her academic progress.

The black adults had very different reactions. They found this child's story "well formed, easy to understand, and interesting, with lots of detail and description." Even though all five of these adults mentioned the "shifts" and "associations" or "nonlinear" quality of the story, they did not find these features distracting. Three of the black adults selected the story as the best of the five they had heard, and all but one judged the child as exceptionally bright, highly verbal, and successful in school.[6]

This is not a story about racism, but one about cultural familiarity. However, when differences in narrative style produce differences in interpretation of competence, the pedagogical implications are evident. If children who produce stories based in differing discourse styles are expected to have trouble reading, and are viewed as having language, family, or emotional problems, as in the case quoted by Cazden, they are unlikely to be viewed as ready for the same challenging instruction awarded students whose language patterns more closely parallel the teacher's.

LEARNING TO READ

Most teachers are particularly concerned about how speaking Ebonics might affect learning to read. There is little evidence that speaking another mutually intelligible language form, per se, negatively affects one's ability to learn to read.[7] For commonsensical proof, one need only reflect on non-Standard-English-speaking Africans who, though enslaved, not only taught themselves to read English, but did so under threat of severe punishment or death.

But children who speak Ebonics do have a more difficult time becoming proficient readers. Why? In part, appropriate instructional methodologies are frequently not adopted. There is ample evidence that children who do not come to school with knowledge about letters, sounds, and symbols need to experience some explicit instruction in these areas in order to become independent readers. Another explanation is that, where teachers' assessments of competence are influenced by the language children speak, teachers may develop low expectations for certain students and subsequently teach them less.[8] A third explanation rests in teachers' confusing the teaching of reading with the teaching of a new language form.

Reading researcher Patricia Cunningham found that teachers across the United States were more likely to correct reading miscues that were "dialect" related ("Here go a table" for "Here is a table") than those that were "nondialect" related ("Here is a dog" for "There is a dog").[9] Seventy-eight percent of the former types of miscues were corrected, compared with only 27% of the latter. He concludes that the teachers were acting out of ignorance, not realizing that "here go" and "here is" represent the same meaning in some black children's language.

In my observations of many classrooms, however, I have come to conclude that even when teachers recognize the similarity of meaning, they are likely to correct Ebonics-related miscues. Consider a typical example:

Text: Yesterday I washed my brother's clothes.

Student's rendition: Yesterday I wash my bruvver close.

The subsequent exchange between student and teacher sounds something like this:

T: Wait, let's go back. What's that word again? [Points at *washed*.]

S: Wash.

T: No. Look at it again. What letters do you see at the end? You see "e-d." Do you remember what we say when we see those letters on the end of the word?

S: "ed."

T: OK, but in this case we say "washed." Can you say that?

S: Wash*ed*.

T: Good. Now read it again.

S: Yesterday I wash*ed* my bruvver . . .

T: Wait a minute, what's that word again? [Points to *brother*.]

S: Bruvver.

T: No. Look at these letters in the middle. [Points to *brother*.] Remember to read what you see. Do you remember how we say that sound? Put your tongue between your teeth and say "th". . . .

The lesson continues in such a fashion, the teacher proceeding to correct the student's Ebonics-influenced pronunciations and grammar, while ignoring that fact that the student had to have comprehended the sentence in order to translate it into her own language. Such instruction occurs daily and blocks reading development in a number of ways. First, because children become better readers by having the opportunity to read, the over-correction exhibited in this lesson means that this child will be less likely to become a fluent reader than other children who are not interrupted so consistently. Second, a complete focus on code and pronunciation blocks children's understanding that reading is essentially a meaning-making process. This child, who understands the text, is led to believe that she is doing something wrong. She is encouraged to think of reading not as something you do to get a message, but something you pronounce. Third, constant corrections by the teacher are likely to cause this student and others like her to resist reading and to resent the teacher.

Language researcher Robert Berdan reports that, after observing the kind of teaching routine described above in a number of settings, he incorporated the teacher behaviors into a reading instruction exercise that he used with students in a college class.[10] He put together sundry rules from a number of American social and regional dialects to create what he called the "language of Atlantis." Students were then called upon to read aloud in this dialect they did not know. When they made errors he interrupted them, using some of the same statements/comments he had heard elementary school teachers routinely make to their students. He concludes:

> The results were rather shocking. By the time these PhD candidates in English or linguistics had read 10-20 words, I could make them sound totally illiterate. . . . The first thing that goes is sentence intonation: They sound like they are reading a list from the telephone book. Comment on their pronunciation a bit more, and they begin to sub-vocalize, rehearsing pronunciations for themselves before they dare to say them out loud. They begin to guess at pronunciations. . . . They switch letters around for no reason. They stumble; they repeat. In short, when I attack them for their failure to conform to my demands for Atlantis English pronunciations, they sound very

much like the worst of the second graders in any of the classrooms I have observed.

They also begin to fidget. They wad up their papers, bite their finger-nails, whisper, and some finally refuse to continue. They do all the things that children do while they are busily failing to learn to read.

The moral of this story is to not confuse learning a new language form with reading comprehension. To do so will only confuse the child, leading her away from those intuitive understandings about language that will promote reading development, and toward a school career of resistance and a lifetime of avoiding reading.

Unlike unplanned oral language or public reading, writing lends itself to editing. While conversational talk is spontaneous and must be respon-sive to an immediate context, writing is a mediated process which may be written and rewritten any number of times before introduced to public scrutiny. Consequently, writing is more amenable to rule application—one may first write freely to get one's thoughts down, and then edit to hone the message and apply specific spelling, syntactical, or punctuation rules. My college students who had such difficulty talking in the "iz" di-alect found writing it, with the rules displayed before them, a relatively easy task.

WHAT TEACHERS MUST DO

To conclude, the teacher's job is to provide access to the national "stan-dard," as well as to understand the language the children speak suffi-ciently to celebrate its beauty. The verbal adroitness, the cogent and quick wit, the brilliant use of metaphor, the facility in rhythm and rhyme evident in the language of Jesse Jackson, Whoopi Goldberg, Toni Morrison, Henry Louis Gates, Tupac Shakur, and Maya Angelou, as well as in that of many inner-city black students, may all be drawn upon to facilitate school learning. The teacher must know how to effec-tively teach reading and writing to students whose culture and language differ from that of the school, and must understand how and why stu-dents decide to add another language form to their repertoire. All we can do is provide students with access to additional language forms. Inevitably, each speaker will make his or her own decision about what to say in any context.

But I must end with a caveat that we keep in mind a simple truth: Despite our necessary efforts to provide access to Standard English, such access will not make any of our students more intelligent. It will not teach them math or science or geography—or, for that matter, compassion, courage, or responsibility. Let us not become so overly concerned with the language *form* that we ignore academic and moral *content*. Access to the standard language may be necessary, but it is definitely *not* sufficient to produce intelligent, competent caretakers of the future.

NOTES

1. Nelson-Barber, S. "Phonologic Variations of Pima English," in R. St. Clair and W. Leap (Eds.), *Language Renewal Among American Indian Tribes: Issues, Problems and Prospects*. Rosslyn, VA: National Clearinghouse for Bilingual Education, 1982.

2. Some of these books include Lucille Clifton, *All Us Come 'Cross the Water* (New York: Holt, Rinehart, and Winston, 1973); Paul Green (aided by Abbe Abbott), *I Am Eskimo—Aknik My Name* (Juneau, AK: Alaska Northwest Publishing, 1959); Howard Jacobs and Jim Rice, *Once Upon a Bayou* (New Orleans, LA: Phideaux Publications, 1983); Tim Elder, *Santa's Cajun Christmas Adventure* (Baton Rouge, LA: Little Cajun Books, 1981); and a series of biographies produced by Yukon-Koyukkuk School District of Alaska and published by Hancock House Publishers in North Vancouver, BC, Canada.

3. Heath, Shirley Brice. *Ways with Words*. Cambridge, England: Cambridge University Press, 1983.

4. Michaels, S. and Cazden, C. B. "Teacher-Child Collaboration on Oral Preparation for Literacy," in B. Schieffer (Ed.), *Acquisition of Literacy: Ethnographic Perspectives*. Norwood, NJ: Ablex, 1986.

5. Cazden, C. B. *Classroom Discourse*. Portsmouth, NH: Heinemann, 1988.

6. *Ibid*.

7. Sims, R. "Dialect and Reading: Toward Redefining the Issues," in J. Langer and M. T. Smith-Burke (Eds.), *Reader Meets Author: Bridging the Gap*. Newark, DE: International Reading Association, 1982.

8. *Ibid.*

9. Cunningham, Patricia M. "Teachers' Correction Responses to Black-Dialect Miscues Which Are Nonmeaning-changing," *Reading Research Quarterly 12* (1976–77).

10. Berdan, Robert. "Knowledge into Practice: Delivering Research to Teachers," in M. F. Whiteman (Ed.), *Reactions to Ann Arbor: Vernacular Black English and Education.* Arlington, VA: Center for Applied Linguistics, 1980.

ALEXANDRA: Just because Ebonics (or black dialect, or African American Vernacular English as it is sometimes called) isn't in the news with the same frequency it once was doesn't mean the issues raised by Lisa Delpit in this article have been resolved. If anything, reductions in bilingual classrooms and laws in some states that mandate teaching in English have made Delpit's keen observation that "forcing speakers to monitor their language typically produces silence" (p. 245) more true than ever. Why do so many Americans continue to denigrate the languages and dialects of others, to isolate themselves from the potential for cultural enrichment, when it is readily apparent that globalization is here to stay and the need for Americans to speak in foreign languages and understand other cultures have never been more urgently important?

Delpit provides multiple ideas for making language awareness meaningful to students and to their learning in classrooms. Teachers must also be made aware of how code switching among African Americans does not just apply to English grammar, as demonstrated by the important research of Sarah Michaels on storytelling forms. The consequences outlined by Delpit when teachers lack cultural familiarity with the students they are charged with teaching, coupled with a tendency to publicly correct children's spoken language, are devastating and no doubt contribute to the persistent presence of an achievement gap between white students and those of color. Most schools and the curriculum they adopt encourage teachers to ignore these issues and stick to narrow definitions of "proper" Standard English. But at what cost? My hope is that teachers and parents will help children, regardless of the color of their skin or their language, to appreciate Virginia Hamilton's lilting prose, the stunning screen presence of Queen Latifah, and countless other artists who celebrate the beauty in African Americans' speech and cultural heritage.

SUGGESTED RESOURCES AND FURTHER READING

http://www.wcwonline.org/seed

http://www.fairtest.org

http://teachingforchange.org

http://rethinkingschools.org

http://www.great-ideas.org/enc.htm (journal entitled *Encounter: Education for Meaning and Social Justice*)

http://www.tolerance.org/index.jsp (journal entitled *Teaching Tolerance*)

http://www.pbs.org (search Eyes on the Prize)

http://www.naacp.org

http://www.virginiahamilton.org

Spike Lee's *4 Little Girls*: http://www.imdb.com/title/tt0118540/

Curtis, C. P. (1996) *The Watsons go to Birmingham*—1963. New York: Doubleday.

Davis, O. (1992). *Just like Martin*. New York: Simon & Schuster.

Dewey, J. (1897). My Pedagogic Creed. *School Journal* 54 (1), 77–80.

■ PART V ■

THE FINAL WORD: PURPOSES OF EDUCATION IN A DEMOCRACY

Democracy, at least as Americans are coming to understand it in the United States, entails embracing plurality. Features such as a multiplicity of views, varied approaches to solving problems, ongoing debate and deliberation, and freedom of expression are considered signs of a healthy democracy. Yet in education we are currently witness to a shift to sameness, to standardization, to single definitions of what is referred to as "best practice." Schools are also becoming more segregated, which is a trend that is likely to become even more problematic given the 2007 Supreme Court decision that rejected the racial diversity plans of school districts in Seattle, Washington, and Louisville, Kentucky. Students are tracked and grouped by questionable measures of ability at the earliest years of schooling in the name of "differentiated instruction." The writers in this last section offer a vision of foundational ideas in education that call for risk taking, a sense of adventure in learning, trust (of students, teachers, parents, and administrators), and coping with uncertainty.

· 17 ·

John Dewey

DEMOCRACY IN EDUCATION*

MAUREEN: John Dewey, an American philosopher and educational reformer, is often praised or excoriated by people who have never even read him. It was not easy, in fact, to choose a representative piece for this volume. His prose is difficult, contradictory, and often dull. At the same time, it is pertinent; one senses the influence it has had in the past as it casts new light on the problems of the present. "Democracy in Education" (not to be confused with his 1916 magnum opus Democracy and Education) *was written over one hundred years ago, yet has a remarkable relevancy for education today.*

Teaching takes an inordinate amount of time, energy, and dedication. Often we never see the results of our endeavors, to weigh their success or failure. There's a loneliness, an emptiness about teaching that's not mentioned in textbooks. We have to accept on faith that our work has been successful, even though we seldom see or hear from our former students. That may make our work seem insignificant, yet most of us believe that it is the single most important work in our society. We are sustained by the conviction that education does, indeed, make a difference. But undemocratic restrictions on the practice of our profession often result in the decrease of well-qualified and dedicated teachers.

When I read this essay, I am moved by Dewey's faith in the ability of the teacher to make decisions about what to teach and how to teach it. When he talks about decisions of that nature being made by people outside the school system who have no expert knowledge of education but are motivated by noneducational motives, I am struck by its applicability to today's headlines. The restrictions placed upon the teacher result in the flight of the truly intelligent

*From John Dewey: The Middle Works 1899–1906, ed. J. A. Boydston (Carbondale, IL: Southern Illinois University Press), 229–239.

and imaginative person who might be attracted to the profession were it not for
the imprisonment of the spirit that the lack of freedom implies.

Modern life means democracy, democracy means freeing intelligence for independent effectiveness—the emancipation of mind as an individual organ to do its own work. We naturally associate democracy, to be sure, with freedom of action, but freedom of action without freed capacity of thought behind it is only chaos. If external authority in action is given up, it must be because internal authority of truth, discovered and known to reason, is substituted.

How does the school stand with reference to this matter? Does the school as an accredited representative exhibit this trait of democracy as a spiritual force? Does it lead and direct the movement? Does it lag behind and work at cross-purpose? I find the fundamental need of the school today dependent upon its limited recognition of the principle of freedom of intelligence. This limitation appears to me to affect both of the elements of school life: teacher and pupil. As to both, the school has lagged behind the general contemporary social movement; and much that is unsatisfactory, much of conflict and of defect, comes from the discrepancy between the relatively undemocratic organization of the school, as it affects the mind of both teacher and pupil, and the growth and extension of the democratic principle in life beyond school doors.

The effort of the last two-thirds of a century has been successful in building up the machinery of a democracy of mind. It has provided the ways and means for housing and equipping intelligence. What remains is that the thought-activity of the individual, whether teacher or student, be permitted and encouraged to take working possession of this machinery: to substitute its rightful lordship for an inherited servility. In truth, our public-school system is but two-thirds of a century old. It dates, so far as such matters can be dated at all, from 1837, the year that Horace Mann became secretary of the state board of Massachusetts; and from 1843, when Henry Barnard began a similar work in Connecticut. At this time began that growing and finally successful warfare against all the influences, social and sectarian, which would prevent or mitigate the sway of public influence over private ecclesiastical and class interests. Between 1837 and 1850 grew up all the most characteristic features of the American public-school system: from this time date state normal schools, city training schools, county and state institutes, teachers' associations, teachers' journals, the institution of city superintendencies, supervisory officers, and the development of state universities as the crown of the public-school system of the commonwealth. From this time date the striving for better schoolhouses and grounds, improved text-books, adequate material equipment in maps, globes, scientific apparatus, etc. As an outcome of the forces thus set in motion, democracy has in principle, subject to relative local restrictions, developed an organized machinery of public education. But when we turn to the aim and method which this magnificent institution serves, we find that our democracy is not yet conscious of the ethical principle upon which it rests—the responsibility and freedom of mind in discovery and proof—and consequently we find confusion where there should be order, darkness where there should be light. The teacher has not the power of initiation and constructive endeavor which is necessary to the fulfillment of the function of teaching. The learner finds conditions antagonistic (or at least lacking) to the development of individual mental power and to adequate responsibility for its use.

1. *As to the teacher.*—If there is a single public-school system in the United States where there is official and constitutional provision made for submitting questions of methods of discipline and teaching, and the questions of the curriculum, text-books, etc., to the discussion and decision of those actually engaged in the work of teaching, that fact has escaped my notice. Indeed, the opposite situation is so common that it seems, as a rule, to be absolutely taken for granted as the normal and final condition of affairs. The number of persons to whom any other course has occurred as desirable, or even possible—to say nothing of necessary—is apparently very limited. But until the public-school system is organized in such a way that every teacher has some regular and representative way in which he or she can register judgment upon matters of educational importance, with the assurance that this judgment will somehow affect the school system, the assertion that the present system is not, from the internal standpoint, democratic seems to be justified.

Either we come here upon some fixed and inherent limitation of the democratic principle, or else we find in this fact an obvious discrepancy between the conduct of the school and the conduct of social life—a discrepancy so great as to demand immediate and persistent effort at reform.

The more enlightened portions of the public have, indeed, become aware of one aspect of this discrepancy. Many reformers are contending against the conditions which place the direction of school affairs, including the selection of text-books, etc., in the hands of a body of men who are outside the school system itself, who have not necessarily any expert knowledge of education and who are moved by non-educational motives. Unfortunately, those who have noted this undemocratic condition of affairs, and who have striven to change it, have, as a rule, conceived of but one remedy, namely, the transfer of authority to the school superintendent. In their zeal to place the centre of gravity inside the school system, in their zeal to decrease the prerogatives of a non-expert school board, and to lessen the opportunities for corruption and private pull which go with that, they have tried to remedy one of the evils of democracy by adopting the principle of autocracy. For no matter how wise, expert, or benevolent the head of the school system, the one-man principle is autocracy.

The logic of the argument goes farther, very much farther, than the reformer of this type sees. The logic which commits him to the idea that the management of the school system must be in the hands of an expert commits him also to the idea that every member of the school system, from the first-grade teacher to the principal of the high school, must have some share in the exercise of educational power. The remedy is not to have one expert dictating educational methods and subject-matter to a body of passive, recipient teachers, but the adoption of intellectual initiative, discussion, and decision throughout the entire school corps. The remedy of the partial evils of democracy, the implication of the school system in municipal politics, is in appeal to a more thorough-going democracy.

The dictation, in theory at least, of the subject-matter to be taught, to the teacher who is to engage in the actual work of instruction, and frequently, under the name of close supervision, the attempt to determine the methods which are to be used in teaching, mean nothing more or less than the deliberate restriction of intelligence, the imprisoning of the spirit. Every well-graded system of schools in this country rejoices in a course of study. It is no uncommon thing to find methods of teaching such subjects as reading, writing, spelling, and arithmetic officially laid down; outline topics in history and geography are provided ready-made for the teacher; gems of literature are fitted to the successive ages of boys and girls. Even the domain of art, songs and methods of singing, subject-matter and technique of drawing and painting, come within the region on which an outside authority lays its sacrilegious hands.

I have stated the theory, which is also true of the practice to a certain extent and in certain places. We may thank our heavens, however, that the practice is rarely as bad as the theory would require. Superintendents and principals often encourage individuality and thoughtfulness in the invention and adoption of methods of teaching; and they wink at departures from the printed manual of study. It remains true, however, that this great advance is personal and informal. It depends upon the wisdom and tact of the individual supervisory official; he may withdraw his concession at any moment; or it may be ruthlessly thrown aside by his successor who has formed a high ideal of "system."

I know it will be said that this state of things, while an evil, is a necessary one; that without it confusion and chaos would reign; that such regulations are the inevitable accompaniments of any graded system. It is said that the average teacher is incompetent to take any part in laying out the course of study or in initiating methods of instruction or discipline. Is not this the type of argument which has been used from time immemorial, and in every department of life, against the advance of democracy? What does democracy mean save that the individual is to have a share in determining the conditions and the aims of his own work; and that, upon the whole, through the free and mutual harmonizing of different individuals, the work of the world is better done than when planned, arranged, and directed by a few, no matter how wise or of how good intent that few? How can we justify our belief in the democratic principle elsewhere, and then go back entirely upon it when we come to education?

Moreover, the argument proves too much. The more it is asserted that the existing corps of teachers is unfit to have voice in the settlement

of important educational matters, and their unfitness to exercise intellectual initiative and to assume the responsibility for constructive work
is emphasized, the more their unfitness to attempt the much more difficult and delicate task of guiding souls appears. If this body is so unfit,
how can it be trusted to carry out the recommendations or the dicta-
tions of the wisest body of experts? If teachers are incapable of the intellectual responsibility which goes with the determination of the methods
they are to use in teaching, how can they employ methods when dic-
tated by others, in other than a mechanical, capricious, and clumsy manner? The argument, I say, proves too much.

Moreover, if the teaching force is as inept and unintelligent and irre-
sponsible as the argument assumes, surely the primary problem is that
of their improvement. Only by sharing in some responsible task does
there come a fitness to share in it. The argument that we must wait
until men and women are fully ready to assume intellectual and social
responsibilities would have defeated every step in the democratic direction that has ever been taken. The prevalence of methods of authority
and of external dictation and direction tends automatically to perpetuate the very conditions of inefficiency, lack of interest, inability to assume positions of self-determination, which constitute the reasons that
are depended upon to justify the régime of authority.

The system which makes no great demands upon originality, upon
invention, upon the continuous expression of individuality, works automatically to put and to keep the more incompetent teachers in the
school. It puts them there because, by a natural law of spiritual gravita-
tion, the best minds are drawn to the places where they can work most
effectively. The best minds are not especially likely to be drawn where
there is danger that they may have to submit to conditions which no
self-respecting intelligence likes to put up with; and where their time
and energy are likely to be so occupied with details of external conformity that they have no opportunity for free and full play of their own
vigor.

I have dwelt at length upon the problem of the recognition of the intellectual and spiritual individuality of the teacher. I have but one ex-
cuse. All other reforms are conditioned upon reform in the quality and
character of those who engage in the teaching profession. The doctrine

of the man behind the gun has become familiar enough, in recent discussion, in every sphere of life. Just because education is the most personal, the most intimate, of all human affairs, there, more than anywhere else, the sole ultimate reliance and final source of power are in the training, character, and intelligence of the individual. If any scheme could be devised which would draw to the calling of teaching persons of force of character, of sympathy with children, and consequent interest in the problems of teaching and of scholarship, no one need be troubled for a moment about other educational reforms, or the solution of other educational problems. But as long as a school organization which is undemocratic in principle tends to repel from all but the higher portions of the school system those of independent force, of intellectual initiative, and of inventive ability, or tends to hamper them in their work after they find their way into the schoolroom, so long all other reforms are compromised at their source and postponed indefinitely for fruition.

2. *As to the learner.*—The undemocratic suppression of the individuality of the teacher goes naturally with the improper restriction of the intelligence of the mind of the child. The mind, to be sure, is that of a child, and yet, after all, it is mind. To subject mind to an outside and ready-made material is a denial of the ideal of democracy, which roots itself ultimately in the principle of moral, self-directing individuality. Misunderstanding regarding the nature of the freedom that is demanded for the child is so common that it may be necessary to emphasize the fact that it is primarily intellectual freedom, free play of mental attitude, and operation which are sought. If individuality were simply a matter of feelings, impulses, and outward acts independent of intelligence, it would be more than a dubious matter to urge a greater degree of freedom for the child in the school. In that case much, and almost exclusive, force would attach to the objections that the principle of individuality is realized in the more exaggerated parts of Rousseau's doctrines: sentimental idealization of the child's immaturity, irrational denial of superior worth in the knowledge and mature experience of the adult, deliberate denial of the worth of the ends and instruments embodied in social organization. Deification of childish whim, unripened fancy, and arbitrary emotion is certainly a piece of pure romanticism. The would-be reformers who emphasize out of due proportion and perspective these aspects of

the principle of individualism betray their own cause. But the heart of the matter lies not there. Reform of education in the direction of greater play for the individuality of the child means the securing of conditions which will give outlet, and hence direction, to a growing intelligence. It is true that this freed power of mind with reference to its own further growth cannot be obtained without a certain leeway, a certain flexibility, in the expression of even immature feelings and fancies. But it is equally true that it is not a riotous loosening of these traits which is needed, but just that kind and degree of freedom from repression which are found to be necessary to secure the full operation of intelligence.

Now, no one need doubt as to what mental activity or the freed expression of intelligence means. No one need doubt as to the conditions which are conducive to it. We do not have to fall back upon what some regard as the uncertain, distracting, and even distressing voice of psychology. Scientific methods, the methods pursued by the scientific inquirer, give us an exact and concrete exhibition of the path which intelligence takes when working most efficiently, under most favorable conditions.

What is primarily required for that direct inquiry which constitutes the essence of science is first-hand experience; an active and vital participation through the medium of all the bodily organs with the means and materials of building up first-hand experience. Contrast this first and most fundamental of all the demands for an effective use of mind with what we find in so many of our elementary and high schools. There first-hand experience is at a discount; in its stead are summaries and formulas of the results of other people. Only very recently has any positive provision been made within the schoolroom for any of the modes of activity and for any of the equipment and arrangement which permit and require the extension of original experiences on the part of the child. The school has literally been dressed out with hand-me-down garments— with intellectual suits which other people have worn.

Secondly, in that freed activity of mind which we term "science" there is always a certain problem which focuses effort, which controls the collecting of facts that bear upon the question, the use of observation to get further data, the employing of memory to supply relevant facts, the calling into play of imagination, to yield fertile suggestion and construct possible solutions of the difficulty.

Turning to the school, we find too largely no counterpart to this mental activity. Just because a second-handed material has been supplied wholesale and retail, but anyway ready-made, the tendency is to reduce the activity of mind to a docile or passive taking in of the material presented—in short, to memorizing, with simply incidental use of judgment and of active research. As is frequently stated, acquiring takes the place of inquiring. It is hardly an exaggeration to say that the sort of mind-activity which is encouraged in the school is a survival from the days in which science had not made much headway; when education was mainly concerned with learning, that is to say, the preservation and handing down of the acquisitions of the past. It is true that more and more appeal is made every day in schools to judgment, reasoning, personal efficiency, and the calling up of personal, as distinct from merely book, experiences. But we have not yet got to the point of reversing the total method. The burden and the stress still fall upon learning in the sense of becoming possessed of the second-hand and ready-made material referred to. As Mrs. Young has recently said, the prevailing ideal is a perfect recitation, an exhibition without mistake, of a lesson learned. Until the emphasis changes to the conditions which make it necessary for the child to take an active share in the personal building up of his own problems and to participate in methods of solving them (even at the expense of experimentation and error), mind is not really freed.

In our schools we have freed individuality in many modes of outer expression without freeing intelligence, which is the vital spring and guarantee of all of these expressions. Consequently we give opportunity to the unconverted to point the finger of scorn, and to clamor for a return to the good old days when the teacher, the representative of social and moral authority, was securely seated in the high places of the school. But the remedy here, as in other phases of our social democracy, is not to turn back, but to go farther—to carry the evolution of the school to a point where it becomes a place for getting and testing experience, as real and adequate to the child upon his existing level as all the resources of laboratory and library afford to the scientific man upon his level. What is needed is not any radical revolution, but rather an organization of agencies already found in the schools. It is hardly too much to say that not a single subject or instrumentality is required which is not already found in many schools of the country. All that is required is to gather these materials and forces together and unify their operation. Too often they are used for a multitude of diverse and often conflicting aims. If a single purpose is provided, that of freeing the processes of mental growth, these agencies will at once fall into their proper classes and re-inforce each other.

A catalogue of the agencies already available would include at least all of the following: Taking the child out of doors, widening and orga-nizing his experience with reference to the world in which he lives; nature study when pursued as a vital observation of forces working under their natural conditions, plants and animals growing in their own homes, in-stead of mere discussion of dead specimens. We have also school gar-dens, the introduction of elementary agriculture, and more especially of horticulture—a movement that is already making great headway in many of the western states. We have also means for the sake of studying physiographic conditions, such as may be found by rivers, ponds or lakes, beaches, quarries, gulleys, hills, etc.

As similar agencies within the school walls, we find a very great vari-ety of instruments for constructive work, or, as it is frequently, but some-what unfortunately termed, "manual training." Under this head come cooking, which can be begun in its simpler form in the kindergarten; sewing, and what is of even greater educational value, weaving, includ-ing designing and the construction of simple apparatus for carrying on various processes of spinning, etc. Then there are also the various forms of tool-work directed upon cardboard, wood, and iron; in addition there are clay-modeling and a variety of ways of manipulating plastic material to gain power and larger experience.

Such matters pass readily over into the simpler forms of scientific ex-perimentation. Every schoolroom from the lowest primary grade up should be supplied with gas, water, certain chemical substances and reagents. To experiment in the sense of trying things or to see what will happen is the most natural business of the child; it is, indeed, his chief concern. It is one which the school has largely either ignored or actually suppressed, so that it has been forced to find outlet in mischief or even in actually destructive ways. This tendency could find outlet in the con-struction of simple apparatus and the making of simple tests, leading constantly into more and more controlled experimentation, with greater insistence upon definiteness of intellectual result and control of logical process.

Add to these three typical modes of active experimenting, various forms of art expression, beginning with music, clay-modeling, and story-telling as foundation elements, and passing on to drawing, painting, de-signing in various mediums, we have a range of forces and materials which connect at every point with the child's natural needs and powers, and which supply the requisites for building up his experience upon all sides. As fast as these various agencies find their way into the schools, the centre of gravity shifts, the régime changes from one of subjection of mind to an external and ready-made material, into the activity of mind directed upon the control of the subject-matter and thereby its own upbuilding.

Politically we have found that this country could not endure half free and half slave. We shall find equally great difficulty in encouraging free-dom, independence, and initiative in every sphere of social life, while perpetuating in the school dependence upon external authority. The forces of social life are already encroaching upon the school institutions which we have inherited from the past, so that many of its main stays are crumbling. Unless the outcome is to be chaotic, we must take hold of the organic, positive principle involved in democracy, and put that in entire possession of the spirit and work of the school.

In education meet the three most powerful motives of human activ-ity. Here are found sympathy and affection, the going out of the emo-tions to the most appealing and the most rewarding object of love—a little child. Here is found also the flowering of the social and institu-tional motive, interest in the welfare of society and in its progress and reform by the surest and shortest means. Here, too, is found the intel-lectual and scientific motive, the interest in knowledge, in scholarship, in truth for its own sake, unhampered and unmixed with any alien ideal. Copartnership of these three motives—of affection, of social growth, and of scientific inquiry—must prove as nearly irresistible as anything human when they are once united. And, above all else, recognition of the spiritual basis of democracy, the efficacy and responsibility of freed intelligence, is necessary to secure this union.

————————

ALEXANDRA: Dewey's opening lines of this essay on democracy and free-
dom may be perplexing to the average reader. What does he mean by describ-
ing democracy as a spiritual force? How can it be deemed unconscious of its
foundational ethical principle? What does any of this have to do with children's
education?

If you were intrigued enough to read on, you discovered prophetic wisdom in
Dewey's writing. He argues for "adoption of intellectual initiative, discussion,
and decision throughout the entire school corps" (p. 262) as the remedy for mis-
guided reform. Reformers often don't empower educators to make necessary
changes and improvements, which can further hamper efforts to build trust.
Dewey also warns of unforeseen dangers in personal and informal acts of subver-
sion to the ready-made teaching scripts that today are becoming so ubiquitous.
He cautions that the "wisdom and tact" of those who "wink at departures from
the printed manual of study" are not reliable and may be overtaken by others
higher up in the power structure. Dewey also explores why teachers are caught
in a vicious circle of external authority that labels them stubbornly resistant to
change and to improvements that others have deemed essential and seek to force
on them: "The prevalence of methods of authority and of external dictation and
direction tends automatically to perpetuate the very conditions of efficiency, lack
of interest, inability to assume positions of self-determination, which constitute
the reasons that are depended upon to justify the régime of authority" (p. 264).

Halfway through this essay you may have found yourself wondering, along
with Dewey, who would even want to teach in a system where teachers' creativ-
ity and autonomy are constantly thwarted and choked. It's not hard to see why
the profession loses half of the new teaching force within five years in urban set-
tings. As Dewey says, "their time and energy are likely to be so occupied with
details of external conformity that they have no opportunity for free and full
play of their own vigor" (p. 264). My students report to me that in the weeks
leading up to high-stakes standardized testing, they are told to drop virtually
all instruction in order to complete test preparation materials made by the Kap-
lan Corporation. Any parent who has had to contend with coercing a child to
complete a dull homework assignment can only imagine what it's like to spend
weeks with thirty children filling in bubble sheets.

Yet Dewey provides a vision of an alternative that does not require ten volumes to explain. In fact, he sums it up in a strikingly simple phrase: "First-hand experience." Why have we lost sight of something we know to be fundamentally true of our own learning? How did we learn to make a family recipe, repair a bicycle tire, or make a decent sound out of a musical instrument? In Dewey's words, we learned not by acquiring, but by inquiring. We can no longer afford to ignore or even suppress the freeing of the mind that humans naturally crave.

· 18 ·

Carla Rinaldi

INFANT-TODDLER CENTERS AND PRESCHOOLS
AS PLACES OF CULTURE*

MAUREEN: In the first section of this book, we included a translation of a poem written by Loris Malaguzzi about the hundred languages of children with which they express themselves. Carla Rinaldi, a colleague of Malaguzzi, has worked in the municipal schools of Reggio Emilia since 1971. She is the president of Reggio Children, former director of the Municipal Infant-toddler Centers and Preschools system, and she is a professor at the Modena-Reggio University in Italy.

In this piece Rinaldi raises questions that lead me to wonder why, among all this potential for diversity of human thought and expression, schools continue to privilege the three languages of reading, writing, and speaking. The undue emphasis on testing is partly to blame for the disappearance of programs in music, art, and dance, and less class time spent on science and social studies. What's missing are discussions and conversations about the value of all traditional areas of the curriculum as we devise tests to increase the accountability of individual schools and districts.

Rinaldi's essay is about values. What, she asks, does each society value, and why and how do societal values affect the education of the young? How do we come to know one another? I believe it is through conversation. We have already seen in other selections in this book that conversation is a vehicle for learning. Here Rinaldi points out that conversations enable self-discovery: "Learning is the emergence of that which was not there before. It is a search for the self as well as for the other and others that surround each individual" (p. 280). Diversity is positive, therefore, and contributes to the dynamic of learning in schools. In learning about others through conversation, we also learn about ourselves.

*From Making Learning Visible: Children as Individual and Group Learners (Reggio Emilia, Italy: Reggio Children and Project Zero, 2001), 38–46.

I find great promise in Rinaldi's belief that we must create schools with a re-newed focus on the meaning of learning, in and outside of school. She asks us to educate ourselves by studying in order to understand the differences among us; she encourages us to let go of absolutes so that we can be more open to possibilities.

As I read her thoughts on the values of subjectivity, difference, participa-tion, democracy, learning, and of play, fun, emotions, and feelings, I notice a contrast with values often found in American schools: competition, merit, and accountability. There are reasons for this contrast, because our cultures and therefore our values are different. Rinaldi writes, "School is a place of culture— that is, a place where a personal and collective culture is developed that influ-ences the social, political, and values context and, in turn, is influenced by this context in a relationship of deep and authentic reciprocity" (p. 274).

School is too often a place where we shy away from discussions of values. In my education courses, I work to develop a personal and collective culture born of such discussions. When my students meet in seminar on their first day of stu-dent teaching, I ask them to think about and list their goals for the semester. The statements of goals become working documents. As the student teachers work with their students in classrooms, they constantly revise and elaborate the list as they share their goals and experiences with one another. They clarify and enhance what is individually valued and what is common to all and can be de-termined as collective values. This sharing of values is, in a sense, the micro-cosm of what might occur in a democracy, and what education is as Rinaldi would define it. Individual ideas, when shared, produce consensus. Consensus creates common values. In a democratic society these values are almost always under scrutiny and debated. Rinaldi celebrates this search for common values and embraces the conversations it engenders, for it is only in open discussions and the sharing of ideas that we can learn from one another. Indeed, Rinaldi would define education as this exchange of ideas—constantly pushing us to new discoveries and broadening our horizons.

————————

I begin with a declaration that I consider to be fundamentally important for more than just the comprehension of this document. The declaration is this: school, including the school for young children, is an educational place, a place of education; a place where we educate and are educated; a place where values and knowledge are transmitted; and above all a place where values and knowledge are constructed. School is a place of culture—that is, a place where a personal and collective culture is developed that influences the social, political, and values context and, in turn, is influenced by this context in a relationship of deep and authentic reciprocity.

Considering school as an educational place is a choice that has always characterized the Reggio Emilia experience, and this choice has assumed topical importance within the contemporary debate regarding the role of the school: Is school a place of education or a place of "formation"?*

Nowadays in Italy, there is often a tendency to favor the use of the term (and concept) of formation. The reasons are not easy to understand. We can suppose that the term formation has been singled out because it is effective in expressing the subjective and self-constructive aspects of education. Or perhaps because it is close—as others maintain—to the concept of professional and vocational training, which is certainly an extremely important element of a scholastic experience, but not the only one. Or perhaps the word formation seems more neutral, more detached from the issue of education in relation to the question of values, which is certainly a pressing issue of our times.

In short, the individual is "formed" and then takes his or her own direction, choosing the values that will sustain the relationships and rapport with the community in which he or she lives.

My personal hope is that the debate will continue, but above all that the concept expressed by the term education can remain strongly tied to the concept and identity of school.

We see school not as the place of instruction or the place of formation (in the vocational/professional sense), but as the place of education. But what do we mean by this? That school, for us, is a place where, first and foremost, values are transmitted, discussed, and constructed. **The term education is therefore closely correlated with the concept of values**, where "to educate" also means—and in certain respects primarily means—to educate the intrinsic values of each individual and each culture, in order to make these values extrinsic, visible, conscious, and shareable. And what is a value? Value is certainly a polysemous word, one of the most polysemous of all, just as education, for-

---

*In Italian, the word *formazione* in the educational context is used in the more general sense of personal "formation" as well as in the sense of vocational or professional training.

mation, and subjectivity are contextual terms; that is, they can only be defined in relation to the cultural, political, and historical context.

One consideration is that the term value seems to come not from the philosophical sphere but from the economic and cultural sphere. A possible definition could be: "Values are the ideals that a person aspires to in his or her life." These values act as a point of reference in our judgments and our conduct, and on this basis we conform (or not) our relationships within the social group of reference (community, society, culture). Values define cultures and are one of the foundations on which society is based.

Others may define values as "what makes the human being more human."

These are appealing definitions—intuitively appealing. But what is, and who is, a "more human" human being? And this presupposes another prior question: "Who is a human being?"

In Reggio Emilia, it is a question with which we are very familiar, because we place it at the core of our pedagogical action (though in a substantially modified form) when we ask ourselves, "What is our image of humanity and of the child?"

Values, therefore, are relative and are correlated with the culture to which they belong: they determine the culture and are determined by it.

This apparent digression is actually a fundamental issue for an institution that wishes to define itself as educational. Certainly, when we talk about assessment, the question of values will return as the subject of our reflections and discussions.

What I would like to put forth are some of the values that have structured our experience, but that have also been expressed and renewed by this experience. **The first is the value of subjectivity, which we view in terms of wholeness and integrity** (a holistic value). I have chosen the term subjectivity from a number of possible others (such as person or individual) because I think it more clearly highlights the correlational and reflexive aspects involved in the construction of the individual subject. Each subject, then, is a construction (self-constructed and socially constructed) that is defined within a specific context and culture.

A number of studies on the brain have quite spectacularly demonstrated the uniqueness and unrepeatability of each individual and of his or her construction as a subject. Much is known about how the individual develops in relation to the environmental context, and about the strong influence of interactional qualities on the destiny of each of us, particularly in the early years of life.

The methodological implications of this value of subjectivity can be seen in our daily strategies in the Reggio schools: observation and documentation, small-group work, the organization of the space, the presence of mini-ateliers,* and so on.

But I would like once again to underscore the importance of this value of subjectivity in the way that we have described it. In my view, the relationship between subjectivity and intersubjectivity is fundamental not only on the cognitive (and psychopedagogical) level, but above all on the political and cultural level.

I believe that this question is virtually important for the future of humanity itself. The relationship between the individual and others, between Self and Other, is a key issue for our futures. To choose whether our individual construction is independent from others or exists *with* others and *through* others, means resolving not only the traditional pedagogical-psychological debate, but also the one regarding different images of the human being and humanity. It is a question of political and economic choices that can influence the entire educational system, and also the social system.

Here we can clearly see how the sciences, and above all pedagogy, are not neutral but are "partisan," and our pedagogy in Reggio Emilia is a pedagogy of partisanship; that is, it holds certain values.

The value of subjectivity, with the related affirmations regarding the uniqueness and unrepeatability of each individual, is strongly connected to **the value of difference**: difference in regard to gender, race, culture, and religion. Difference because we are individuals, because we are all, in fact, different.

---

*The mini-atelier is a small studio space connected to each classroom.

But difference per se is not a value. It can become one if we are able to create a context, a culture, a strategy, and a school of differences.

Dealing with differences is difficult and requires commitment and hard work. In confronting differences, we are faced with otherness, but also with "outsideness" (extraneousness). Differences are sometimes painful, and always challenging. We tend to be more attracted by the idea of sameness, by that which makes us the same. But this is a great risk, and the questions consequently raised are of vital importance:

- What do we do with the differences?
- How do we avoid the risks of homogenization or standardization?
- Are all differences acceptable? If not, which ones are not?
- What is the aim of an educational project that seeks to be open to differences? Is it to standardize them?
- What concept of equality are we developing?
- Is the aim to make everyone equal, or to give everyone opportunities to develop his or her own subjectivity (and thus difference) by interacting with others, where this includes elements in common as well as elements that are different?

These questions are of substantial importance at both the pedagogical and the political levels. The inherent risks involve not only education but Western culture in general, which is experiencing massive migration of people, races, cultures, religions.

Globalization, which is fostered by our extraordinary communication systems (television and the Internet, for example), has the potential to create a widespread phenomenon of standardization and encourage the formation of cultural stereotypes. Schools, however, can do an equal amount of damage by encouraging a "culture of normality"; that is, fueling the desire for "normality," for "norms" or "standards," which is so pervasive nowadays.

In my opinion, the only perspective that can translate differences into values is that of integration, but by integration I do not mean fundamentalism. We cannot move toward creating a harmonious unity if this means an overpowering will to impose a single vision, a single way of thinking, a sort of homogeneity without doubts or defeats. Integration is based on multiplicity, and we cannot expect to encounter one single reality without the contrasts and contradictions that are always present in a reality composed of different visions.

The risk that we run, in Italy as elsewhere, is that of fundamentalism and extremism.

In all our lives, somewhat instinctively and without educational input, at some point we begin to recognize otherness. Soon after, in relation to certain others who are "more other," more extraneous, we tend to develop a concept of "others" who are "less other." We are all potentially subject to this attitude, even those who consider themselves to be "above reproach."

The term integration has many possible meanings, and often in daily use it has a meaning and a policy that is very close to the term conformism (for example, having all the children do the same thing based on a principle, or a value, of equality).

In order to educate ourselves, we must try to understand the differences rather than having any pretensions to eliminate them. This means approaching each individual with great sensitivity in terms of his or her particular background and personal history. It means "listening" to the differences (we talk about the "pedagogy of listening"), but also listening to and accepting the changes that take place within us which are generated by our relationships and particularly by our interactions with others. It means letting go of any truths we consider to be absolute and being open to doubt, giving value to negotiation as a "strategy of the possible."

All this means—or can mean—greater possibilities for us to change, without feeling divided.

In this definition of the value of differences, we find a richer and more contemporary definition of **the value of participation, or, participation as a value**. In the Reggio educational experience, we have always maintained that participation (feeling a sense of belonging and partaking) is not limited just to the families, though family participation is absolutely crucial. It is a value and a quality of the school as a whole. This means providing for spaces, languages, and, more generally, organizational methods and strategies that make this kind of participation possible, which we have always worked toward in our experience. It means that the educational and pedagogical aims must be clearly stated, but at the same time, participation requires a certain sense of indefiniteness and ample spaces of possibility.

These reflections lead to the affirmation of another value that is part of our experience: **the value of democracy**, which is embedded in the concept of participation.

Once again, the relationship between the individual and the community in which he or she lives can be regulated and oriented in such a way as to exalt either active participation or participation by delegation. The debate is affecting our country as well as each of us individually.

This extremely important issue deserves at least a brief mention, because we must not forget how closely the school is connected to the society in which it is situated. The recurring question is whether the school is limited to transmitting culture or can be, as we in Reggio Emilia strive toward, a place where culture is constructed and democracy is put into practice.

I would also like to mention another value, **the value of learning**. Though some may question the concept of learning as a value, I feel it is essential for our experience, and in a certain sense is its founding principle.

Learning *is* and *can be* a value if we are aware that learning—which is decided by each individual in times and ways that cannot be programmed—is a "relational place" that makes us reflect on the meaning of education itself and leads us to search for new paths in educating and in personal and professional formation.

In educational practice, this means being open to the complex, conflictual, and unpredictable nature of human learning wherever it takes place, both inside and outside the institutional contexts directly involved in education and formation. The entire Italian school system today—with great effort, many contradictions, and many risks—is enmeshed in this process of evolution from a school of teaching to a school of learning.

Learning is the emergence of that which was not there before. It is a search for the self as well as for the other and others that surround each individual.

Educating is thus modified in relation to learning. It means placing the world in front of us, creating an event, and living the various situations. It means educating ourselves.

When we participate in an educational process, in fact, we bring our own growth and development into play, and we do this on the basis of our own expectations and our own designs. There is a constant relational reciprocity between those who educate and those who are educated, between those who teach and those who are taught. There is participation, passion, compassion, emotion. There is aesthetics. There is an aesthetic relationship, as described by Gregory Bateson: aesthetics as a quality of knowledge-building (aesthetics as a value) and, we might add, the value of change, of becoming, and so on.

Then there is **the value of play, of fun, of emotions, of feelings**, which we see as essential elements of any authentic cognitive and educational process.

Learning thus becomes a value because of its power to bring about a synthesis between the individual and his or her context, in a warm relationship between those who learn and that which is being learned, a relationship filled with emotion, curiosity, and humor.

For each of us, the cognitive act becomes a creative act, involving the assumption of responsibility as well as autonomy and freedom.

Knowledge, or better, subjective understanding, becomes an individual responsibility and, in order to be realized to the fullest, a sense of optimism and of the future is needed.

What, then, constitutes formation for us as teachers? It is simply learning: the job of teachers is to learn, because they are teachers. It means keeping our distance from any overriding sense of balance, from that which has already been decided, preconstituted, or considered to be certain. It means staying close to the interweaving of objects and thoughts, of doing and reflecting, theory and practice, emotion and knowledge.

Our task, perhaps, is to seek constantly (though not necessarily ever to find) a balance between the inherent rules and restrictions (some of which are indispensable) and the real emotion and passion of learning.

We are talking about formation for teachers and children alike, rejecting the idea of formation as "modeling," as a passage from one state to another, from various "ways of being" to another "way of being." The aim of this kind of formation is to think and act with reference to the process of becoming, of change. It is an ongoing activity, a permanent process, a quality that must pervade the scholastic institution and that the school, in turn, must grant to all the subjects involved.

Formation toward change, and formation as change.

All of this takes place by means of a choral effort, with the participation of everyone, in full awareness of the restrictions and limits of the institution itself (restrictions of timetables, spaces, and resources), with a commitment that does not delegate to others that which is inherent in formation, which is above all self-formation and group formation.

The scholastic institution thus emerges as the privileged place of education—not the only one, but a special one. Schools must overcome the conflict between the expectation and desire to belong (the sense of belonging) and the need for autonomy and self-affirmation that each of us experiences.

These two aspects, which may seem contradictory and ambiguous, can be extremely generative. Formation for teachers (weekly staff development meetings, for instance) can be a context in which other views can represent both an opportunity and a potential threat, but where negotiation and cooperation can be the ultimate outcome.

It is for this reason that in Reggio Emilia the primary contexts of professional development are inside the schools themselves or in the system-wide professional development program. Not as "contexts" in which one simply describes to the others what he or she has learned, but as places where we can reflect on what has happened inside (as well as outside) the school, in order to self-assess and assess the quality and quantity of learning opportunities that we offer the children, the families, and the teachers themselves—opportunities for learning and sharing values.

What kind of culture should we be working toward and build?

This is a crucial question for all, and particularly for those who work in the educational field.

- Where is the future?
- Where does the "new" reside?
- What kind of future can we construct together?

Because we are now in a phase of increasing globalization, we are inundated with information and kept abreast of events across the entire planet in real time. We are spectators, more than authors, of an extraordinary technical-scientific revolution that is changing the quality of human relationships, the definition of personal identity, and the construction of cognitive processes. New issues will certainly emerge regarding the concepts of privacy, ethics, space, and time.

So is the "new" to be found in the media explosion? I think not, or at least not *only* there. The media revolution will be just one of the possible futures, provided we are able to produce another "revolution"; that is, the new is and will be found where individuals are able to overturn every rigid barrier of culture, class, ethnic group, and wealth.

We will find the new and the future in those places where new forms of human coexistence, participation, and co-participation are tried out, along with the hybridization of codes and emotions. New languages will be generated: planetary languages.

Today's youth are already doing this. Young people are the great precursors and authors of these hybridizations: in music, in fashion, in design, creating new forms and new freedoms. Young people are extremely capable and sensitive in finding these common roots in different universes of thought.

It is necessary for us to learn this unity in diversity, and this diversity in unity. We need the involvement of each diversity in the "pluriverse" of our planet: a cultural and linguistic pluriverse.

Now more than ever, the concept of "the hundred languages of children" seems to be an extraordinary intuition, as well as an obligation for all of us.

How can we make the languages truly one hundred in a "project of alliance" with this cultural pluriverse that surrounds us? What can help us is the now-mature awareness of the unfinished nature of every tradition and of each of us (the value of incompleteness).

The construction of self, of the individual, becomes increasingly defined as a point of intersection and of multiple identities. More and more, the individual will express an intercultural, intersubjective identity. So the quantity and quality of his or her encounters and experiences will become increasingly important. Intercultural education thus represents one of the essential guidelines for defining the quality of our future, to the extent that the interaction between cultures is not only a political issue, but above all a cultural and cognitive issue.

Cultural education is not a separate discipline, nor is it simply the illustration of the customs and religions of a country, though these are certainly important. It is more than this: it is primarily a style of educational-relational thinking. It is what we call "project-based thinking" (*pensiero progettuale*), a way of thinking that is open to others, that is open to doubt and to the awareness and acceptance of error and uncertainty. It is the interweaving of multiple cultural codes, multiple languages, "contagion," hybridization. It plays on boundaries, not as marginal zones (center versus boundary), but as places that generate the new that is born of contagion and interchange.

The new thus seems to lie in promoting an educational process based on the values of human dignity, participation, and freedom.

ALEXANDRA: Carla Rinaldi's essay is a challenging piece of writing, perhaps one of the most difficult in this anthology. It is challenging for several reasons. The most obvious is that it is translated from the Italian, and as in any translation, finding word equivalents is not always possible, and this can mean obscuring the meaning and intent of the author. But it is also challenging in that the ideas put forth by Rinaldi turn some of our most deeply rooted ways of thinking about education upside down. We are not often provoked to make explicit the values that inform how we think about education. It's far safer to measure and compare test outcomes, speak of reading levels, and assess academic performance by arbitrary notions of what is normal. The values explored here by Rinaldi, such as subjectivity, difference, participation, democracy, learning, and play, are not always found in American public discourse regarding education and schools.

That dialogue and debate are essential to a healthy democracy is widely accepted in the United States. Yet how often do we see practices in our schools that reflect the idea that discussing different points of view or conversing to exchange ideas is as important as absorbing and memorizing facts? What has become of a democratic process of evaluation that entails multiple perspectives, a variety of evidence, and documentation that considers process as well as product, when we find that politicians impose policies to retain young children for a second year in the same grade based solely on test score results?

Rinaldi challenges her readers to take on the task of seeking a balance "between the inherent rules and restrictions (some of which are indispensable) and the real emotion and passion of learning" (p. 281). Educational institutions have the unique ability, and indeed the moral obligation, to grant people space, time, resources, and permission to freely pursue their own interests and those of their communities in the making, the microdemocracies that begin in the classroom, and spread to the school and to the culture we are all in the process of creating. John Dewey likened democracy to "a mode of associated living, or conjoint communicated *experience" (1944, p. 87). We are constantly in the process of identity formation, of becoming what we are not yet, both on our own and in the company of others. We must all endeavor, therefore, to both hear and be heard, to better understand what makes us different and where we share common ground, to find ways to participate in making meaning and in finding both private and public personal fulfillment.*

· 19 ·

Joseph Featherstone

LETTER TO A YOUNG TEACHER*

ALEXANDRA: Joseph Featherstone is Professor of Teacher Education at Michigan State University in the College of Education. His interests in education are broad and include social policy, history of education, issues of democracy and justice in education, the work of John Dewey, and progressive education. Perhaps my favorite piece of writing to share with my graduate students, Featherstone's heartfelt letter is filled with wisdom about the political commitment and powerful vision of a strengthened democracy that he feels teachers must cultivate to sustain themselves in the challenging work of teaching the young. When we discuss this piece, we brainstorm together what we feel are the essential purposes of public education in a democracy, particularly in the urban context in which my students teach, and are often surprised at the eloquence and range of ideas expressed in our list that are rarely heard in conversations in schools. The more we talk about and elaborate on those purposes, the more we come to value the central ideas about community and the inherently political nature of teaching that Featherstone brings to life in this unique letter.

At the same time that we are energized by our discussion and the generation of our list, we often express sadness at the current state of affairs in schools. We wonder aloud why it is all too rare to see students excitedly engaged in controversial discussions, or as Featherstone notes, moving "back and forth from their experience to the experiences embodied in poems" (p. 293) and in other works of art and cultural artifacts. Teachers seem to know that their lofty goals of helping students find their voices, know how they will make their contribution to society, learn to develop crucial habits of mind, and forge meaningful relationships with others can easily get lost in the daily grind, especially

---

*From "Dear Josie": Witnessing the Hopes and Failures of Democratic Education, ed. J. Featherstone et al. (New York: Teachers College Press, 1995), 163–172.

when there are external forces mercilessly pressing in on them to raise test scores.

Perhaps I am an eternal optimist, but in my work in New York City schools I see glimmers of hope. Recently I was invited into the fourth- and fifth-grade classroom of a teacher named Otis Kriegel, where students had taken on the role of senators debating the issue of free public transportation for city employees. Actively engaged in crafting the perfect language for a bill and in convincing other senators to sign it, students were buzzing with an infectious enthusiasm for the political process, even though in the discussion that followed, they admitted that getting others to sign a bill was hard work. They described the importance of compromise, of listening carefully, and of being open-minded and flexible. It's worth noting that although this school has a familiar rule—no running—students are allowed to skip down the hallways instead. The feeling you get when you step inside is that this is a place where learning is a joyful process. Featherstone's wisdom reminds us that all schools have the potential to be that way.

Dear Josie,

You asked me for some advice about starting out as a teacher and what popped into my head first is an image of my grandmother. I never met her, but she remains a strong presence. She was the principal of a small, mostly immigrant elementary school in the Pennsylvania coal country. The stories of her teaching got buried with her, as so many teachers' stories do. She was one of many urban Irish Catholics who took part in the progressive educational and political movements of her day. I know that she was ambitious about kids' learning. The immigrant coal miners' children, whose families were often out of work, were to read high-class literature and poetry—she had a weakness for the English poet Robert Browning. She also checked to see that kids brushed their teeth. She was a force in local and state politics, fighting for labor rights, pioneering in women's rights, and leading the movement to end child labor. She was the first woman elected to the state Democratic committee in Pennsylvania. I think she saw a direct link between politics and her practice in education. Both had as their aim the general progress of ordinary people. She was on the people's side, creating an expansive democratic vision of education based on the idea of a country that would work for everybody, not just for the rich.

This seems to me a perspective—a tradition, really—worth reminding ourselves about in a confused political time. Fewer teachers now put matters in terms of politics, although it seems to me that teaching in the United States today more than ever involves a political commitment. I would argue that, like my grandmother, you should think of yourself as a recruit on the people's side, working to build a democracy that doesn't yet exist but is part of the American promise. My grandmother would surely point out that there is important work to be done both in and out of classrooms, and that sometimes school matters get framed by wider social issues. I'm sure that my grandmother would say that teachers today have a vital stake in a national health care system, for she always saw the connection between kids' learning and good health. Brushing your teeth and Browning were inseparable.

Thinking of her reminds me that society and its schools are both battlegrounds, on which different sides fight for rival visions of America and its possibilities. The real basics in education, she would argue, flow from the kind of country you want the kids to make when they grow up. She was voting for a real, rather than a paper, democracy. And she thought that teachers had a role to play in helping the people become more powerful.

New teachers often don't realize that there are sides to take, and that they are called upon to choose. The old idea that education is above politics is a useful half-truth—it helps keep the schools from being politicized. But it conceals the essentially political character of choices we make for kids. Do we see the children we teach today as low-paid workers for the global economy, or as the reserve army of the unemployed? If so, why be ambitious for their hearts and minds? Alternatively, we can frame fundamental aims: that we are creating a first-rate education for everybody's kids, so that as grown-ups they can make a democracy happen. My grandmother and many in her generation would say that schools should offer what students need to take part in a democratic society and its culture—a complex package for everybody's children that would equip them for full participation in work, culture, and liberty.

This is clearly an ambitious goal, rarely achieved in world history, let alone in America. Schools alone can never accomplish it. Still, our sense of the purpose of education matters, and for a long while too many of our schools have not believed in educating all of the people. The old Greeks said that some were born gold and others brass, and they designed education accordingly. A slave or a woman would not get a free man's education. Over the centuries around the planet, a lot of the human race has agreed, establishing separate educations for rulers and ruled. Hewers of wood and drawers of water would not read Jane Austen in advanced placement English classes. In a democracy, however, the people are supposed to rule. They are, the old phrase has it, the equal of kings. So the people need an education commensurate with their potential political, economic, and cultural power. To give the children of ordinary people the kind of education once reserved for the children of the elites—to do this for the first time in history—is the dream of the builders of U.S. education like Horace Mann and my grandmother and thousands of others who triumphed and struggled and died in obscurity.

You are a newcomer to a historic struggle. Some of this you may have learned already, just by keeping your eyes open. You probably know that the United States has always been a deeply flawed democracy and that education has always mirrored the systematic inequality of society. There was no golden age when the United States did right by everybody's kids. This society still has vastly different expectations for well-off and poor kids. The gap seems to be growing, not shrinking. We are two educational nations. The schools for poor kids that you may visit and teach in will often look like schools in a desperately poor nation, not in the world's most powerful country. Textbooks are old, the roof leaks, and there is a shortage of paper. People of color and women and immigrants had to fight their way into the educational feast and are still kept at the margins in many schools. But you also need to know that in each generation, strong teachers like my grandmother have worked with parents and communities to make democracy happen. Her ghost is silently cheering you on.

My grandmother was not alone in thinking that schools have a special responsibility for the progress of the people's culture. In taking a large, ambitious, ample—democratic—view of education's aims, she was opposing minimalist views that reduce children to tiny gears in the nation's great economic machine. She was opposing the oldest human superstition of all, the belief in fundamental inequality. She was also laying rude hands on the second oldest superstition, the belief that because there is never enough to go around, existing unfairness must be endured. My grandparents' generation had a healthy respect for policies that generate jobs for the people, but they never made the mistake of thinking that all of life is embraced by the equations of economists or the maxims of bankers and investors. The economy should serve human life and its needs, not the other way around. There is, the old progressives argued, no real wealth but life. Making a living ought to be a means to a wider end: making a life. And in fact, students educated to fit narrow economic grooves—management's view of what will suffice for today's workforce—will never be equipped to take part in debates and movements to change society and build a democratic economy in which everybody has a fair share and basic security.

The capacity to participate—in work, in politics, in the thought of the times—is really in the end a matter of cultural development. The key to the people's success will be the quality of their characters and their minds—the quality of their culture. It is this hardheaded grasp of the radical importance of culture that makes the progressives of my grandmother's generation worth listening to again today. Symbols and ideas and understanding have to become the property of the people if they are to ever gain any control over their lives and the lives of their children. Symbols and ideas and words and culture are no replacement for jobs or political power, but without them, people will easily lose their way. Many in my grandmother's generation admired Eugene Debs, who once said that he would not lead the people to the promised land, because if he could take them there, some other leader could convince them to leave.

In a democracy, people should be educated to be powerful, to tell their stories, to make their own voices heard, and to act together to defend and expand their rights. Culture might be said to be a shorthand word for all the ways that people and their imaginations and identities grow—how we construct the world and make ourselves at home in it, and then reinvent it fresh.

School teachers of my grandmother's era had an almost mystical reverence for the word *growth*. This is how you can tell that, for all their toughness (my aunt Mary had my grandmother in the fourth grade and said that she was really strict), they were Romantics under the skin. In tough times, against heavy odds, with huge polyglot classes, they kept alive an idea of democratic education itself as a romance. This language doesn't fit our current skeptical mood and circumstance. It has an extravagant and sentimental sound—it's the language of possibility, democratic hope. The old progressives believed in a version of true romance. Some got these ideas from politics, some from religion, and some from poetry, believe it or not. My grandmother mixed her poetry and her politics into a potent brew. One of her favorite Romantic poets, John Keats, put the argument for a Romantic, democratic view of culture this way: Now the human race looks like low bushes with here and there a big tree; spin from imaginative experience an "airy citadel" like the spider's web, "filling the air with beautiful circuiting," and every human might become great; in the right educational and cultural environment, everybody would grow to the full height, and humanity "instead of being a wide heath of furze and briars with here and there a remote pine or oak, would become a grand democracy of forest trees."

A forest of oak trees: This democratic and Romantic view of a people's culture—articulated in the nineteenth century by poets like Keats and Walt Whitman and dreamers like Margaret Fuller, Elizabeth Cady Stanton, Margaret Haley, Jane Addams, W. E. B. Du Bois, Eugene Debs, and John Dewey—insists that the goal for which we struggle is a democratic culture in which everyone can grow to full height and take part in the world of ideas, books, art, and music as well as work and politics. To hardheaded teachers like my grandmother, this was a version of true romance—true, because they knew that no kid grows on a diet of dry academic splinters and stunted expectations. If you teach kids just minimalist stuff—isolated skills, for example—they never get to practice and enact the real thing, culture itself. They get slices of the animal but not the whole live hog. They lose what Emily Dickinson called the thing with feathers—hope. In today's hard times, ruled by bastard pragmatism, it is important to insist that beauty is a human necessity, like water and food and love and work. The multiplication tables need memorizing. So do the French verbs. Not all learning is fun. My grandmother and her husband knew all about the virtues and necessities of hard work. But an idea of learning that leaves out grace and poetry and laughter will never take root in kids' hearts and souls. Education is in the end a movement of the spirit. This is the realism behind the old vision of education as true romance. Children require, finally, things that cannot be bought and sold, accomplishments that last a lifetime. They are asking for bread. Too many of our schools are giving them stones instead. From our point of view today, the school culture of my grandmother's generation may have been too genteel—a White schoolmarm culture that often ignored or disdained the experience of immigrants, women, and people of color. It was a monochromatic culture, tied into the many weaknesses of gentility. But what is impressive today about it is the depth of its democratic aspirations: the assumption that everyone will rise up on the wings of hope.

As today, Americans in the past argued over whose version of culture to teach. The tug-of-war over today's (quite recent) canons of literature and history is an inevitable aspect of being what Whitman called a people of peoples. I believe—though my grandmother might disagree— that such tugging and pulling is a sign of cultural vitality, part of a process of democratic change that Whitman described as "lawless as snowflakes." The arguments over whose version of culture to teach will properly go on until the republic closes shop. A democracy educates itself by arguing over what to teach the next generation. But as grown-up groups struggle for each generation's balance of pride and recognition and representation and inclusion, we need to keep in mind how important it is for kids to be allowed to make and do culture, to participate in enacting live meanings and symbols. Opening up the school curriculum to the world's rainbows of cultures is a necessary step toward becoming a people of peoples, a real democracy—creating an education that helps kids become good citizens not only of their own country, but of the world. But it will not be much of a gain to substitute a new multicultural and multiracial orthodoxy for an older cultural orthodoxy. Nobody's version of the canon will matter if kids don't start reading real books sometime. Unless kids get a chance to make cultural meaning, and not passively absorb it, nothing will come alive. Anybody's version of culture can be delivered secondhand and dead. The real challenge is to help kids make cultural meanings come alive here and now, to act as creators and critics of culture, armed with the skills and discipline to—as Emerson put it—marry form and power. And what holds for kids surely holds for teachers too.

A Romantic and democratic vision of human possibility may in the end be a practical thing for teachers—as real as radium, and more valuable. Teaching is, after all, more like taking part in a religion or a political movement than anything else—the whole thing rests on what the old theologians called the virtue of hope. Its loss kills more kids than guns and drugs. The technocratic lingo of the educational managers and the boredom of today's colleges of education do no service to a profession that in the end requires true romance, the stuff that lights up the soul. Who would rise up on a cold, dark morning and go out to teach if the only goal were to raise the SAT scores? A democratic vision helps you not only in rethinking your purposes, in choosing the curriculum, for example, but also in making it through those February days when the radiators are banging and teaching school feels like the dark night of the soul. It says on the Liberty Bell, across the crack, that the people without vision shall perish. This should be a warning to us in an educational era dominated by dull experts, squinty-eyed economists, and frightened politicians. You will never survive your years as a teacher by listening to what passes for vision now in the United States.

Teachers and the rest of us need to start reimagining an expansive and democratic vision of education as true romance—not the romance of sentimentality and fakery and escape (the media have stuffed us all with too many such lies) but the true romance that knows that the heart is the toughest human muscle, the romance of respect for the people and what their children's minds are capable of.

To enact this true romance, we need to do many things. We need a democratic version of the humanities and the liberal arts from kindergarten through the university. At the university level, as in the schools, the older traditions of the "liberal arts" and the "humanities" and elite science and math are often preserves for privilege, crusted over with the practices and superstitions of human inequality. But the people's children deserve the best, and such subjects and traditions need to be rescued for them. Culture needs to be democratized, not abandoned. The people have a right to claim their heritage and take possession of what generations of leisure have given the privileged. Poor kids deserve the kind of education rich kids get.

Underlying the daily work in schools, then, is the task of creating a democratic culture, a task that may take generations. Of course, a genuine people's culture, when it emerges, will look very different from the oily "people's cultures" concocted by the commissars in totalitarian regimes. To begin such work, teachers need to be able to see "culture" in its several meanings: what used to be called the "high" culture, the traditional symbols of academic learning, the great books and works of art and music; newcomers to the canon; and also the local webs of meaning and tradition arising out of the lives of students and communities. Today we want to interrogate the old "high" culture and ask whom it included and whom it left out. But in the end, we also want our kids to get access, to break into the old vaults as well as savor new treasures.

Instead of thinking of culture as a separate realm of "high" experience, an elite commodity, we want to show our kids the common continuum of human experience that reaches from the great works of art of all times and cultures to children's talk and imagining right now, to help students move back and forth from their experience to the experiences embodied in poems, artworks, and textbooks. Skills matter, but they need to connect to a vision. Unlike my grandmother's generation, we want the visions of culture offered in our schools to be true rainbow bridges that the children crisscross daily in both directions—the home and neighborhood cultures on one end, and the wider worlds of culture on the other.

My grandmother had a vision of a teacher going forth to bring culture to the people. What we might add to that today is the image of the people and their children giving something back in a true exchange of gifts. Today we might be in a better position to see that culture-making in the schools has to be a two-way street. The idea of culture embraced by the school must also reach out to embrace the cultures of the students and their families.

As a teacher on the side of the people, you need to make yourself a careful student of the care and feeding of small, provisional human communities, for these are where people learn to make cultural meaning together, to practice and create the people's culture. This is why John Dewey called schools "embryonic democracies" and why some of the old reformers called them "little commonwealths." Classroom communities require certain elements: learning to talk the talk, learning to listen respectfully, finding a voice, learning to make and criticize knowledge in a group, giving and taking, finding the blend of intellectual and emotional support that a good classroom group can provide, valuing the habits and skills of reading and writing that arise when speakers and writers and artists get responses from audiences and listeners and readers. The discipline that lasts comes from participation, and it is the discipline of freedom.

In practice, then, helping the people progress in cultural terms means the ongoing creation of provisional forms of community. In good schools, students are learning not only skills but how to use them to make culture—the kind of broad, powerful, and purposeful meanings we associate with intellectual, artistic, scientific, and democratic communities— and to forge links between the kind of culture they are enacting in school and the cultures of their communities. In school subjects, they learn the discourse of many of the smaller worlds that make up the large world of culture, literacy, and the languages of math and science and the arts, as well as the logic of action required to go on making, remaking, and criticizing different kinds of community over a lifetime.

With her union background, my grandmother would warn you about the need for solidarity as an educational ideal. The elites who manage today's schools want you to stay isolated and to think of education and politics as mainly a matter of competition between individuals. My grandmother would tell you something different: that we are brothers and sisters, that we learn from one another, and that we will have to work out a common fate on a troubled and threatened planet. Not only that, but to the extent that we remain isolated, the Gradgrinds will prevail. Look at the way they used the racial issue to divide the forces of American democracy throughout the 20th century.

Although individual students make the meanings, the business of taking part in culture always means participation in some kind of community, real or imagined. You are part of a music community, even when you play the guitar alone. Math skills and ideas have as their aim participation in the community of those who make, who "do," math. The old Greeks emphasized the communal side of math when they called it a performance art and—to our astonishment today—linked it with such communal arts as theater and dancing. They would be amazed to hear that we make kids study math solo, rather than reasoning together as a group.

I emphasize the community angle not to slight the individual—all education has to balance individual and social aims—but to stress the way that the individuality we prize so deeply in our students emerges from what they learn through community encounters with others, their families, peers, and teachers. But students who haven't learned to listen won't have much of a chance of finding their distinctive voices; nor will students who have never spoken in class about something that really matters to them or made some significant choices at some important points about their own learning.

My grandmother's generation was in love with the idea of growth. It's easy to see the importance of growth for students, but how about for you? When you start teaching, you do not know enough, but you are also not culturally developed enough to be a model for your students. This might be particularly true if you come from a family that never had much access to "high" culture. Even if you got a lot of "culture," is it really yours, or is it a ragbag of secondhand experiences and unexplained views? How do you help your kids build the rainbow bridges back and forth? How can you sell them on literacy if you yourself don't read much and don't enjoy books? What about your identity as a teacher? What about the struggle for democracy? You might like the picture of the teacher going out to meet the people, but what do you really have to offer? This is a harsh question, but you have a big responsibility if you are signing up as a teacher. How do you start the lifetime work of becoming a practical intellectual who can help the people progress culturally?

The question of your own cultural development may in the end be the big question about your future as a teacher. With some attention, I think that you can begin to see how democracy is the underlying issue in our society today, and how education reflects a wider, worldwide struggle. It may be more difficult to see the democratic cultural challenge; to see that a lively discussion of *Frog and Toad* in the second grade is one step toward a people's culture. A vision helps, but it needs to come alive daily in your teaching practice. How can you start to become a practical intellectual who is able to bring culture to the people's children and able to accept their gifts back? This will never be easy. But don't despair, you aren't dead yet. There are lots of ways to begin expanding your own possession of culture, ranging from exploring your roots to developing your own literacies and your acquaintance with ideas, traditions, and symbols in a host of realms. My grandmother, with her message of solidarity, would urge you not to go it alone, to join up with other teachers and reach out to people in your community. Your own ability to nourish a learning community in your classrooms will be helped immeasurably if you yourself inhabit—and help create—genuine learning communities outside of class. The things you want for your students—the development of skills, culture, interests, identities, and a voice—are all things you need as a teacher. One or two genuine interests to share with kids are worth their weight in gold. Finding one or two ways to link your teaching to the wider struggle for democracy will show you the meaning of your work. Read Herbert Kohl's great essay "The Good Old Days . . ." in his collection *Should We Burn Babar* to begin to get a sense that history and democratic tradition are resources to draw on in the work of teaching. Learn something about your own history, because that can give you an important angle on where you stand in relation to culture making.

Culture is like—is another name for—growth and development and education itself. Like history, it has no end. Generations of thoughtful teachers have taken part in the long struggle. Now, just your luck, it's your turn. All the best.

Joseph Featherstone

P.S. I call you "Josie" because that's what W.E.B. Du Bois calls his student in his sketch of himself as a teacher in the rural South in *The Souls of Black Folk*. Josie represents all the life and vitality of the people and craves a formal education, which she never gets, dying young. Du Bois was the young teacher going out to meet the people, and Josie was the people meeting the teacher. Both had something to offer in the exchange. The result for Du Bois was the complex educational agenda embodied in *The Souls of Black Folk*[1]; to learn the ways and the powers of the wider culture represented by school learning and the classics, but to keep your soul and know your roots. Du Bois was the spiritual grand-daddy of the civil rights generation—he died in exile just as the 1963 March on Washington was taking place—but his vision of a democratic culture awaits our work. I know that the dreadful premature harvest of young Josies has not stopped, but I like to think that some are making their way into teaching, like you.

NOTE

1. This passage was quoted, significantly, by that Romantic John Dewey (1934) in *Art as Experience*, his great argument for a democratic approach to art and culture.

———————

MAUREEN: Featherstone's letter of encouragement to an imaginary new teacher strikes a sensitive chord with me. When I was a new teacher, I often felt insecure and exhausted. I often questioned my own understanding of the goals of education and my ability to oversee the emotional, social, and political aspects of my work.

Now as a teacher educator, in an even more complex climate, I listen to my students voice many of the same insecurities I felt more than fifty years ago. New teachers go from college or graduate school after months or even years of observing and participating in classrooms where they receive meaningful feed-back from the teachers who have volunteered to assist in educating them. They are also supported by college supervisors, who direct their student teaching, by their professors, and by their peers in the program.

But as neophytes, there is often no way for them to know how they are pro-gressing in their chosen profession. The lucky ones sometimes are assigned a mentor teacher, or have supportive administrators who do more than a few for-mal observations. Parents can help bridge this gap. Teachers are hungry for feedback from parents. They want to know how their children talk about school when they are at home. What do they especially like about school? What do they need or have trouble with? What are their passions and pastimes? What can the teachers do to help? Too often parent-teacher conferences are one-sided affairs. They should be conversations—an open sharing of ideas about children and how they grow and learn.

Featherstone wisely reminds us that "a diet of dry academic splinters and stunted expectations" (p. 290) is inadequate for growth in a democratic society. We must all remember that kids have a natural love of learning, and they flourish in an academic environment that furnishes them with broad exposure to the richness of many cultures. "An idea of learning that leaves out grace and poetry and laughter will never take root in kids' hearts and souls" (p. 291). Parents and teachers together can seek the balance required for an education that is both challenging and exciting: "They are asking for bread. Too many of our schools are giving them stones instead" (p. 291).

As a practitioner of fifty-seven years who still finds teaching exciting, challenging, and rewarding, I can bear witness to the efficacy of choosing the adventure rather than conformity. I often think back to Dewey's notion that the kindergarten teacher in the block corner must know physics or Paley's emphasis on fantasy, fairness, and friendship. I think too of Maxine Greene's courage and tolerance for ambiguity. I am reminded that I must be an advocate for uncertainty. If I want my students to be explorers, I too must be willing to risk a venture into the unknown. For teachers are, first and foremost, role models. We must embrace the adventure if we hope to inspire our students to be adventurous.

ABOUT THE AUTHORS

The authors and editors of this collection are two teacher educators, a mother and her daughter, who teach prospective and practicing elementary teachers at the graduate and undergraduate levels. Dr. Maureen Miletta, who earned a B.A. from Barnard College, an M.A. and an Ed.D. from Teachers College, Columbia University, taught in the Great Neck Public Schools for most of her career, where she started an innovative multiage program for upper elementary grades with two colleagues. Author of *A Multiage Classroom: Choice and Possibility* (1996), she taught at Hofstra University in the Department of Curriculum and Teaching for twenty-four years. Dr. Alexandra Miletta taught fifth and sixth grade in Edmonds, Washington, for four years, and has a B.A. from Wellesley College and an M.A. from Syracuse University in art history. She completed her Ph.D. in Educational Studies at the University of Michigan. She currently teaches in the Department of Childhood Education at the City College of New York, City University of New York.

PERMISSIONS

pervision and Curriculum Development is a worldwide community of educators advocating sound policies and sharing best practices to achieve the success of each learner. To learn more, visit ASCD at www.ascd.org.

Lisa Delpit, "Ebonics and Culturally Responsive Instruction," from *Rethinking School Reform: Views from the Classroom*, ed. L. Christensen and S. Karp (Milwaukee, WI: Rethinking Schools, 2003), 79–88. Reprinted with the permission of the author.

John Dewey, "Democracy in Education," from *John Dewey: The Middle Works 1899–1906*, ed. J.A. Boydston (Carbondale, IL: Southern Illinois University Press), 229–239.

Carla Rinaldi, "Infant-Toddler Centers and Preschools as Places of Culture," from *Making Learning Visible: Children as Individual and Group Learners* (Reggio Emilia, Italy: Reggio Children and Project Zero, 2001), 38–46. Copyright © Reggio Children, the President and Fellows of Harvard College, and the Municipality of Reggio Emilia, published by Reggio Children 2001. Reprinted with the permission of Reggio Children, Via Bligny 1/a-C.P. 91 Succursale 2, 42100 Reggio Emilia, Italy, www.reggiochildren.it.

Joseph Featherstone, "Letter to a Young Teacher," from *"Dear Josie": Witnessing the Hopes and Failures of Democratic Education*, ed. J. Featherstone et al. (New York: Teachers College Press, 1995), 163–172. Copyright © 1995. Reprinted with the permission of Teachers College Press.

INDEX

CITY KIDS, CITY SCHOOLS
More Reports from the Front Row
Edited by William Ayers, Gloria Ladson-Billings, Gregory Michie, and Pedro A. Noguera

This new and timely collection has been compiled by four of the country's most prominent urban educators to provide some of the best writing on life in city schools and neighborhoods.

978-1-59558-338-3 (pb)

CITY KIDS, CITY TEACHERS
Reports from the Front Row
Edited by William Ayers and Patricia Ford

A classic collection exploding the stereotypes of city schools, reissued as a companion to *City Kids, City Schools*.

978-1-56584-051-5 (pb)

COMING OF AGE AROUND THE WORLD
A Multicultural Anthology
Edited by Faith Adiele and Mary Frosch

Twenty-four stories by renowned international authors chronicle the modern struggle for identity among young people around the globe.

978-1-59558-080-1 (pb)

COMING OF AGE IN AMERICA
A Multicultural Anthology
Edited by Mary Frosch with a foreword by Gary Soto

The acne and ecstasy of adolescence, a multicultural collection of short stories and fiction excerpts that *Library Journal* calls "wonderfully diverse from the standard fare," in a beautiful new edition.

978-1-56584-147-5 (pb)

COMING OF AGE IN THE 21st CENTURY
Growing Up in America Today
Edited by Mary Frosch

A follow-up to the multicultural collection of stories about growing up in America—updated for the new century.

978-1-59558-055-9 (pb)

CONSUMING KIDS
The Hostile Takeover of Childhood
Susan Linn

In this shocking exposé, Susan Linn takes a comprehensive and unsparing look at the demographic advertisers call "the kid market," taking readers on a compelling and disconcerting journey through modern childhood as envisioned by commercial interests.

978-1-56584-783-5 (hc)

CROSSING THE TRACKS
How "Untracking" Can Save America's Schools
Anne Wheelock

A groundbreaking survey of schools around the country that have successfully "crossed the tracks" and reintegrated their classrooms.

978-1-56584-038-6 (pb)

DIARY OF A HARLEM SCHOOLTEACHER
Jim Haskins

Called "a weapon—cold, blunt, painful," by the *New York Times*, this classic work recounts the experiences of an African American teacher during his first year working in a Harlem elementary school in the 1960s.

978-1-59558-339-0 (pb)

DISMANTLING DESEGREGATION
The Quiet Reversal of Brown v. Board of Education
Gary Orfield and Susan E. Eaton

"Powerful case studies . . . the authors convincingly argue that the ideal of desegregation is disappearing."   —*Kirkus Reviews*

978-1-56584-401-8 (pb)

EVERYDAY ANTIRACISM
Getting Real About Race in School
Edited by Mica Pollock

Leading experts offer concrete and realistic strategies for dealing with race in schools in a groundbreaking book that should become required reading for every teacher in the country.

978-1-59558-054-2 (pb)

FINAL TEST
The Battle for Adequacy in America's Schools
Peter Schrag

An in-depth look at school finance and the latest struggle for equality in public education.

978-1-59558-026-3 (pb)

FIRES IN THE MIDDLE SCHOOL BATHROOM
Advice to Teachers from Middle Schoolers
Kathleen Cushman and Laura Rogers

Following on the heels of the bestselling *Fires in the Bathroom*, which brought the insights of high school students to teachers and parents, Kathleen Cushman now turns her attention to the crucial and challenging middle grades, joining forces with adolescent psychologist Laura Rogers.

978-1-59558-111-2 (hc)

FIRES IN THE BATHROOM
Advice to Teachers from High School Students
Kathleen Cushman

This groundbreaking book offers original insights into teaching teenagers in today's hard-pressed urban high schools from the point of view of the students themselves. It speaks to both new and established teachers, giving them first-hand information about who their students are and what they need to succeed.

978-1-56584-996-9 (pb)

FULLER'S EARTH
A Day with Bucky and the Kids
Richard J. Brenneman

Perhaps the most lovable and personal portrait ever produced of visionary Buckminster Fuller—the man who has been called "the planet's friendly genius."

978-1-59558-405-2 (pb)

GROWING UP GAY/GROWING UP LESBIAN
A Literary Anthology
Edited by Bennett L. Singer

The first literary anthology geared specifically to gay and lesbian youth. *A Library Journal* Notable Book of the Year.

978-1-56584-103-1 (pb)

THE HERB KOHL READER
Awakening the Heart of Teaching
Herbert Kohl

The best writing from a lifetime in the trenches and at the typewriter, from the much-beloved National Book Award winner, with a foreword by William Ayers.

978-1-59558-420-5 (pb)

HOW KINDERGARTEN CAME TO AMERICA
Friedrich Froebel's Radical Vision of Early Childhood Education
Bertha von Marenholtz-Bülow

An enchanting 1894 account of the inventor of kindergartens, introduced to a new generation of educators and parents by Herbert Kohl.

978-1-59558-154-9 (pb)

"I WON'T LEARN FROM YOU"
And Other Thoughts on Creative Maladjustment
Herbert Kohl

The now-classic piece on refusing to learn, as well as other landmark Kohl essays.

978-1-56584-096-6 (pb)

MADE IN AMERICA
Immigrant Students in Our Public Schools
Laurie Olsen

With a new preface by the author, this timely reissue probes the challenges facing teachers and immigrant students in our public schools.

978-1-59558-349-9 (pb)

THE NEW EDUCATION
Progressive Education One Hundred Years Ago Today
Scott Nearing

Classic vignettes, interviews, and speculations on school restructuring, curriculum development, and educational reform by a high-profile public advocate, with a foreword by Herbert Kohl.

978-1-59558-209-6 (pb)

THE NEW PRESS EDUCATION READER
Leading Educators Speak Out
Edited by Ellen Gordon Reeves

The *New Press Education Reader* brings together the work of progressive writers and educators—among them Lisa Delpit, Herbert Kohl, William Ayers, and Maxine Greene—to discuss the most pressing and challenging issues now facing us, including schools and social justice, equity issues, tracking and testing, combating racism and homophobia, and more.

978-1-59558-110-5 (pb)

OTHER PEOPLE'S CHILDREN
Cultural Conflict in the Classroom
Lisa Delpit

In this anniversary edition of a classic, MacArthur Award–winning author Lisa Delpit develops ideas about ways teachers can be better "cultural transmitters" in the classroom, where prejudice, stereotypes, and cultural assumptions breed ineffective education.

978-1-59558-074-0 (pb)

THE PUBLIC SCHOOL AND THE PRIVATE VISION
A Search for America in Education and Literature
Maxine Greene

A newly updated edition of the celebrated educational philosopher's first masterpiece, with a foreword by Herbert Kohl.

978-1-59558-153-2 (pb)

RACE
How Blacks and Whites Think and Feel about the American Obsession
Studs Terkel

Based on interviews with over 100 Americans, this book is a rare and revealing look at how people feel about race in the United States.

978-1-56584-989-1 (pb)

RACISM EXPLAINED TO MY DAUGHTER
Tahar Ben Jelloun

The prizewinning book of advice about racism from a bestselling author to his daughter, introduced by Bill Cosby. The paperback version includes responses from William Ayers, Lisa Delpit, and Patricia Williams.

978-1-59558-029-0 (pb)

RETHINKING SCHOOLS
An Agenda for Change
Edited by David Levine, Robert Lowe, Robert Peterson, and Rita Tenorio

The country's leading education reformers propose ways to change our schools.

978-1-56584-215-1 (pb)

A SCHOOLMASTER OF THE GREAT CITY
A Progressive Educator's Pioneering Vision for Urban Schools
Angelo Patri

Angelo Patri's eloquent 1917 chronicle of multicultural education in the inner city remains as relevant today as it was ninety years ago, with a foreword by Herbert Kohl.

978-1-59558-212-6 (pb)

SHE WOULD NOT BE MOVED
How We Tell the Story of Rosa Parks and the Montgomery Bus Boycott
Herbert Kohl

From a prizewinning educator, a meditation that reveals the misleading way generations of children have been taught the story of Rosa Parks, offering guidance on how to present the Civil Rights movement to young students.

978-1-59558-127-3 (pb)

SHOULD WE BURN BABAR?
Essays on Children's Literature and the Power of Stories
Herbert Kohl

The prizewinning educator's thoughts on the politics of children's litertuare.

978-1-59558-130-3 (pb)

THE SKIN THAT WE SPEAK
Thoughts on Language and Culture in the Classroom
Edited by Lisa Delpit and Joanne Kilgour Dowdy

A collection that gets to the heart of the relationship between language and power in the classroom.

978-1-59558-350-5 (pb)

STUPIDITY AND TEARS
Teaching and Learning in Troubled Times
Herbert Kohl

"Vintage Kohl—incisive, funny, reflective, profound . . . a provocation to educators to better teach all our children."
                    —Norman Fruchter, NYU Institute of Education and Social Policy

978-1-56584-982-2 (pb)

TEACHERS HAVE IT EASY
The Big Sacrifices and Small Salaries of America's Teachers
Daniel Moulthrop, Níninve Clements Calegari, and Dave Eggers

A startling call to action for improving the working lives of public school teachers.

978-1-59558-128-0 (pb)

TEACHING FOR SOCIAL JUSTICE
A Democracy and Education Reader
Edited by William Ayers, Jean Ann Hunt, and Therese Quinn
Published in conjunction with Teachers College Press

A popular handbook on teaching for social justice for parents and educators.

978-1-56584-420-9 (pb)

THE USE OF EXPLOSIVE IDEAS IN EDUCATION
Culture, Class, and Evolution
Theodore Brameld

Using three "explosive ideas" of the past century—culture, class, and evolution—Brameld brings both philosophy and the liberal arts to bear upon the myriad activities of classrooms, playgrounds, and administrative offices.

978-1-59558-421-2 (pb)

THE VIEW FROM THE OAK
The Private Worlds of Other Creatures
Herbert Kohl with Judith Kohl

The National Book Award–winning book on ethology: the study of the way animals perceive their environment.

978-1-56584-636-4 (pb)

WELCOME TO THE AQUARIUM
A Year in the Lives of Children
Julie Diamond

Told through the eyes of a veteran kindergarten teacher, this book presents what life is like in an elementary school classroom.

978-1-59558-171-6 (hc)